T
Who Skipped

by Jeff Adkins

Jeff Adkins

Dedicated to Miss Carol "CC" Combs

"We've done so much for so long with so little, we believe we can now do anything...with nothing!" - Carol Combs

The Boy Who Skipped

ISBN 978-0-557-53497-5

Chapter Index

Acknowledgments and Introduction

In the spring of 2007, I received a note from a friend of mine, Marni Berendsen, asking if it would be "all right" if she nominated me for a teaching award, called the Amgen Award for Excellence in Science Education. I said sure, why not? There was a cash award attached that I could use in my astronomy education program at my school. I am a teacher in a large suburban high school in California.

I, along with several other teachers from California, received the award and was asked to visit the Amgen campus as part of the recognition. The company asked me to attend a banquet and make a speech about why I became a teacher. They politely requested that we submit these speeches in advance. There were six winners from the state of California.

I dutifully wrote my speech, and in it I said the teacher who had had the greatest influence on me was my high school speech and drama teacher, Carol Combs.

Over the years, the story of how Miss Combs inspired me has stayed in the background of my life, influencing how I make presentations and teach. I always thought it was an interesting story that others might benefit from and enjoy. In fact, I'd started writing the story of her program four or five times, only to stall out after 30 or 40 pages. I couldn't seem to make any headway until recently, when I began making connections with old friends I hadn't spoken to in many years.

Many people assisted me by sharing stories about those days, filling in gaps in my memory or correcting things that I misinterpreted. My sister Joyce told me some of the history of the program before I joined, and reminded me of some things we did together while she was still in school. My sister Barbara, and my father Asble remembered things about those days as well, and shared them with me even as I was writing.

I am indebted to my friends and colleagues who took the time to read this manuscript and listen to my stories in various stages of completion. My good friends Raymond Kuntz, Genie and Russell Christoff, and Allison Weihe were very gracious and provided advice and independent comments that helped insure that people who weren't there during the events described would "get" the message I am trying to deliver. Genie shared with me the remarkable book *The Glass Castle* by Jeannette Walls, which I read with intense interest and not a few newly dredged up memories. Other friends who read early versions and offered advice were Lori Adkins, Karen Del Purgatorio, Maria McClain, Jerome Larsen, Peggy O'Neill, Nicole Santa Maria, Steve Kish, Bruce Hemp and Mike Johnson. I considered all of their suggestions carefully. The final decisions of how to approach this story and what to leave in and what to add are my own, but the best parts definitely owe part of their existence to the excellent advice I received.

Authors Homer Hickam and Julie Czerneda gave me valuable advice, which I used as I began writing. It astonishes me how generous they are with their time and advice with a first-time author. I also received useful advice from Julie's friend Mindy Klasky. I would also like to acknowledge my friend Marni Berendsen, who nominated me for the award that eventually set in motion the events that led me to write this book.

I also obtained many stories from my former teacher and mentor Miss Carol Combs, to whom this book and related projects are dedicated. She taught me the value of hard work, unflinching dedication and purpose, and if truth be told, served as my surrogate mother in some ways, during those times I spent under her supervision. She taught me excellence, persistence, an appreciation for the arts and inspired me as a student and a teacher. She taught me how to have a vision that exceeded the limits of what I could see.

Most of all, however, I must acknowledge the assistance and cooperation of Sheri Lyn "Greylyn" Gregory, who befriended me, was the my muse and inspiration in high school and who gave me the confidence to go on to make whatever I wanted out of myself.

She asked to read it; after she did she encouraged me to continue. She reminded me of all the things that happened to me – to *us*– my freshman year in high school. Suddenly, as if I had a *blinding glimpse of the obvious*, I knew what the plot should be, and how to proceed. That was about six months ago. Lyn read all of these words as they were written, and shared personal stories and gave me permission to use them. As she always was, she was open and honest, loving and caring, and I owe her more than she can ever know. I have made a good honest effort to tell her through the writing of this book. Maybe she does know, now. I hope so.

This is the story of what happened to us, mostly during my freshman year of high school. It's not an autobiographical history. Strictly speaking, it's become a novel based on real events. I've changed and edited and flat-out made up some stuff to try to tell a more compelling story. It's deviated far enough from what really happened that we decided it would be best to change the names of people and some places.

Some people were combined into one character, events were placed out of sequence, conversations were created to explain things that we knew, but don't remember how we learned. Ultimately the story took on a life of its own, and what you are about to read is the result of the negotiations between myself, the story, my memories and my friends. I think it falls into the category of *novoir* as defined by Homer Hickam, author of *Rocket Boys*.

With regards to what happened in our hearts during the 1976-1977 school year there in Eastern Kentucky... every word is true. I hope you enjoy it.

October 16, 2007 - June 30, 2010
Antioch, California

The Pool Hall

One hot, humid day approaching the end my seventh year in school, my principal Mr. Caldwell suddenly appeared at the door to my class-room and called me out of class. The other students in the room had never seen me extracted from class for anything before, so of course they said, "You're in truuuuuubullllll," as seventh-graders are wont to do.

"Get your stuff." he said curtly, although he did have a tiny smile on his lips. *Probably not a good thing*, I thought. He pushed back the shock of black hair suspended above his forehead. His hair always looked like it was reaching forward as if it were somewhat dissatisfied with its current arrangements and was seeking a new home.

"What for?" I gulped. I didn't know how to interpret what he said. Naturally, I assumed I was in trouble since I was talking to the princi-pal, the Keeper of the Paddle. I didn't know how to react to being in trouble, especially when I was fairly certain I had done nothing wrong. Pretty sure, anyway.

"You'll see. I already called your mom," he said. He jerked his head to the side, indicating the door. This gave his pompadour permission to resume its attempt to escape.

"OoooooOOOOOHHHH," resumed the seventh graders, fulfilling their role. I got up. I was nearly as tall as he was, which was more of a testament to his short stature than to my height. I looked at my teacher, who shrugged noncommittally. So we turned and left. As we walked down the lone hallway bisecting the elementary school he said, off-handedly, "We're going to town." I looked at him in query but he did not pick up on the cue.

We went outside into the humid spring afternoon air. The school was surrounded on all sides by hills covered in trees, broad leafy green leaves alternating with smothering knots of kudzu. We got into his car, a nondescript four-door sedan you might expect an elementary school principal to drive. He turned off the radio, which had started wailing some country tune as the car engine sputtered to life. When I was done buckling my seat belt, he took off down the winding road that followed the river into Hazard. Actually, the road went *up* at first onto the narrow unlined two-lane road that was etched into the side of the steep hills surrounding the school.

It was 1975.

Hazard was about a half-hour trip from school. In those days Hazard was a small town of some 7,000 souls, give or take a few, depending on whether or not it was the first of the month and the government checks had come in. The Dukes had not yet made an appearance on television, so people in other parts of the country had no sense of where the town was or what was in it. (Not that the television show gave them any sense of what the town was like even when the show was on.) It was the location of the county office of education, universally known throughout all school systems as "the downtown office." At least, that's where I *assumed* we were going.

The principal didn't offer an explanation. It never occurred to me to call home to verify that he'd spoken to my mother or that no field trip forms or paperwork had been issued. He was the principal, like the boss; and as a student I dutifully followed directions. This was the 1970's and the kind of precautions parents and students take for granted today would have seemed insulting then. Along the way we chatted about inconsequential things, like school and grades and such. I finally got the nerve to ask him where we were going. All I got in return was a cryptic "You'll see soon enough."

Once we arrived in town we stopped in front of the only pool hall in town, at one end of Main Street. *Odell's Place,* declared a slightly unleveled sign hand-painted and suspended from a rusty chain attached to a rusty pipe extruding from a rust-stained whitewashed concrete block wall. A hand-drawn sign attached with decaying tape on the window declared *No chilldren alowed.* Rusted metal Coke and Bud signs clung to the walls and a neon COLDBEER fixture sputtered in the darkened window. Inside, the pool hall was a dank, dark, smoke-filled room populated by men with tattoos and enormous bellies alternating places with scrawny, gangly fellows sporting beards desperately seeking the ground, wearing half-length sleeveless t-shirts that exposed their ribs. These men trudged around the pool tables, faces lined with concentration, cigarettes hanging loosely from their lips, hair slicked back, shirts clinging to them due to the humid air. In the back the *ching-ching-ching* of mechanical pinball machines was only interrupted by the occasional cursing of a patron who missed a shot. One or two of them grinned at us, and revealed a competition between existing and missing teeth for space. No one seemed to notice it was strange to have an underage boy in the place, despite the fact that bottled beer was being sold from a cooler on the side of the room with a lid that slid sideways, like the ice cream cooler at the peanut store near my house.

"Mr. Caldwell," I said, finally summoning the courage to ask, "Wh-why are we *here*?"

"I want you to meet someone," he replied. "Louis Newberry." He beckoned me to follow.

What could I do? Run for help? Scream?

I followed.

We worked our way to the back of the pool hall, where we found a pair of bluejean-clad legs, connected to feet, protruding from the open face of a pinball machine. It looked as if the pinball machine was an alligator eating someone alive. *Alligator jaws open upward. Crocodile jaws open downward,* said a voice in my head.

"Louis," he said, poking the fellow's ankle. "Louis. *Lou.* It's me. I brought that boy I told you about." *Ching-ding* said the pinball machine as he extracted himself.

Louis Newberry was one of those fidgety fellows who looked like he was always a bit nervous about something he wouldn't divulge even if you asked. His pockets were stuffed with things, *too many* things that made them bulge uncomfortably. He lifted his head from the innards of the machine and stared at me. His eye twitched as he looked me over. Too much caffeine, or other substances, probably. He had yellowish grease spots all over his shirt, and bits of wire insulation suspended in his hair. He extricated himself from the pinball machine and hopped to the floor.

"OK," he said, nodding at Caldwell. "I'll take it from here."

I *still* didn't know what was going on, and then Mr. Caldwell suddenly decided he had to be somewhere else.

"I've got to go downtown to the district office," he said. This was about a block away from our current location. "I'll be back in twenty minutes or so to pick you up."

I started to ask him again what was going on, but he turned on his heel and left.

"Come on, boy," said Newberry. "We're going upstairs."

I swallowed my doubts and followed him into a narrow, twisting stairwell that turned this way and that and grew narrower as we climbed, until we arrived into a loft-like area above the pool hall. *What the heck is going on?* I thought to myself. In a different era I would have run away and called to strangers for help. Heck, if it had gotten any weirder, I would have done it *then.*

"What are you waiting on?" he said. "Come on, I don't have much time."

Calling for help might have been an option. But not then, and not there. I followed.

12

At the top of the stairs I realized that the loft wasn't a living space–it was a *workshop*, containing boxes of parts–pinball machine parts– and electrical equipment.

My guide extracted a cardboard box and pulled out a large black box with a needle on the front accompanied by a large knob. The case was made of bakelite, I think. Wires dangled from connections on the front.

"This here's a multi-meter," he said. "See, you turn this knob, and this is how you get your Ohms, and your Amps, and your Volts."

"It measures electricity," I said.

"Yup," he said. "It's a 'lectrician's best friend. I use one all the time. This one here's gettin' a little old. " He put it in a cardboard box. "Now over here are switches, and knobs and pots," he said, gesturing. "wires, and light bulbs and sockets, 'gator clips and such. Help your-self. Fill up the box and come on downstairs."

I'm getting stuff to experiment with? I thought, incredulously. Mul-timeters like this were expensive. "Do I get to borrow this stuff?"

He nodded.

"How long can I keep this stuff to work with it?" I asked.

"I dunno," he replied as he returned to the pool hall. "A couple of months, maybe. Just bring it back when you're done."

What was I supposed to do with it? I thought, as I filled the box with resistors and wires and knife switches.

Downstairs, he was again wrestling with the guts of the pinball ma-chine.

"Look here," said Newberry. "Down here, this is your actuator, and this is your momentary single-pole switch on the bumper. And this here is the relay that triggers the score counter when you go through that whirlygig there."

I didn't understand much of what he was saying, but I could see the chains of devices linked together, all wired together like a rat's nest of copper wiring. "How does it know you put money in?"

"There's a trigger over here from the coin box, see," he said, pointing. "A coin makes it through the filter, it triggers this reed switch right here, an' that starts up the game and resets the score with this line right here."

"What's wrong with it? Why do you have it open?"

"One of the flappers over here warn't triggering the bonus it was 'spose to," he replied. "But I fixed it." With that he closed the lid on the pinball machine.

The closing lid revealed that Mr. Caldwell was there, waiting for me to finish asking questions. I looked at him, holding my box of electrical treasures.

"You ready?" he said. I nodded. "Thanks," he said to Newberry, who waved as we left the pool hall.

"No problem," said Newberry. He was already fishing around in his pockets for some sort of a tool, on to the next task.

It never occurred to me to ask him how he knew Newberry, or if he made a habit of hanging around in smoky pool halls.

In the car on the way back to school, I pondered what had happened as the steep hillsides blanketed with trees alternately shaded us and revealed the sun. Vines completely covered one side of the road and were making a break for the other side via a power cable. Finally I asked him, "Mr. Caldwell, what am I supposed to do with this stuff?"

"Figure out how it works," he said simply. "Play with it. You'll think of something."

"Why did you pick me to do this? Why not some other kid?"

"Jeff, we all know you're capable of doing more than we have time to give you," he replied. "There's the potential in you to do great things. I was talking to your teacher and your mom, and we just decided to give you a little nudge today. Don't know if it'll lead anywhere. Might not. But if we never try to challenge you– and *especially* if you don't challenge yourself– you won't ever find out what you can really do."

He looked at me with a little lopsided grin. Kind of made him look like Elvis.

"Don't ever settle for just doing what your teachers ask you to do. That's just a test to see who's paying attention."

I thought about that for a long time, and resolved to try to do *something* with the opportunity that had been handed to me.

For several weeks I tried different combinations of parts, and eventually figured out the essentials of Ohm's law connecting voltage, current, and resistance. I learned to connect an ammeter in series and a voltmeter in parallel. My classmates were impressed when I showed them how to use an Ohmmeter as a lie detector; the conductivity of human skin changes when you sweat, and the theory is you sweat when you lie.

You would think that such an opportunity would have turned itself into a science fair project, but that never occurred to me. I was just playing catch-up with things that were already known. I was in no position to make new discoveries with the multimeter, and I knew it.

On the other hand, I did learn enough about electricity I was able to construct a quiz-box that buzzed and blinked when you connected the answer to the question. I learned enough about soldering to disassemble a broken radio and install its indicator lights in the eye sockets of a plastic skull that had an unfortunate encounter with my sister's fist late one night. I learned to test batteries, and to see if electrical outlets were live, and a lot of other fact-based things. The real effect it had on me was when I went to college I gravitated towards things electrical in my physics courses. I learned what I could on my own, and eventually returned the kit to its owner.

There was another side effect of the visit to the pool hall. I knew people were watching me, and expected me to do more than just get good grades. Eventually, I realized that that was more important than understanding Ohm's Law.

The Boy Who Skipped

There's an old joke that goes: *When the world comes to an end, I'm moving to Kentucky, because everything happens 20 years later there.* Like many of the other infuriating jokes at the expense of "hillbillies," this one has a kernel of truth in it. I became aware of this because my family moved from Ohio to Kentucky halfway through my 6th grade year in the early 1970's, and I had entered Viper Elementary in Perry County, Kentucky.

It quickly became obvious that the school I attended in Kentucky was not moving kids along as quickly as my school had in Ohio.

I remember learning about degrees and angles and protractors in the fifth grade in Ohio. The topic didn't get introduced into our education in Viper, Kentucky until the sixth grade. *Late* in the sixth. Seventh grade found me so far ahead of my peers, and annoying everyone (students and teachers) by answering all of the questions, blowing the curves, and being a little rude about the slow pace that one day, I was called into the hall outside the classroom to have a "conversation" about it.

At first it was just a knock on the door. My teacher suspended the lesson and answered the door. Then he turned back to the room and gestured to me. "Jeff Mason," he said, as I looked up in surprise. *Again?*

This time Mr. Caldwell and my *mother* were in the hallway. When the rest of the class saw her and the principal waiting for me in the hall, there was the traditional rolling chorus of "ooooOOOHHHoooo!" I rolled my eyes as I left. *I didn't do anything wrong. It's probably something else.*

The hallway was only six or seven classrooms long, but it seemed to stretch on forever, notably empty and silent except for murmurs from classrooms and the hum of fans futilely attempting to redistribute the heat of the day. Mr. Caldwell stood beside my mother, and my teacher stepped into the hall and joined us. I think my teacher was Bobby John

Combs, who was also my bus driver, but I'm not completely sure I remember who my teacher was that year.

"Son, we've decided that going to the 8th grade here is a waste of time for you," the principal said. He always wore a tie with a short-sleeve buttoned white shirt even on the hottest of the humid, sticky days of early summer, and true to form he was wearing one today. He was also wearing a smile, which confused me.

I raised my eyebrows, but said nothing. Was I being kicked out of class? Why was he smiling?

"What we were thinking is that it might be in your best interests to go on to Devitt H. Caudill Memorial High School next year. What do you think about that, Jeffery?"

Skip the eighth grade? I thought. *But I'm not ready!* Thoughts of the slow pace and the ease of work I'd encountered so far vanished from my mind. I'd go from being a year ahead of everyone academically to being a year behind chronologically. What did that mean to me personally? My mind whirled.

"Um, what about the stuff I'll miss in 8th grade?"

"Your teachers tell me that you're basically a year ahead in every subject and reading at 11th grade to college level already," replied the principal. My teacher nodded. I was surprised. This was the first time anyone had said anything formal to me about being more advanced than the rest of my class. I didn't *feel* advanced. Just... focused.

"He read that Carl Sagan book in less than a week," said my teacher.

I had read *Intelligent Life in the Universe* in long marathon reading sessions over several days, and eventually learned how to use the formulas in the back to compute the Schwartzchild radius of a black hole (and taught myself from my calculator manual how to use scientific notation to finish the problems); but once again I was reticent. No one

18

I knew, except maybe a kid down the road named Don I played with sometimes, even knew what a black hole *was*. I learned about novas and nebulas, and probably got my initial interest in science and astronomy, from sneaking downstairs at midnight when we lived in Ohio to watch reruns of *Star Trek* (the original version) after carefully twisting our old black-and-white television away from the open bedroom door where my mother snored and my father slept fitfully trying to ignore it. I got caught once when I inched the volume up too loud, and got yelled at for waking up my parents and being up without permission.

None of the television stations we could pick up in Hazard transmitted *Star Trek.* They went off the air at midnight, right after a brief newscast out of Lexington and the obligatory rendition of the Star Spangled Banner. Reruns were limited to *Gunsmoke* and *The Little Rascals.*

"He did win that science fair, too," said my mother. I had won the 6th grade science fair shortly after joining the school with a design for a cryogenically-frozen perpetual motion machine I had imagined after reading a library book on low-temperature physics– not a textbook or a graduate level thing, that would not have been in the school library in the first place–but an age-appropriate science book written for middle schoolers. I had been the first student to check it out, I noted. The design was based on the idea that cryogenically frozen wires had no electrical resistance and thus no loss of energy. Certain mechanical parts had been demonstrated to be frictionless under those conditions as well. Why not use a cryogenic motor to turn a cryogenic generator, which powers the cryogenic motor? With no friction, and no energy loss in the wires (the wires in my makeshift electrical kit would sometimes get *hot)* the thing should run *forever.* A perpetual motion machine. It won't work–I learned years later–because of the conservation of energy and the fact the thing would radiate buckets of electromagnetic energy– but as this is not a physics text, I'm going to have to let that go for now.

One of the judges said, "I don't know what you're talking about, but you sure as heck did your homework on this one," as a cluster of people surrounded my simple hand-lettered poster, flanked by the traditional clay volcano filled with baking soda, baby rabbits in cages, and coal-stained shirts soaking in different brands of detergent.

"Well, son?" said Caldwell. "What do you want to do?"

I looked at my mother. She was a small, wiry woman, already hunched over from years of hard work and worry. At age twelve I was already taller than she was. Like my sister, she had coal-black hair, worn straight and simple. Today she was dressed in a brown polyester pants suit, the same thing she wore when paying bills or going to town for some official purpose. Serious business.

She shrugged, peered at me with her hands shoved into her jacket pockets, and said, "It's up to you."

I was a little worried about the academic preparation issues, but I'd been through similar transitions before (by this time in my academic career I had already attended five different schools in four districts) and I didn't think it would be a big deal. What about social issues? My only real friend was Don, and he was held distant from me by my mother ever since she had been offended that Don's parents made me dig weeds in the potato garden for several hours when I stayed overnight to visit once.

"Kids ought not to have to work all the time," my mother had said. "They need time to be kids now, or they never will be. Believe you me, I know what it means to lose your childhood."

This went back to her hard and laborious upbringing during the depression years. Mom worked in the fields and kitchens and yard and such since she was old enough to lift a hand. Such were the conditions in Eastern Kentucky that the Depression came and went and the region hardly noticed; for a time, the rest of the country came down to our level, then, later, most of the nation prospered as the people in the hollows and bottoms of Kentucky went on, unperturbed, unchanged and unnoticed. The same thing, I noted some years ago, happened again during the dot-com boom.

Maybe in high school I could make some *new* friends. I had never had many, and the few I had enjoyed the most I had left behind when we evacuated from Ohio. (I know you want to know why we evacuated, but I'm going to have to save that story for a little later.)

If I had been a little more worldly, or thought about it for a long time, I would have considered the equation

one year younger than everyone +
short kid+
from ohio+
academically gifted+
no friends
= high school misery

and said *no*. But, once in a while, I figured, you either step through the door to a new adventure, or you wonder the rest of your life what it would have been like if you had.

I imagined my future self looking back, trying to talk to me through some esoteric time portal. *Why the heck didn't you jump on this when you had the chance,* said the sad, older me, shaking his head. *Instead you just wasted your time. There's only so much time to learn things in a human lifetime. Get started now!*

So I said *yes*, but I wasn't as confident as my voice claimed to be.

Caldwell produced an envelope from his jacket pocket. "Here's your 8th grade diploma," he said. "I already signed it."

He must have known what I would do, I thought. *Or,* I thought, *if I had said no he could have just tossed it. It's just a piece of paper.* "Do I get to go to the 8th grade graduation this year?" Viper held a formal graduation ceremony for students leaving eighth grade. It never occurred to me that for some of my classmates it might be the last diploma they ever earned. Some of them didn't even earn *that.*

"I'm afraid not," he said. "We should keep this a little quiet from your classmates here at Viper, because otherwise every Tom, Dick and Delmer will want to skip 8th grade too. And frankly, there's not many of them as could do it. You're the first one we've had in a while now." *So there were other skippers.*

I nodded, and he shook my hand and handed me the 8th grade diploma.

"Congratulations, son, you've just graduated 8th grade," he said. He shook Mom's hand, swept his thick shock of black hair back from his forehead. He smiled, slapped me on the back and departed. I turned to go back in the classroom.

"Where you going?" she asked. "You heard the man, you've graduated from Viper. You're done." She grinned at me, her false teeth flashing white. She didn't smile much, probably a learned habit from years of having bad teeth until she surrendered and had the remaining teeth removed in favor of an entirely artificial upper plate.

I'm going to miss the last three days of school? I thought. *But what about my grades?* Then I realized it didn't matter; I'd *already* graduated. I had the diploma in my hand. No one in high school cares about your middle school GPA. Once you're done, it's done. I looked at my mom, who was obviously proud of me, and smiled. For some reason, the thought came to my mind that I had just saved her an entire year's worth of money on food, clothing, school supplies, and field trips. I doubt she ever thought of it that way. She probably thought I was stealing away one more year of living at home with the family, if she considered it at all.

All my life, for nearly as long as I can remember, people have told me how smart I was. I *liked* being smart. I got special privileges. My parents pampered me by letting me pursue my interests, even against their better judgement. The thing is, though, I've never really, down deep in my heart, *felt* smart. If someone asked me, "What's it like to be a gen-

22

ius?" I wouldn't know what to say. People *have* asked me that–mostly people I knew from school, but still.

Most people don't know how much front-end work it takes to *appear* to be smart. Not to mention the fact that I personally considered the root of my academic success lay 400 miles to the north, because it was mainly due to the slower pace of schools in Kentucky relative to those I attended in Ohio that I gained a real reputation for being bright in the first place.

Because I had a kick-start like that, I've always felt as if I'm somewhat of a sham in that respect; as if someone really smart is going to come along and expose me for the fraud I've been all these years. And of course whenever I admit that to people they don't believe me, or consider it a false modesty, and then they start in with that whole "you're a genius" claptrap again, so for the most part, I keep my uncertainties to myself.

I've met some *really* smart people in my time. When I have a conversation, today, with a PhD about how to interpret space probe data and set up observations with my students, it can take me a week to decompress the amount of information coming my way in an afternoon. College provided me with my first true academic challenges, and it damn near overwhelmed me. My attitude had always been that I just attacked academic problems early, without procrastination, and got help when I needed it. I forgot that for a while, and I suffered mightily in my sophomore year of college because of it. The risk to my major saved my collegiate academic career by making me *focus* again. Ironic, if you think about it.

Some people meet that challenge much earlier in their academic careers. Some people meet it much later. Some who fail to conquer the challenge of perhaps *not being quite smart enough* never recover, and never find out what might have been.

Most of the kids I went to school with weren't dumb. Some suffered from the lack of opportunity or enthusiasm of some of their teachers.

Some suffered from the lack of personal vision or having a mission, a niche for themselves in the larger world. They were perfectly capable of doing the work, but they didn't see the work as having any purpose, and without purpose or goals, it would be boring and a waste of time to learn *anything* the teacher tried to teach.

What made the difference for me was that I had had it drilled into me since I was small that schooling was my ticket out of poverty. "Work with your head, not with your back," my Dad would say. "Your back won't last. But your brain will."

Still, it's hard to keep an even keel when you're surrounded by people you love and respect, and all you hear is how smart you are, how gifted, how talented, how .... *everything*. The day you start believing everything people say when they praise you beyond your ability is the day you stop wanting to learn new things. Once you stop growing and having adventures, what fun would that be?

Complacency is the *enemy*. Taking the easy way out of school work is a *death sentence* for your brain.

I stepped back into the doorway and looked back in my 7th grade classroom. Already it seemed small, in the way that elementary school rooms seem small when adults go back to visit. That wasn't the first or last time I had a sense of being displaced in time, conscious of what my future self would think when confronted with a memory that was still happening. Kids were still looking at me, wondering if I had finally managed to get myself in trouble. I got my books, told a couple of people I knew that I was going home, nodded in the teacher's general direction, and left.

Simple as that.

That's how I became the Boy Who Skipped 8th Grade, and one of the reasons I wound up in Miss Caudill's English and Drama classes a year early, just in time to meet Lyn Anderson, the most beautiful girl I had ever seen, the first girl I ever loved with all my heart, and who changed my life forever.

My Freshman Year Begins

My first day of high school was somewhat nerve-wracking, as I suppose it is for everyone. Devitt Caudill High School, by most people's standards, was not a large place, but it was probably one of the largest buildings I had ever visited at the time. It was more than twice the size of Viper, although it housed only half as many grade levels. It was perched halfway up a hill on the edge of the moderately expansive bottom land that flattened out the wrinkled hillsides a little as various hollows fed into the North Fork of the Kentucky River. It was located in the small town of Jeff (no, I wasn't named for it) that had a single stop sign, a gas station, a post office, a church and a couple of other nondescript businesses of less than permanent character. Kentucky Route 7 intersects the main road (Ky. 15) that goes through the town. "Fi-teen" was the closest four-lane road to my parent's home.

I had trouble finding classrooms despite the tiny size of the school. I was shorter than most of the boys, but not dramatically shorter. I was slender in those days, with dark brown hair, and an innocent face that some said made me look like a Beatle wannabe. I had to maneuver my way around giant upperclassmen, which I suppose most freshmen have had to endure.

I barely understood my schedule; in Viper the school was K-8 (and still is), and while we did shift between rooms a bit, we all did it together, as a unit, and all of the rooms were less than 20 feet apart. I kept checking my pocket to make sure that I hadn't lost the handwritten schedule that told me which room to look for next. The last-minute schedule, not in the regular sequence of events because I missed the 8th grader registration and orientation, had been handed to me by a harried school secretary who had no time for explanations. This was the first time, I remember thinking, that I figured out that rooms that all start with 100- were on the *first* floor, and rooms with 200- were on the *second* floor.

Our high school was small, only about 400 students total. My graduating class was 77 people. We were crowded into a 1950's era brick schoolhouse consisting of a long hallway about 7 or 8 classrooms long, two stories tall, with an adjacent band room and a permanent "portable" classroom added later for special education. Colonel Devitt Hayword Caudill Memorial High School was named after a school board member instrumental (I assume) in getting funding to build the school in the first place. It was what is known as a consolidated school because it brought together the students from several different, smaller schools and allowed them to share the benefits of a larger school such as a greater variety of courses and a bigger pool of people from which to select athletic teams. (The real reason, of course, is that it is cheaper to pay one principal to work twice as hard than pay two principals each with a manageable job.) Whatever preceded it must have been *much* smaller. In the present day, it has been absorbed into a still larger school which effectively serves much of the entire county. The Devitt H. Caudill building itself is used as an office building now, what fragment of schoolyard there was now dedicated to parking, the wooden staircase winding down the hill to the store at the foot of the hill decayed and abandoned, half lost among the tall grass that grows in the summer.

"You'll be fine," said Mom. "You're smarter then half of them teachers down there at Devitt what gets paid for jes' setting around on their *ass* all day." When Mom wasn't angry or shouting, the few curse words she uttered she sort of squeezed out like toothpaste; sparingly, and with effort. Sometimes you could barely hear them; when she said *ass* all you could really hear was the hissing of the s'es: *sss.*

Somehow I doubted my high school teachers would share the my mother's opinion. I know *I* didn't.

I was terrified of making some mistake, such as the time when I was put into the 8th grade spelling bee as a 7th grader and I was the first one out (*glacier* doesn't follow the i-before-e-except-after-c rule). "You weren't so smart as you thought you were," said my classmates. Another time a fifth grade teacher had asked me a series of questions attempting to find some vocabulary word I didn't know. "Ontogeny recapitulates phylogeny!" he barked at me. "Whazzat mean, boy?" I had no idea what he was talking about, which made him snicker. "Y'see, boy? Y'don't know *everything*."

I allowed as I had never claimed to, and there were *huge* amounts of things I didn't know, but he never did acknowledge that I was attempting to be the very humble person he was ridiculing me for not being.

Entering the 8th grade bee wasn't *my* idea in the first place, but I *had* agreed to it. These memories burned in my mind as I worked my way down the hall that first day. Skipping the 8th grade wasn't my idea, either, but once again, I'd *agreed* to the scheme.

I navigated carefully through the beginning of my freshman year, amused and embarrassed at the attention for skipping 8th grade for about a month. I was introduced to the principal as the "That Boy From Viper Who Skipped 8th Grade," and that made me sympathetic with Harry Potter years later. I dutifully spent my days taking notes and filling in fill-in-the-blank questions from Mrs. (Wilhelmina) Caudill's science classroom chalkboard, plodding my way through Health & PE, cranking out equations in Miss (Mary) Caudill's Algebra I, and diagramming sentences for Miss (Cheryl) Caudill. Perhaps a quarter of our teachers were one variety of Caudill or another. Harold, Halford, Byron, Wilhelmina, Cheryl, Nervis, Dary, Pauline and Loretta and God knows who else. Heck, even our *school* was named after Col. Devitt H. Caudill. (You pronounce Devitt with emphasis on the second syllable, De-VITT.) For those of you who don't know, a Kentucky Colonel is a title bestowed by the governor on pretty much anyone who ever had any connections whatsoever with the Old Boys Network, was owed a favor by the governor, was remotely famous, in some cases infamous, or relatively wealthy.

Mr. (Byron) Caudill, the principal, didn't think much of me when he first met me. "Too short for basketball, ain'tcha boy," was his first comment to my face.

"Yes, sir," I replied. In Kentucky we always called our elders "sir" even when they insulted us.

"Well, I sure hope you're as smart as everyone says you are," he said. "You sure ain't gonna get an athal-letic scholarship." He grinned at me. I didn't know what to make of that; wasn't the point of high school to get an education to get ready for college, rather than seeking an athletic scholarship as an end unto itself? Or rather, wasn't the point of an athletic scholarship to get an education, and if you were going to get an education anyway without the assistance of basketball, why bother with the whole bouncing-running-throwing-keeping score part?

"Are you sure you're up to high-school work, son?" he said. He peered at me over the top of semicircular reading glasses perched on the end of his nose. He was probably in his 40's or 50's, about the same age as my parents, but without the worldworn, weary look of what my father would call a *"real* workin' man." He had a rim of hair bravely defending the open territory on the top of his head. Whenever I spoke to him, he made me feel as if I was being tested and I didn't even know what the questions were really about. "I have had my doubts about them cutting out the eighth grade for some of these students," he continued before I could compose an answer. "I don't really think most of them are ready for it. They're not mature enough yet." *I wonder who the other skippers were,* I thought. *But I'm the only one from Viper this year.* "Well?"

"I don't know if I am or not," I said. "I've never done high school work, so I can't rightly judge whether or not I'm ready to do it."

He looked at me with his mouth twisted to one side, trying to decide if this was a serious answer or some sort of smart-alecky remark.

"Well, boy," he said, folding his arms on his chest, "I reckon you're about to find out. Good luck." He dismissed me with twitch of his head. I left, wiping sweat from my forehead. *That could have gone better,* I thought.

I had had few friends at Viper, and was invisible to the former 8th graders who were now my classmates. None of the people in my classes were my friends, or were inclined to be. *Yer not from around here, are ye boy?* was a phrase I'd heard more than once, despite the fact I had been born in Perry County like the majority of my classmates. Except for my older sister and a couple of cousins older than I, with whom I shared no classes, I didn't know anyone. It's nearly impossible to go to school in Eastern Kentucky and not be related to *someone*.

The high school had several feeder elementary schools, and those few faces I recognized were absorbed into the mass of people who crowded the hall at every class change. Even a small school can seem crowded when you put everyone into two narrow hallways simultaneously.

I'd always made some friends among the slide-rule set whenever we made one of our frequent school district shifts in Ohio; but it's different in high school. An outsider behaving as an outgoing person, introducing themselves to strangers, is considered *odd*, a curiosity almost.

I was so anxious to prove myself, and so used to being on my own in a new school, that I think I was kind of numb to the isolation and loneliness I had brought upon myself, and just accepted it as part of the Smart Kid's Burden, just another thing that had to be endured like Finding A Way To Keep The Obnoxious Bully From Copying Your Homework and Always Getting Picked Dead Last For P.E. Teams.

Days would pass when, if I didn't answer a question for a teacher, I wouldn't speak to anyone, about anything, all day long. Sometimes days at a time would pass where I would issue only one word, curt responses in social settings. I was terribly lonely and had no idea at all what to do about it. Once you start off in a group of people as shy and reserved, it's really hard to break out of it and show your true colors. Your classmates will either think you're weird, on drugs, in love, or something worse. So those first few impressions were critical. And mine were: quiet, unassuming, loner, nerdy. Like millions of other bright, but socially isolated kids, in every community in the country, I felt trapped by the first impressions that other people held of me.

I've been a teacher long enough that I know that happens to a *lot* of people. Not everyone. But more than you think.

Anyway, to give you a taste of high school life in that time and place: I even had a study hall. In those days we could schedule an hour to study, and during that hour you could do special things like practice basketball if you were on the team, or sleep, or get all of your homework done so you didn't have anything to actually do at home. You can guess which of those three I did. When I finished I doodled cartoon aliens zooming around the universe. Endless drawings of the Starship *Enterprise* adorned my notebooks and binder covers.

These days we don't have study hall because the adults are frightened of what an oversized class of teenagers with no specific assignment might do. They might organize, form a mob or some whole new gang no one's ever heard of before with some distorted spanish-sounding name ending in a vowel, or perform identify theft with their cell phones. I guess it was a more innocent time then, although we didn't feel particularly innocent. Probably everyone feels that way about their childhood.

To Be or Not

One October day during my freshman year I was sitting in health class, having finished all of my homework in the period of time between lectures. I had read the chapter we were currently studying, which was sufficient preparation for the worksheets and quizzes we would be offered later. There was a timid knock at the door, and my older sister Jane appeared.

Jane is three years older than I. Like mom she had long straight black hair. Unlike mom she would often grin widely, with an infectious smile that made you want to grin whenever you were blessed enough to see it. She had a big gap between the front teeth of her toothy grin. I thought she was secretly self-conscious of the gap, but she never complained about it that I remember hearing. She had no middle name, which I guess is pretty unusual, especially in the South. (I don't have a middle name either. I like to tell my astronomy students that my middle name is "Space.") Jane was a good student, and often helped me with my homework, especially when I was younger. Simply because she was a good student, not a party girl or a druggie, that reduced her circle of friends to a few good kids and a number of acquaintances. She was somewhat heavy then, and I teased her mercilessly about it as brothers do. That's one of the things that led me to believe in karma, because now she's much smaller than I am. What goes around, comes around.

Jane entered the room and asked our teacher C.J. Holt if he minded if I went with her somewhere. Holt was a career P.E. teacher, destined for some assistant principalship or associate superintendent of something or other in the future. If you were an athlete, you called him "C.J.," and if you were anyone else, it was "Mr. Holt." He was a thin man with jet-black hair, with a coach's air of worldliness and wisdom (as seen from a 13 year old's perspective). He also had this way of walking that was almost *languid.* He just sort of flowed along the floor, like spilled mercury crawling along the top of a table (don't ask.) I got along well enough with him because I didn't talk back and attempted to do what I was told without complaining or whining, which was sufficiently rare, apparently, to be noteworthy in his mind.

He gave me a discerning look, and said "You got your work done, son?" I nodded, surprised he needed to ask. "All right, but don't make a habit out of it," he said, *languidly* rippling his entire arm at me in dismissal. Jane waved at me (*Cmon!*), and I motioned her over to my desk.

"What's going on?" I asked.

"Miss Caudill wants to see you," she replied.

My English teacher? Did I forget to turn something in? I asked, "What for?"

"She wants you to help read a play."

"You mean act? On a stage?"

"Yeah."

"No thanks." I started to put my head down on my desk where it had been before my sister arrived. Mr. Holt looked at us, with a *What's taking so long?* look in his eyes. I swear it took him all of three seconds just to turn his head towards us.

"Oh, come on, you'll *love* it," she said, pleading with her eyes.

I shook my head *no* again.

"I *promised* her you'd come."

Huh. On consideration it seemed a small price to pay to keep the peace with Jane at home, and it *would* get me out of Health. In another one of those odd moments of clarity I thought: Would I have to answer to my future self if I passed an opportunity to do something new and interesting instead of filling out worksheets and dozing in a chair? Why else had I agreed to go to high school early in the first place?

I got up and nodded at the coach. He grunted in reply, smoothly tilting his chin slightly upward and somehow aiming it at the door at the same time.

I reluctantly followed her down the hall. A few days ago I was standing talking to Jane in the hall when someone asked her if I was her little brother. She allowed that I was, reluctantly it seemed to me. In a little jab of little brother vengeance, I commented to Jane and her friend that by the time she graduated, people would ask *her* if she were *my* older sister. Later I regretted the jibe as she really hadn't done anything to deserve it, but she took it in stride even as she recalled it, and told me it came true, before she graduated. We were three years apart in age, but because I skipped a year, I was a freshman while she was a junior.

Miss (Cheryl) Caudill was my freshman English teacher. She and everyone else pronounced her name *Shur-ull*. She was currently teaching us sentence diagramming, which was close enough to graphing that it made me really enjoy English. Frankly, I don't remember much else I learned in freshman English; unlike most people, I don't view that as equivalent to not learning anything. Like most of my other classes, freshman English was not inspirational to me but it became part of the general background knowledge I operate with on a daily basis. As far as sentence diagramming goes, I am sure that was vanishingly rare then, and even more so now because it is "pedagogically unsound" to teach sentence diagramming these days.

Miss Caudill ran a reasonably tight ship in freshman English. I remember we had to start each class by carefully lining up the feet of our desks on designated cracks and rows in the tile floor; when papers were written and ready to turn in they had to be folded *lengthwise*, no staples (because none were provided for teachers by the office) with name, assignment title, class period, and date on the outside of the left edge of the paper. She kept papers bundled with rubber bands, bundling them like stacks of money to be deposited in a safe somewhere. Grading was done in red pencil with the final score circled in a swirl.

A few steps away from my PE class I arrived at Miss Caudill's class-room. It was dramatically different than the sparse container of desks and sleeping students I had just left. They had recently renovated the school by painting all the rooms, adding drop ceilings, and fixing window locks, etc. The door was covered with paint, too, bright orange and yellow and red, and looked like there had been fingerpainting and even feet walking up the side of the wall. My sister told me Athena Hamnill had been lifted by some of the boys as she walked up the door with paint on her feet. Every teacher was allowed to select the color for their room. Mr. Simmons (a redhead) picked green. Mrs. Hayword (Senior English and all that implies) selected bright orange, the better to keep her students awake, or possibly just stunned. Miss (Cheryl) Caudill's room, on the inside, was primarily blue. Even the floor tile had been colored to match the decor. In today's more corporate school environments such personal choices would never be allowed.

As I arrived in Miss (Cheryl) Caudill's room, I looked at the pair of happy-sad faces (*Comedy* and *Tragedy*, I learned later) that were painted on a segment of plastered wall between two windows, one of which was open. There was, of course, no air conditioning, and few fans. A tattered carpet covered the rear third of the room, and a beat-up couch resided there as if it had been there forever. From the smell of it, it probably had. Strange sparkling fabrics and expandable hosiery, feather boas, hats and other costuming materials were strewn about. In fact, the room looked like a tornado had struck, in contrast to the neatly organized room I inhabited during the day during freshman English.

The desks which were normally set into rigid lines during the day were scattered almost randomly about leaving a large empty space in the center front of the room. The room contained perhaps a dozen upper-classmen lounging around holding small folded-up copies of what I presumed were *scripts*. I walked into the room and maneuvered be-tween the jumbled desks to get out of the way. There was, I noted, someone sitting on the floor on the opposite side of Miss Caudill's desk.

Sitting cross-legged, perusing a script held in both hands, was the most beautiful girl I had ever seen. She was wearing close-fitting jeans, sandals, and a blue blouse. I glanced at her and glanced away and then back, as if my brain were unable to decide if it was socially acceptable to stare.

Miss Caudill was talking to someone, and that afforded me the opportunity to look again at the girl, whose golden blonde hair flowed off of her shoulders, framing her face. She looked up and saw me, and *smiled.*

Her eyes were blue, and her lips were covered in some sort of lipstick. Her hair was feathered in the style of the time, swept back from her face, which had rounded cheeks, a smallish chin, and an impish button nose. As she noted me staring at her, her smile widened slightly. *Her clothes match her eye color*, I thought. *Why is this the first time in my life I've ever noticed someone's eye color matching their clothes?*

Other incoherent thoughts raged through my head as my past, present, and future incarnations argued for priority.

Then Jane nudged me, and the moment, as they say, was lost. *What? Whaaat?* I started to say, but then saw Miss Caudill looking at me.

Miss Caudill was perched on *top* of her desk, legs crossed, directing students as if she were directing traffic, with her hands. This was considerably different than her behavior during English, where she directed the class mostly from behind her desk and often from a seated position. Miss Caudill smiled at me, and hopped off the desk.

"There you are, Mason," she said. She often referred to us by our last names. She asked, "Have you ever been in a play?"

36

"Not really." I replied. Would I just be a person carrying a cardboard tree, like in an elementary school pageant?

"That's all right," she said. "You can learn as you go." She picked up a copy of a paperback book and rifled through the pages. "Here we go. Now let me explain what is happening here."

"Benny here plays Petruchio," she said, pointing at a tall, dark haired upperclassman. He stood with his arms folded, as if he might spontaneously decide to leave, hopping in a car or on the back of a motorcycle, departing for parts unknown. He had hair that covered his neck and hung below his collar, cut tapered in rock-star fashion. Mostly it hung straight down. He had these long bangs that nearly reached his eyes, which I always though looked cool but would be annoying in practice. It seemed to me that he had been around the block a few times, most likely at excessive rates of speed. He looked like he might be one of those new crop of guys popular in the early disco era who spent time on his hair beyond just washing and drying it. Defined muscles flexed at where his biceps emerged from his black short sleeve shirt. *Best not irritate this fellow,* I thought.

"Petruchio is a young wealthy aristocrat who is looking for a bride," said Miss Caudill, pointing at Benny. "You, on the other hand, will be Grumio, his manservant."

"Man...servant?" I said. "Like a butler?"

She chuckled. "Not exactly. More like ... a sidekick." OK, *sidekick* any thirteen-year-old boy could understand. I nodded. I noted out of the corner of my eye the blonde-headed girl was looking at us. When she saw me look back at her, she rose, and I couldn't help but notice the tightness of her jeans and the ...*interesting* curvature they revealed. She retreated to the back of the room. I followed her progress as long as I could without turning away from Miss Caudill.

"A lazy ne'er-do-well drinking buddy sidekick," Miss Caudill continued. "Not an assistant as much as much as loyal servant that is just competent enough to keep his job. Raynard, give him your script," she continued. Raynard Smith, a tall junior with a crop of poorly-controlled red hair and a loping (not *languid)* gait, handed over his script. Handwritten at the top of the script was the word "Grumio" in Miss Caudill's elaborately tilted script, along with strange coded notations such as XUSR, USL, Face DSR, and so on. Bits and pieces of the Shakespearean dialog were crossed out with lines through the text. On a somewhat more ominous note, there were signs of extensive, and repeated, erasures.

"Stand there," said Miss Caudill. She was a large woman, with dark coppery-colored hair set high on her forehead. She had moved behind her desk after arranging us, and now was sitting astride a chair turned backwards as a man would. She was also graceful for a large woman. I noted how she pointed her toes as she walked, and seemed to *glide* along the floor as she moved. (I know it seems I'm a little overly concerned with how people moved, but believe me I didn't think about it at the time. It's something you sort of notice in retrospect once you learn *how* to walk... ask any dancer and they'll know what I mean.) She usually wore pants suits and that was true that day. I remember thinking her favorite color was brown since so many of her clothes were that color. She was leaning over the back of the chair making it tilt up forward on two legs in the fashion that would have caused any other teacher to smack a ruler on a desk and declare that a toppling was imminent. She pointed at an X marked on the floor in masking tape.

Standing on an adjacent X was Benny. It was probably the first time he had ever laid eyes on me, even in a school of 400. That could have been due to the fact that the top of my head was even with the bottom of his chin, more or less.

"You can't be serious, Caudill," he said. He always called Miss Caudill "Caudill." As if she were the only one.

"I'm dead serious," she said. "You need someone smaller than you to play against, and Raynard is too big, so he can be Biondello instead.

We tried to cast Pat as Grumio, but she dropped out because it's a man's part. Hoss here is a small fellow. *He* can be Grumio." She said, looking at me but speaking to Benny, "Start reading at the top of page twelve." She looked at me again. "He is going to get you to try to knock on the door, but you think he means for you to hit *him* instead. That's the joke." She waved her hands in little excited circles as she talked. She seemed so *animated* about it all. This was completely unlike her behavior in English class, where she was much more business-like, less friendly, always behind the desk, and... less *cheerful.*

"Here, sirrah, knock me here and knock me soundly," Benny said, in what seemed to me to be a fair facsimile of a British accent. There was no door to knock upon, but Benny gestured to the wall, as if a door were there.

"Uh," I said, looking around. I was still trying to wrap my head around why she referred to me as *Hoss* when Hoss Cartwright was a great big strapping fellow. "What am I supposed to do?"

"Just read the words next to where it says 'Grumio'," she said.

"Oh," I said. "Knock sir, whom should I knock? Grumio assumes a fighting stance," I said, in what must have been the worst possible delivery of that line in theatrical history. Everyone laughed, but they were quickly *shushed.*

"Don't read the part in the brackets, child," said Miss Caudill. "Those are directions that tell you what to do with your body."

"Oh. Uh, sorry." *Duh. That's obvious. Why am I having so much trouble engaging my brain?* I thought. Not realizing what would be the simplest explanation, my next thought was *Where's that girl?*

"Villain, you shall knock me here and knock me soundly!" shouted Benny. I was so startled I almost dropped my script. *Focus.*

"Why, master, has any man here... refused your worship?" I read haltingly.

"Stop," said Miss Caudill. "It says 'rebused,' not 'refused.'"

"Caudill, this ain't gonna work–" began Benny. He was speaking to her, but looking at me.

"*Hush*," she commanded, and surprisingly, he did. We went through about two pages of the lines, haltingly, and then did it again, more smoothly. I wasn't quite so befuddled as the first time. Just when I was starting to feel as if I was getting the hang of the pronunciation of the words, she stopped us again. She looked at my sister. "You said he was funny. He's not funny." She looked at me. "You're not funny, Hoss."

My sister, arms crossed across her chest and one knee bent, knew her reputation was at stake, so she gave me a stare worthy of Lucy Van Pelt as she said, "Use one of your funny voices."

"Which one?" I said. I wasn't, as they say these days, quite with the program yet.

At home I liked to imitate famous people, and was a big fan of Rich Little. Most of my impressions were my impression of Rich Little doing people I'd never seen for myself. (*"Will you shut up talking with those God-damn stupid voices! I work hard all day and don't need to hear that–"*) My father's opinions didn't stop me, though. He didn't like it when I whistled, either. *That damn pucker makes you look like you got an asshole in your face,* he would say occasionally. I honestly don't think he was deliberately trying to be mean to me; he never called me *stupid* or, God forbid, *lazy.* He was just tired and grumpy from working so hard building houses and pouring concrete and driving untold miles to and from work.

I viewed him as a force of nature, not controllable or solvable, but avoidable. I took to whistling when I was alone.

"Richard Nixon," Jane said.

I shook my face to make my cheeks rattle to drop into "Richard Nixon" mode. Using my best impression of Rich Little's version of the gravelly president, I said "Why, master, has any man here rebused your worship?"

"No," said Miss Caudill. Now she was holding her head in her hands. "Can you make up a voice for someone who isn't too bright, sounds funny, but doesn't sound like someone on TV?"

I considered this and responded with a nasal sort of doofus voice, with a sort of hyuk-hyuk quality to it, an exaggerated goofy voice. At the last moment I added a lisp. "Knock, thir? Whom thould I knock?"

"That'll do for now," she said. We read a few more lines and she said, "I can't understand you now, tone it down," and I did. A few more lines later, she said "Your diction needs work. You're not enunciating when you say 'Has any man...'." She waved her hand in a circle to indicate she meant to include the entire line.

"My diction is fine, thank you very much," I said in a faux British accent. I thought I was smart for knowing what diction was, and confused knowing a definition with being able to do it. "I sound very educated, don't I?" I continued. However, when I said "don't I?" it came out without the "t"; which is why Miss Caudill said–

"*Donii* is the plural of *doughnut*. You mean to say "don'*t* I." Try again."

I felt the heat of my flushed face, and to add insult to injury, I dropped my script. As I picked it up somehow managed to twist around and noted the blonde girl– a young *woman*, really– was facing the back of the room and hadn't witnessed my minor humiliation at the hands of my English teacher. *Concentrate.* I repeated the line, enunciating the *t*.

"Better," she said. "Now say your line again with the funny voice."

"Why, Mathter, hath any man rebuthed your worthip?" I smiled broadly, finally letting the idea connect in my head that this was a *comedy* and I was being instructed to be *funny*. My brain felt like it finally managed to slip out of neutral and shift into a forward moving gear. I bugged my eyes out and feigned innocent indignation, raising my fists and gyrating them wildly.

"You're hired." She turned to my sister. "Go tell C.J. to let him stay down here the rest of the period, and I'll talk to him after school." She said, almost muttering, intended for Jane's ears alone, "He's pretty bad but at least he follows directions." That was the first time, but not the last, that I learned being able to take direction was more important than being talented.

"Um," I said.

"Yes, child?" she replied.

"Um, what am I hired for?" Everyone looked at me as if I were mad. Miss Caudill merely smiled.

"You're going to be in a play," Miss Caudill said. "Shakespeare. *The Taming of the Shrew*."

"Oh." *William Shakespeare,* my mind said to me. *To be or not to be.* Memory flashed; I had a sudden vision of myself reclined on my brother Bill's leather couch, reading encylopedia volumes for fun, thinking *some day you'll need to know almost everything you'll ever read.* I remembered a photo, a photo of a bust of Shakespeare on the page with the entry. He was bald on top with a rim of hair below, like our principal. *English playwright and poet. 1600's. Wrote a bunch of famous plays. Romeo and Juliet. Hamlet.* I didn't know anything about *Taming of the Shrew*, but I suspected it wasn't about training small rodents.

If it got me out of health class and the piercing stares of C.J. Holt, that was good enough for me. Not that I was actually asked what I wanted. As it turned out, I had plenty of other motivations for coming to rehearsal.

As we rode the bus home that evening, I sat next to my sister Jane. Her long black hair flipped in and out of the window we had lowered when the ride began.

"Well," said Jane. "What did you think of your first day of drama?"

"It was all right," I said. "I get to act goofy and no one tells me to stop."

"I didn't realize you would be such a ham," she said.

I looked at her and snorted like a pig. That made her laugh. I looked at her again, and after a couple of moments worked up the courage to ask, "Who was that girl?"

"What girl?"

What girl? "The girl, the *girl*, the blonde-headed girl in Miss Caudill's room," I managed to squeak. Oh, that wasn't smooth at *all.*

"Oh, that's Lyn Anderson," said my sister. "She's Miss Caudill's niece." My sister looked at me as if she was noting that it was the first time in my entire thirteen trips around the sun I had ever asked her about a girl. In all likelihood, it was. She raised an eyebrow at me. "She's a senior. She's nice."

Nice. "Um, yeah. I *thought* she looked older." She looked like a college student to me, or could pass for one easily enough.

"Why do you ask?"

A slight hesitation, less than a tenth of a second; still too long, though.

"No reason. Just curious."

Riiight said my sister's eyes. "She plays Katherine, who is in a lot of scenes with Petruchio. You're going to see a lot more of her. Petruchio and Kate and *Grumio* have a lot of scenes together." She pulled in her wayward hair from the open window and tied it into a ponytail with a rubber band. Watching me the entire time.

"Mmm," I grunted, noncommittally. My heart and my mind engaged in a high-speed race and kept me silent for the rest of the ride home. I pulled out the script Miss Caudill had given me to study and began reading the play from the first scene. The words on the page, curiously, did not match the words running through my mind at all. *If I get a chance to talk to her,* I thought, *what could I possibly say that she would find interesting?*

I had absolutely no idea. None of the various permutations and combinations of who I might be in the future had any bright ideas, either.

Story Tell

Editors and friends asked me why I decided to write this book, and what took me so long to start it. I guess I'm trying to figure out if I have fulfilled some of my childhood goals, and what my motivations were and what they should be today. Consequently I am sometimes telling a story so you can follow what I'm trying to delicately thread together, and other times, I'm sort of talking to myself and you're along for the ride. For the longest time I viewed storytelling as merely a means of delivering information to my students, or a form of entertainment; I never thought about storytelling in the larger context. Upon reflection, I think there's more going on than simple one-way communication.

Stories, it is said, can sometimes come alive. I believe this to be true. Not in the fantasy sense where a mythical creature can appear in your driveway and lead you to an enchanted forest, but in the sense where a story itself becomes a kind of living creature, reproducing itself through retelling, and evolving to become part of a cultural history. A living story influences the development of other stories, and minds, and lives. A story you tell yourself, repeated often enough, can even influence your own behavior, beliefs, and memories.

It's also said that everyone has a story that's simply waiting to be told. When a story can't wait to be told any longer, it emerges, unbidden, sometimes pleasantly, sometimes humorously, and sometimes tragically. I've held mine in me as long as the story will allow, and now it wants out to see the larger world of stories, to see if it can hold your attention, and be related to others, and perhaps have a small influence in the world.

This next part gets a little metacognitive and perhaps a bit preachy. Sorry about that; there's just some stuff I need to get off my chest that will help you understand the motivations for why this story exists and why I have to write it this way. Just bear with me, and it'll be over soon, I promise.

Our world today has changed almost without our noticing. The connected threads of our lives and the events beyond our own personal experiences have become interwoven into the daily cycles of our lives. In the past, it might have been possible to live in a town so isolated from the rest of society that there would be differences between our cultures so dramatic as to be startling.

That is no longer true. Continuing a process started with the town crier, the newspaper, radio and television, the internet beckons us to reach beyond our grasp. Almost every house has a television; finding one without is newsworthy and notable. Stories of multiple families sharing a phone line are now several generations in the past for many families; indeed, the entire concept of a party line must usually be explained to modern students by their grandparents, if they hear of it at all. Outhouses, drinking gourds, home canning, hand-dug wells, applesauce made from apples you picked yourself (cooked then squeezed through a clean cotton pillowcase), patchwork quilts, coal-fired furnaces and hot water available only from a stovetop all seem to be inventions of the distant past, as far removed from the experiences of today's youth as musket rifles and log cabins.

I am only 44 years old, and yet I once lived in such a time and place.

Even as I did, I knew my experiences were so rare as to be uncommon at the time; a subject of derision, of ridicule, or worse. Southerners of my generation were sharply aware that the division in the nation started in the Civil War extended into the mid-20th century and beyond. The most visible sign understandable to people not from the area is the fact that it is *still* politically correct to laugh at the antics of rural Appalachian white men. Of which I am one. As has been pointed out to me by African American friends, I can lose the accent, but they can't lose the skin color. Losing the accent, though, turned out to be a little more traumatic for me than almost anyone who knows me would guess.

As I have grown and had the opportunity to travel across America, it is obvious to me that the disassembly of our small towns continues, with town after town essentially decapitated—when its school is absorbed into a larger unit, when the post office closed in the face of efficiency, when the mom and pop "peanut" stores too expensive to compete even with the cost of driving fifteen miles or more to the nearest Wal-Mart close. We're in the process of losing something vital as we continue this process. In part, this book's purpose is to remind those people who read it, just a little, of what it was we once had. Our school was so small that there are many concrete, tangible, and financial reasons that it made perfect sense to consolidate it into the county school in the 1990's. The intangible things we had, a sense of friendship, of family, of history and purpose, now lost or forgotten, can't be measured quantitatively but they were nonetheless real.

There is, however, a price to be paid for having a small school. Our school was too small to wield a football team, and even our mighty basketball team did not even have its own enclosed basketball court—only half an asphalt basketball court with a single hoop, the other end occupied by the portable special education classroom which I don't recall entering in four years of high school.

Daily practices were sometimes held on this half-court, but the team regularly got on a bus and drove to the nearby town of Hazard, Kentucky to practice in the old Memorial Gymnasium. This is also where the team played (and lost) basketball games. There was a team back in the 1950's, I think, which had actually made it to the state championship in our division, but as far as I knew the team of my era never came close to winning anything except permission to run up and down the hallways without passes. Not that I paid that much attention to the basketball team. They didn't pay much attention to me, either. No one else did either, except in drama class, as far as that went.

In fact, my only real exposure to organized sports had come in the 5th grade in Ohio. I went out on the football field as instructed on the first day I attended that school and found my new teacher, the middle school football coach, organizing the team. I sat on the sideline.

"Get off yer butt and get over here, son," he grunted.

"Uh, Coach," I stammered. "I don't know how to play football."

"That's why you're here, son." Despite this promise of lessons and explanations, none ever came. In fact, the ability to quote that line is the only tangible benefit I remember gaining from that particular teacher. By 5th grade in north central Ohio, where we lived at the time, I suppose it was just assumed you knew how to play football through osmosis. Eventually, I and another physically inept boy were assigned the task of repeatedly crashing into each other, primarily to keep us busy while the real football game moved off elsewhere.

Eventually I started figuring things out. We didn't watch football, or any other sport, in my home. I'd never seen a game. But through simple observation it was pretty straightforward to see what the point was. The boy starting with the ball gives it to another boy, the quarterback. The quarterback, now possessing the ball, runs, and tries to avoid the other team, to deliver the ball to the goal post. Sometimes he throws it to another person, who carries it for him. If you touch the ball-carrier with both hands, play stops, and that is a desired outcome. Even in football-mad Ohio we didn't play tackle football in 5th grade.

One day, the star quarterback, an entire head taller than I was, decided to keep the ball and just flat out outrun the rest of the class. We were all well aware he was capable of it. To gain room to maneuver, he inscribed a wide, circular path from the center of the field around to the edge. All the other boys, except me and my erstwhile opponent, took off running after the quarterback, all following along in a large, circular pattern that would, if the quarterback continued on his present course, lead him within just a few feet of...me.

"Excuse me," I said to my opposite, and stepped aside to watch him miss our synchronized collision, and fall on his face on the ground with an *oomph!*

I trotted over to intercept the quarterback, who was looking anywhere but in my direction. Every other player on the team was pounding turf, trying to catch him.

As I approached the quarterback, the same boys who were trying to tag him– even the ones on the opposite side of the temporary teams formed for class play–were screaming at him to *look out! look behind you!* but he thought this was a trick and kept his focus on the nearest pursuers. For the most part, his own side was being singularly ineffective at stopping anyone from reaching him. The only thing saving him from being tagged was the other boys were all equally matched and all equally slow; no one in class could catch him, and he knew it.

Except, just that one time, *me.*

I ran toward him to intercept. He still approached me, facing backward and watching the boys from the real football game chase him. At the last moment he saw me, attempted to change course, and almost stumbled.

I adjusted course and tagged the quarterback solidly in the chest with both hands.

I wanted there there to be no question that I managed to actually do the dirty deed. The larger boy *squealed* in surprise, leapt aside, tripped, and fell down out of sheer astonishment. The ball fell to the ground. A whistle blew to stop playing. He had, in fact, *lost* a yard or two overall in the maneuver.

Everyone stopped running, still spread out in an elongated crescent curling around the field. Several of the boys gaped at me in amazement. The fellow I was assigned to "keep from moving from this here spot," my erstwhile opponent, still sat on the grass where I had left him. Our quarterback cast panicked glances at me, and at the grinning boys scattered downfield.

"What do you think you're doing?" he yelled at me, leaping to his feet.

"Tagging you," said the coach, who proceeded to ream out the quarterback for not being aware of his surroundings, yelling as coaches are wont to do, gesticulating wildly and stomping back and forth.

A few of the smaller players in the class came over and clapped me on the back. "He'll never get over being tagged by the slowest kid in the class," said one. I didn't know whether or not that was actually a compliment, but shrugged. *Why hadn't any of the other boys cut across the arc? They could easily have boxed him in and tagged him first,* I thought.

The next day, the coach said it would be O.K. if I sat out on the practice if I wanted to, and I cracked open a book and took advantage of the free time. The quarterback glared at me, outran the rest of the class repeatedly, and never spoke to me again.

If they'd give both sides one of those funny shaped balls then they wouldn't have to fight over the one they've got, I thought. That was effectively my last voluntary participation in organized sports. My attitude has matured, and I've known many fine student athletes and coaches who teach the value of teamwork, who keep themselves in good physical shape, and who try to motivate as many people on the team as can legally play to give kids purpose in school. But for me, at that time, at that age, it seemed pretty pointless; if you couldn't use strategy to defeat your opponent, I was essentially bored and not interested.

I didn't miss participating. I never did well with sports, lacking the coordination to hit, dribble, throw or catch the ball well. I have no idea if I was incapable of it or merely lacked opportunity and practice time. I didn't run fast, wasn't terribly strong and was probably a little under average height. I succeeded at dodge-ball only because I was considered a target unworthy of attention. I never won, but came in 2nd regularly, winning meaning you dodged all the balls and were the last one eliminated. The only sports I ever enjoyed in high school were dodgeball and kickball–kick a ball I could do, sailing it over the arms of

50

even the tallest boys in the class. I couldn't run fast enough to beat anyone in a foot-race, but if I kicked the ball hard enough and high enough, I didn't need to.

My father made no effort whatsoever to get me to participate in sports. His attitude was, all that energy could be better spent working to make money for the family. He would have called it a waste of time and effort.

"Must be nice to have the energy to run up and down the field like that," my father would have said. "I been working in *real* fields since I was 12, and I never had no time for such like that."

It was in this context that I sat through my winter physical education class my freshman year in high school, unable to go to a gym to play indoor sports because we didn't have an indoor gym and because bus rides to town were reserved for our basketball team. In all of my high school career I think I witnessed one basketball game–a girl's game, at that, and the only reason I was there was because one of my friends was playing. Not that I'd do anything other than what was required even if we had a real gym.

So, in the late fall and winter time we studied health. A little anatomy, a little stuff about communicable diseases (worms spread through the use of outhouses was illustrated in our book, which advised us to build the outhouses downhill from or at least a good distance away from the house and to never run barefoot in the dirt near the outhouse). At my home, we didn't have indoor plumbing (other than cold water from a ground well, which was deposited unceremoniously on the hillside after passing through the sink drain), so we dutifully built our outhouse near the edge of our property line, as far from the house as possible. Read into that whatever you will.

If you look at this minor digression in our larger tale in the context of storytelling, you can see that this relatively minor event in the life of a certain fifth grader was one of the many small influences that seemingly reached into his life and guided him, nudging him this way and that, choosing the path less travelled, as it were.

It made a difference in that it helped me to be ready for drama class, in that place, at that time. Sports held no interest for me, so drama filled the void.

All of us can point to events that would have changed their lives significantly had they turned out differently. There were many disparate threads that led our little troupe together for a few weeks in the fall of 1977, and none of us were quite the same afterward.

I'm still trying to figure out exactly how it happened.

You Can't Look It Up

I spent most of my childhood in Ohio, but I was actually born in Kentucky. The hospital where I was born, like so many other physical manifestations of my early life, no longer exists. We moved from Kentucky to Ohio before I was old enough to remember as part of a large-scale cultural migration of people leaving Eastern Kentucky looking for work, a sort of artificial selection that continues to this day.
We moved around a lot when I was young. I never went to kindergarten–in those days it was optional, and while I never really discussed it with my mother, I don't think it even really occurred to her. Kindergarten was something that rich people did, kind of like preschool is for kids today.

Before I started school, in Ohio, we lived in a trailer at the top of a hill behind a family named Dorfman. I have a distinct memory of telling my mother that I was *not* going to go to school, but somehow she managed to persuade me.

Later on, when I was in the first grade, the Dorfmans moved away to Pennsylvania (which, my sister assured me, was a land *really* far away) and let us rent the house, which we referred to as the Dorfman house from that point onward. I used to watch spectacular thunderstorms from the porch of that house, with lightning and thunder that would most likely make the evening news in weather-starved California today.

When I was in the second grade we moved to a different house at the top of a tall hill near a town in Ohio called Sparta. I don't remember a lot about that house except that the boys across the street fired off model rockets and I would watch them, from a distance. I was eight and too shy to walk across the road and introduce myself so I could see the rockets better. There was also an abandoned telescope in this house left over from the previous tenant. It wasn't much of a telescope, just a small 3-inch mirror mounted on the end of a cardboard tube using a ball-and-socket joint–probably an old Spitz moon scope. I couldn't make it work (because it was missing its eyepiece) so eventually I tore it apart and used the mirror for "experiments." These were not real experiments, but the kind that any eight-year old might do, focusing light on a piece of paper, looking at the distorted images of things in the mirror at various distances, just playing to learn or learning to play, I'm not sure which.

When I was halfway through the second grade we moved again, and I attended elementary school for half a year in a little town called Chesterville. The only thing I distinctly remember about this school is that I couldn't remember which bus I was on when the school day ended, so I had to look for the driver who was wearing a cowboy hat. I do remember a classmate of mine saying his father worked at Perkins Observatory in Ohio. I asked what that was, and he told me it was a place where they used telescopes to look at planets. I begged and pleaded with my parents to go visit the place, but they didn't see the point. Occasionally, on the bus, I could see a tiny white dome on a low hill in the distance. I wondered what it was like inside.

In the third grade we returned to the Fredericktown district, and I attended school at Fredericktown Elementary. We stayed there for a while, and I completed two and a half years of education at that particular school. That was where I first began to realize I was working faster than my peers. I remember learning to spell all the days of the week and the months of the year in second grade. That was kind of a big deal at the time, but of course now helicopter parents are drilling such spelling lessons into students before they even reach kindergarten. In third grade, I remember doing primitive algebra equations–the kind with missing boxes instead of variables.

This was in 1972, and the U.S. was nearly finished with the moon landings. I watched these with rapt attention although I am ashamed to admit that while I was old enough to remember the first moon landing, I don't remember watching it or hearing about it. I do remember the later missions where they used the rover to drive around, and the early Skylab missions that followed the abrupt closure of the Apollo program. This was about the same time as I snuck downstairs to watch

Star Trek reruns at midnight. In 1972 *Star Trek* was fresh enough that it still looked like it had high-quality special effects.

In February we had a Valentine's party and everyone was supposed to bring a box–but no one told me to decorate it. Apparently the rest of the class already knew. I remember how all the other kids had elaborate boxes, some of them decorated with crepe paper and flowers, and all I had was a plain shoebox. Since I was relatively new to them, I got only a few valentines in my box even though the teacher had instructed the class to make one for everyone. At least I didn't get a rock like Charlie Brown at Halloween.

Third grade is also where I began learning about astronomy. I bought a thin book called "Fun with Astronomy" by Mae and Ira Freeman at a book fair. It had the latest pictures of the planets from Mt. Palomar Observatory in California – which, by today's standards, were grainy and lacked detail. It explained how to set up a scale model solar system using pushpins and string to draw enormous arcs. It even showed how to make a pinhole camera with which you could measure the size of the sun. Pretty cool stuff for a 3rd grader. I worked through all the suggested activities and figured out how to scale the model solar system to make it larger so it would fit on a giant piece of poster paper for a school project. I just took all the measurements in the book and multiplied them by two.

I memorized the diameters and distances of the planets from the table in the book, and knew the names of the larger moons, including Titan and Ganymede, both larger than the planet Mercury. Why? Just because knowing a lot of things made me feel smart, I guess.

It always has seemed to me that the large Galilean moons and the larger moons of the solar system have been given short shrift. Many of them are larger than Pluto, and Pluto (until recently) was considered a planet since its discovery. I always thought that it seemed kind of prejudicial to allow Mercury to be called a planet, whereas Io, which is a much more interesting and active place, is relegated to obscure status as a moon of Jupiter. If it orbited the sun we wouldn't hesitate to call it a planet.

I suppose there's some sort of subtle message here in that I always felt less certain of myself because of what other people thought when they found out *where* I was born (*Appalachia? How ever did you survive, dear?*) and so I thought it seemed unfair that these interesting worlds are relegated to footnotes and tabular data instead of getting the attention they should in schools. I guess that's sort of silly since they are inanimate objects, but I suppose that speaks more to my thinking about myself than any emotional attachment to the moons of the solar system.

With respect to the recent brouhaha about the status of Pluto, I suppose you can tell I'm in the leave-well-enough-alone-and-let's-add-new-discoveries-to-the-list-of-planets camp. Don't get me started about Plutinos.

My favorite teacher in those years was my fourth grade teacher Esther Weller, who was really nice to me and encouraged me.

Among other things she did for me was obtain some lithographs from her son, who was an engineer who knew other engineers who worked for NASA. I remember one in particular was a picture of a hand controller for maneuvering thrusters on board the Apollo capsule used to deliver astronauts to Skylab, the first space station the United States had back in the early 1970's. I kept that picture for years, and even included it as decoration on a science fair poster I did some years later on space station design. I wrote letters to her for years, including one when I graduated high school.

During these years of my life, I was fairly isolated from affairs of national significance; my world consisted of my home and school, and we did not discuss such events of importance at either venue. I knew nothing of Vietnam, or Kent State for that matter despite the fact I was living in the state where it occurred at the time; I knew of the space program only because that was part of the evening news. What was said about matters Presidential or about the war was shielded from my eyes; war news and news of protests and civil rights was not fit for children, and my mother would turn off the news when these things came on, saying that the television stations had no respect for families. What I knew of the counterculture movement was distorted and made into caricatures by such shows as *Gomer Pyle* and even *Star Trek*, which always spoke about things that other shows avoided, if only through the mechanism of allegory and metaphor.

I had a great time in 6th grade in the fall of 1974, there in little Fredericktown, Ohio, especially in Mr. Cameron's class in the first half of the sixth grade. He reinforced my interest in astronomy by having a round-robin work day where we had to go to stations to learn about each planet. One question, in the Saturn station, said, "Does Saturn have seasons?" I looked in the book, and couldn't find the answer. I asked Mr. Cameron who said, "You can't look up that answer. You have to figure it out."

I never knew there were answers not contained in a book *somewhere*. It was probably the greatest lesson I ever learned from him.

Things were going great. Three other advanced students and I were given half an hour a day to attempt to teach ourselves Spanish with a record-based self-teaching class. I learned to play trombone enough to participate in the winter band concert. I developed enough hair to become somewhat embarrassed when I dressed out for gym. I had a couple of friends by then, and had even visited a few of the neighboring kids' homes, but that ended when they didn't come to my house, which my mother took as a slight against us; her rule was we couldn't go visit a kid who hadn't been over to visit us. That even applied to my cousins from the next county over.

Then, halfway through my sixth grade year, my older half-brother Ida died.

My mother had been married to a man named Combs before she married my father, and had given birth to two sons during that time. One was Bill and the other was Ida. Both boys were "born to be wild" and got involved with things which would leave my mother weeping at night in her later years. Ida paid the price (so did Bill, eventually) when he died suddenly in his late 30's of liver failure, undoubtedly brought on by excessive drinking. Ida is the reason I am a teetotaler to this day. Not because of what drinking did to Ida; rather, because of what his drinking did to our *mother*.

It's a hard thing to watch your mother weep, night after night.

Consequently, Mom wanted to move immediately from Ohio *back* to Kentucky, where both sons of her unhappy union with "that man" had lived and one still survived. Her reasoning was that if she had been around she could have kept Ida out of trouble, therefore, she should move "back home" to keep Bill straightened out.

It didn't help that Bill had gone AWOL from the Vietnam draft and spent some time in the penitentiary. He didn't dodge the draft out of some objection to the war; he just didn't want to fight, as far as I knew. I myself was too young to be worried about the draft in Vietnam, too old to be concerned with the Bush wars. I was born at the trailing edge of the baby boomer generation and the leading edge of Generation X. I was in high school when disco music ruled the airwaves, even if our access to discotheques with mirrored balls and flashing lights in the floor was limited in Perry County. Even if I had been from a more mainstream American family (whatever that means) from somewhere else in the country, I think I'd *still* feel culturally misplaced, if only because the 'top-40" music we heard on the radio, slotted between Bible-thumping sermons and Bluegrass twangs, was not much more than a brief fad on the American landscape. Baby boomers think we are too young to be of their generation; Gen-Xers think we are too old. Perhaps we need a new category; *Tweeners*, best symbolized by the movie *Airplane!* with its cultural in-jokes and parodies mirroring our cynical views about the significance of cultural generations in the first place.

Bill liked his beers as well as the next guy, at least at first. Later on, he liked them a lot *more*. In my younger years he was healthy and vital and had a little boy, my only nephew. Kept a little garden, as we did, and grew enough food to make a difference in the budget. Played the guitar. He used to play the *Batman* theme song for me when I asked. He kept a neat and well-decorated house, with nice leather couches that I liked to sleep on when I visited. He was a skilled carpenter like my father, and built several houses and worked in construction for many years. Eventually, though, poor choices in friends, worse choices for drugs (oxycontin, called *hillbilly heroin* by those who write about those who use it and *oxy-tocin* by my brother not realizing that was another substance entirely) finally precipitated his downfall. He used to keep his stash in multiple layers of plastic bags in the drop ceiling space above his bedroom, on the theory that drug sniffing dogs couldn't smell it because it was too far from their noses.

Repeated falls from grace, wildly fluctuating temper tantrums, declining health driven by the abuse and neglect, his never-ending put-downs and disparagement of his wife and son so obviously a reflection of his own lack of self esteem, led to near-total estrangement from everyone in the family. People like that–drug users, alcoholics, gamblers– are like an energy black hole, sucking in and demanding all the time and money and energy of everyone around them until there's nothing left, all forgiveness depleted, all last chances expended. Eventually no one could, or would, dedicate the energy necessary to keep him alive; thus he died as my brother Ida had all those years ago, albeit in a much more drawn out and torturous way.

So halfway through my sixth grade year, we *evacuated* during Christmas break from Ohio and moved to Kentucky. We knew we were moving only about a week before school dismissed for Christmas break. My father agreed to the move only on the condition that we never move again--he was tired of endlessly shifting our furniture from house to house. My little sister Brenda cried for *days*–she was in the first grade when we moved. Her biggest complaint was that we had left the swing-set behind, because it wouldn't fit on the aging Ford pickup truck. Dad refused to make the eight-hour trip necessary just to get the swing-set. She was angry about that for *years*.

I wondered what it would be like to live in Kentucky. My classmates teased me that I would wind up marrying my cousins and that kids in Eastern Kentucky had legs of different length to better accommodate the hilly terrain. We owned a small house there, a house perched on the edge of a ledge painfully scraped from the hillside, a house that would be considered a *shack* by my adult friends in California today. These are the same well-meaning and friendly people who drop the phrase *white trash* without a second thought–repeatedly– and pontificate about the sociological effects of poverty and the tendency of families in poverty to have misplaced priorities, while never having actually experienced the condition for themselves.

Our Kentucky home had no siding, little insulation, and a tin roof for many years. The ground wasn't quite level so the house stood suspended on several 4x4 pylons that made it look like some sort of beach house on a cliff from a distance. We stored lumber and coal under the house until we got around to digging out the basement and making the house a two story home many years later. When we moved in from Ohio the house had kuzdu vine that had crawled across the hillside from my grandmother's house over the hill, across a couple of trees and fences, and halfway up the side of the house.

Our first week was spent hacking and chopping at the stubborn vine to make a path to the outhouse that perched on the edge of the ridge a short distance away. I thought the weed was dead, but it was merely dormant in the winter. In the springtime the vines returned with a vengeance, with a large dark green leaf that scraped your skin uncomfortably if you let it. The ropy vines were difficult to cut in the first place, and my mother warned us that kudzu, originally imported from Japan during the Depression to help combat soil erosion, was so tenacious that if you merely threw a piece of cut plant on the open ground it would take root and start spreading overnight. You couldn't literally see the stuff grow but it was rather like watching the hour hand of a clock; walk away and come back and you might actually notice the growth. During that time I read a science fiction story about some astronauts who accidentally bring home a fungus from Venus that grows so fast it starts covering cars, houses, even sleeping dogs; a theme that is spooky enough it appears in War of the Worlds and in the if-you-find-a-meteor-in-your-field-don't-touch-it story that Stephen King did for *Creepshow*. Our version, featuring *cuzzy vine* in the starring role, would be called *Creekshow*, I imagine.

I've always considered it the height of irony that in Eastern Kentucky, the rich people lived in the expensive, flat bottom land, and poor people lived perched on the side of hills, while in the San Francisco Bay Area (where I live now) the exact opposite is true. The difference, though, is that in the Oakland Hills the roads are much better. In Perry County you would often find yourself on the edge of a road with a 150-foot cliff on one side, and an overloaded coal truck more than half the width of the road on the other. The roads had guardrails only occasionally, and no lines appeared to guide your choice of lanes until you got all the way to Viper. Sometimes you could stick your arm out of the window and have it suspended literally over a hundred foot drop or more. Our bus driver once accidentally forced a coal truck off the road because both our vehicles wouldn't fit on the narrow, winding road.

My story insists this particular digression is over, and it's time to tell of magic, and the willing suspension of disbelief, and love, of doors opening and closing and of the hard choices that must sometimes be made in life. That's the thing about storytelling; it's a negotiation between the teller and the story on behalf of the audience, and the teller must listen to the story's cues if communication is going to occur.

Thus, during Christmas break of my 6th grade year, we left, my mother weeping nearly every day over her lost son. And so I eventually wound up in Miss Caudill's drama class, rehearsing a play written by some English guy, dead and buried hundreds of years ago.

Screwed

As it turned out Benny wasn't the only one who had a nickname for our drama teacher–drama "coach" was the term she preferred, a perverse way of protesting the extra resources and attention diverted to our mighty basketball team. The other students called her "C.C.," for her first name was "Cheryl." My sister, Raynard Smith, and the other upperclassmen called her "CC". Benny Doherty steadfastly called her "Caudill," and I, as the youngest cast member by two years at least, dutifully called her "Miss Caudill," which I think she accepted as a function of my status within the group. I hadn't put enough time in to really be one of the "in" crowd. All the rest were veterans of previous plays–multiple previous plays–and I was the only person who hadn't ever been in a play. (Well, there was that one time in 3rd grade, but that's a story fragment for a later point in time than this.) Later on, as we added more supporting characters, some other younger students were added.

Even Lyn called Miss Caudill "C.C.," not "aunt Cheryl," which is what you would have expected. Unless she was in trouble or wanted Miss Caudill to pay close attention to what she was saying.

Throughout the next few weeks we practiced reading through the script, working on difficult words, stopping for clarification when necessary. Even Miss Caudill admitted that she didn't know what some of the phrases meant–it had been so long since Shakespeare's day, perhaps no one knew. We learned that scholars believed the word "soud," which Petruchio repeatedly shouts in one scene, probably means "food." All of us were startled to find out exactly how bawdy "Shrew" was, and snickered at the fact we were essentially getting away with saying bad words and sex jokes in front of other people who probably didn't quite follow what we were saying. All sorts of stuff about cocks and tongues and such actually went over my head at first, and it took Benny Doherty five minutes to recover from laughing when I asked him to interpret it for me during a break.

Since Grumio and Petruchio spent much of the play on stage together, Doherty sort of took me under his wing. He helped me learn how to turn toward the audience when turning around instead of away from the audience. What he forgot to show me Miss Caudill didn't hesitate to add. *Look at Benny, don't look at her while performing. Chin up, stop hanging your hands like hams! PROJECT! Stay focused. Where are you right now? Don't tap your foot or rock back and forth on your feet. Get your hands out of your pockets. Just stand there* and more. He was a strong enough actor he didn't mind surrendering to the fact that I was getting laughs when he was playing the straight man –another term that needed to be explained to me– to Grumio's silliness. He got the scenes with Katherine, played by Miss Caudill's lovely niece Lyn, and in my judgment he came out ahead in the deal.

At the beginning, she barely knew I existed, but she was polite to me. As far as that goes, I saw her being polite and friendly to *everyone.* Because she was Miss Caudill's niece, a senior, and afforded the relative freedom to come and go as needed for various errands, I occasionally even saw her during English class, where she would sometimes sit in a little desk off to the side and process multiple-choice and fill-in-the-blank papers for her aunt. She never got credit for doing any of this work; as far as I could detect she was just doing it because it was a thing that needed doing.

I told my mother once that she treated me like a little brother the entire time I knew her. In truth, it wasn't exactly like a little brother. Certainly my own sister never went out of her way to compliment me, or ask how I was doing even on a day when I wasn't depressed about some 13 year-old's issue of the day. But it wasn't like a boyfriend, either. She is probably the only person from high school that never made an effort to tease me or make me feel out of place even when I was deliberately being weird. (And I was pretty weird. All the time.) She even patted me on the top of the head occasionally, which invariably made me blush. She never laughed about *that*, either.

I always paid close attention to her whenever she was in the room, but after all, I said to myself, I was a *freshman* and she was a *senior.* She might as well have been a movie star as far as I was concerned. I know my chest tightened a little whenever she was in the room, and I also knew how little chance a *boy* like myself had with someone who was a hairsbreadth away from being a full fledged *woman*. She might as well have been on the far side of the moon.

We rehearsed–*practiced* was a verboten term for us, with its basketball connotations–nearly every day, several hours at a stretch. I still wince when I hear high school students talk about *play practice*. At first, it worked out for Dad to pick us up on the way home from his construction jobs. As long as it was convenient, we didn't hear much more than what we were doing was a waste of time and effort and *it had better NOT interfere with your grades because getting a good grades was sure-in-hell the ONLY way you're going to college and get a job that doesn't break your back the way mine does me and if you ever FORGET that I'll cut out this stupid GOD-DAM SHIT faster than you can spit a watermelon seed.*

And that was on a *convenient* day.

We never knew if he was going to make good on this threat to make us drop out of theatre. He certainly threatened to often enough. We knew he didn't approve but helped us because he thought he was supposed to do the things he did. It wasn't always a happy event, getting picked up after *God-damn play practice*. These days, after the world has been wussified sufficiently, he'd probably be investigated for child abuse, but he never hit us unless we deserved it, and only after Mom demanded it. He put food on the table, toys under the tree at Christmas, heat in the winter and a roof to keep out the rain. He did what all men of his generation did and what good men of our generation do: he did right by his kids. We knew it; he knew we knew; but we yelled and cried and screamed about missing rehearsal anyway. And he cussed and pouted and yelled and ... drove us around a lot.

There were times, though, lying awake at night listening to my parents' shouted bedtime arguments about our futures, twitching at the slammed doors, crying when my mother could be heard sobbing about

64

finances, her lost son, and the hard life she'd lived, when I wondered whether or not I was doing the right thing in taking a stand and insisting that we be allowed to continue to work with Miss Caudill.

There just wasn't anyone else at school who *pushed* us hard enough that we had to push *back* just to keep up. I don't mean that in the sense that we opposed her (otherwise we wouldn't have been there in the first place). I mean in a sort of a Newton's Third Law sort of way. She provided the traction that made all of us feel as if we were actually making progress, going *somewhere* even if we weren't sure where we were headed.

We didn't have a theatre in which to practice; as I said we didn't even have a basketball court, and if our school would have had any money to spare it would have first gone to a few hundred square feet of freshly scraped hillside and a layer of asphalt with two hoops instead of one. We had no stage, no sets, few props and rags and tatters for costumes. Our makeup kit (there was only one) fit in a tackle box. What we had for a stage was a raised platform about two feet above the floor at one end of a long room used for study hall. It was room 111.

There's a phrase you sometimes see on cute placards at truck-stop gift shops, that goes something like this: "We've done so much, for so long, with so little, it is now possible for us to do anything–with nothing!" I personally believe Miss Caudill coined this phrase, and if she didn't, she owned the copyright on it.

In those days there were so few courses offered and so few politically-driven graduation requirements you could actually have an hour a day to do homework. As I already mentioned, we called it study hall–and my primary experience was sitting in a desk and doing work, watching the teacher observe us from the raised platform at the far end. I believed the platform's purpose was simply make the teacher more visible to us and us to them. We thought the room was crowded when there were 40 or 50 students in study hall, but these days they'll cram that many math or English students into a classroom half that size in

California and call it world-class education. I got pulled out of study hall so many times by Miss Caudill I eventually stopped going; instead I reported directly to Miss Caudill, who would send a note to the study hall teacher asking where I was if I didn't show up, thus assuring the daily accounting of my whereabouts was accurate.

After school we moved the teacher desk off the platform (at 3 PM it was a stage; during the day it was a platform) and started working. Our lighting system was two switches on the wall. Costume changes were in the bathrooms at the end of the hall. Miss Caudill believed that actors projected voices as necessary; even if microphones had been available, we wouldn't have used them.

Standing on the platform you got a better view of the forest of pencils stuck into the aging ceiling tile like a forest of stripped trees in Tunguska or Mount St. Helens. A stack of milk-crates provided steps on stage right (the right side of the stage as you face the audience). Stage left had a luxury– built in steps. We couldn't even darken the room for scene changes– the windows had no curtains.

"Can you throw him down the steps?" asked Miss Caudill, rocking gently back on two legs of a chair, which was recently inhabiting the platform. I gobbled and gaped at Benny, who was looking at me like a side of beef he'd rather not have to touch if he could avoid it.

"Sure thing," he finally said, shrugging nonchalantly. Miss Caudill nodded. *Go for it.*

"*Waitaminit*," I managed to spit out, before he lifted me in quite a competent fireman's carry, twirled me around, and set me back down. "No problem," he said. I wasn't quite the imposing figure I cut today. In those days, I was a year younger than my peers and smaller than average. Benny was several inches taller and in better shape. No wonder he could pick me up like a rag doll.

"OK," said Miss Caudill, astride the teacher's study hall chair a few feet back from the edge of the stage. "Let's do this nice and slow,

Benny, we can't give him a concussion." She looked at my sister, who was serving as stage manager as well as the role of Curtis, the house manager for Petruchio. "We don't have time to replace him again." A squinty look at me. "You ready, Hoss?"

I don't remember answering.

A few dozen tries later, Benny was essentially rolling me down the steps like a human bowling ball, carefully choreographed like a dance move. We did it exactly the same way every time, and I rolled in such a way that my head never came near a step and I wound up sprawled flat at the bottom of the steps.

"That'll work," said Miss Caudill. "During the play, Ben, don't get excited and throw him into the audience."

"Riiiight," said Benny, somewhat unconvincingly, I thought. He grinned at me, wolfishly. *I might do it anyway,* that grin said.

My costume was modernized, as was everyone else's because we couldn't afford Elizabethan-style costumes. So everyone wore ordinary street clothes, jeans, t-shirts, sometimes with little accents.

I took up the issue with my mother, who had always patched all of our clothes and used them when they were worn out to make quilts. Mom was a child of the Depression, and she never threw anything away; you might need it someday.

She was peeling potatoes when I asked. Come to think of it, there were significant fractions of her life when she was *always* peeling potatoes. I loved her fried potatoes, made midwestern-style with nothing on them but salt, and not much of that. "Will you make me a costume for the play?" I asked. "And can I have some fried taters before supper?"

"Well, I might make you a costume," she said, carefully pouring the peeled and chopped potatoes into a cast iron skillet coated with melted lard, shielding herself from the spattering grease with careful positioning of the potato bowl. "As for the taters, if you keep eatin' them like you do, you'll get foundered on 'em." *Foundered* means eating so much of a thing you get tired of it. "What's this costume supposed to look like?"

You should understand that my mother had an authentic Eastern Kentucky accent, and she didn't actually talk the way I am writing. She would have said, literally, "I reckon I might," and "Wha's 'is costume s'posa look lahk?" while carefully not moving her jaw more than necessary. I don't think I can pull off phonetic spelling consistently, so I think I'll just do what I did when one of my girlfriends from Ohio met my mother for the first time: I'll *translate*. It's not just the accent, it's the word choice. For example, if my mom didn't know an answer to a question, she'd say *it's un-tellin'*. 'Help' became *hope*. 'Improvising' was *jinn t'gether*. 'Not one' was *naryun*. Children are *young'uns*. This was not funny or weird to us, because we grew up with it. People have said the language from Eastern Kentucky was descended from the kind of English spoken in the 1600's, when the first settlers in the area arrived. (We knew our most distant ancestor arrived from France in 1611; his name was Benjamin Brasseur, which became distorted to the modern *Brashear*.) Maybe that made it easier for us to catch on to the cadence of Shakespeare. It's *un-tellin'*.

People who have just met me often say, "You don't *sound* like you're from Kentucky." Usually I just say, "There's a reason for that," and leave it at that. Hours of drills and listening to phonograph records and tape recording my own voice and Miss Caudill's unending scrawls on long yellow pads are left unmentioned.

"Well," I said to my mother, "I'm not exactly sure. This character, he's kind of a goofball."

"Huh, that there's a perfect part for you then," she said, grinning. "Something funny," she said matter-of-factly, as if that defined the problem. "Go get your old jeans, the ones that are a little short on you."

I got the jeans and found her coming back into the house from the outside, carrying some leaves.

"Now how about this," she said, holding up the leaves.

"You want to glue leaves on my pants?" I asked.

"No, I want to cut out fabric shaped like leaves and *sew* the fabric leaves on your pants."

I gaped at my mother, who obviously was *getting* whatever it was that needed *got*.

"Perfect."

The other half of my costume was a floppy hat she had made for me. It was shaped like a cloth bowl, and was reversible. One side was multicolored and filled with odd designs and contrasting patterns such as paisley and stripes together. That was the Grumio Side. The other side was blank white, and that was the Jeff Side. She stitched an Apollo space capsule with flames shooting out of it's retro-rocket pack on the heat shield (following a sketch I made for her) but everyone thought it was a mushroom. That's why it became known as my Mushroom Hat. You could flip the front up to make it look like Larry Storch's hat on F-Troop or you could flip up the brim all the way around to look like Gilligan's cap on Gilligan's Island. Both associations worked for me, so whenever I wore that hat I flipped it up a different way when I went on stage. Oddly enough I don't remember anyone ever mentioning that they noticed.

When my father saw the get-up he nearly exploded.

"There ain't no son of MINE gonna go out lookin' like some bum wearing GOD-damn STUPID-looking SHIT like that!" he boomed. While my parents, and in particular my father, cussed a blue streak whenever they were even the slightest bit agitated, my sisters and I never uttered a curse word in their presence. Not if we wanted to live to see another sunrise.

I couldn't cuss back or out shout him. All I could do was try to placate him.

"It's just a *costume*, Dad," I pleaded. "I'm not wearing it out in *public. It's just for school.* " Which, technically, was a lie, but Dad didn't need to know that.

"Well, why do you have to wear that God-damn ugly thing around the house?" He snatched it from my head and held it in front of my face. "Cain't you just wear a regular ball-cap like a regular boy?" Dad was seldom seen in pubic (or private for that matter) without a grimy ball cap bearing some unlikely logo such as for some restaurant out in New York or a sports team he'd never seen, or, more typically, a blank slate-grey work cap carrying the sawdust of dozens of houses and jobs wormed into the cracks between the seams. It probably never occurred to him that he might hurt mom's feelings by putting down the appearance of the hat. I was alert enough to know if your *mother* makes you a hat, you wear it and *say* you like it even if you don't, just because she's your *mother.*

Truth be told, I actually *liked* the hat, anyway. It was *different.*

"He ain't *raglar*," said my mother. "He don't backtalk you like Jane ner do them drugs and drinkin' and smokin' like most of them boys do." *Like my own two older boys did, and the one still alive still does.* "He gets good grades in school an' I don't see what you're so worked up about."

"Why do you always have to take up his side on everything?" growled my father, tossing the hat on the kitchen table, stomping out the front door and jamming his own rumpled cap down on his thick black hair. He marched out of the house, not for the first time, muttering something about how he "had no say about nothing," because he always, somehow, wound up deferring to my mother in the end. I retrieved my hat and folded it like a rocket parachute, folded in thirds as a narrow cone and rolled into a tube from the bottom up. and stuffed it into my back pocket.

One more thing I would have to edit about myself while I was around the house.

"Don't worry," said Mom. "He'll come 'round."

"Mom," I said, "Does it bug you sometimes that I don't want to work in the mines or fix cars or build houses, whatever it takes to make some real money someday?"

"Well that's what I reckon is buggin' your Dad," she replied. "Though neither one of us would wish the mines on nobody, for no amount of money. " She closed her eyes tightly and shook her head. "I cain't see how any mother can let her young'uns go down in that mine ever day. I couldn't take it. I'd get sick ever single day from worrying." She opened her eyes and stared at me. *One of my boys dead before me is already one too many* flitted across her eyes. She started washing dishes and shifting pots and pans around the kitchen, which is what she did when she was nervous or upset. "As far as me," she continued, "Neither me ner your Dad finished school, and we've paid for it all our lives. I don't even know enough about what you do to give you advice anymore."

She paused long enough to fix me with a squinty eye. "I reckon the best thing I can do for you is get out of your way." She looked at me as if assessing my potential for digging ditches. "Are you sure you want to spend your time on this drama?"

"Yes," I replied. "I think it helps me be more confident about myself. Good for public speaking. "

"Well, then," she said, "Go, and do." She returned a pan to the shelf she had just removed it from with a *clank*. "I'll deal with Tad." *Tad* was my dad's nickname.

And so I obtained a costume and continued working in drama, for the time being at least.

Miss Caudill told me, years later after I became a teacher myself, that I wasn't the only one that struggled against their parents' better judgement to stay in drama. Nearly all of us did. Even Benny.

Benny wore a black t-shirt and jeans. Lyn wore jeans with a tie-dyed t-shirt that fascinated me more for the curvature it revealed than the colors it displayed.

I was developing a *serious* crush on this girl. I'd never really had a crush on a girl before, at least one where I let my interest show enough so that other people could tell. More than once she caught me staring at her, and she smiled when I pretended to look away or to look at something behind her.

Think about it– here was the prettiest girl I'd ever met, and not only was she tolerant of me, she was a nice person, and *smart* as well. She never seemed to have trouble learning her lines. Even Benny struggled with memorizing lines, and she often drilled him with a copy of the script she always seemed to have on her person. Later on she didn't need that, and memorized most of the lines everyone had in her scenes and would provide gentle prompts when Miss Caudill would let her get away with it. She was a role model for many of the younger students because she acted like theatre was serious business– no goofing off (at least where Miss Caudill could see it), always prepared, helping other students rehearse, fetching things, working on costumes, constantly in motion. She put more hours in than anyone involved, except possibly Miss Caudill herself.

She must have known I had a crush on her all along, but eventually I made it painfully obvious by overcoming my rational voice (that told me she'd never consider having anything to do with me romantically) and asking her (a senior) out on a date with me–a freshman one year younger than his peers. She patted me on the head and told me I was sweet. Well, I was supposedly in puppy love (at least that's what everyone *thought*), but I wasn't *entirely* stupid, and I knew what my chances of success would be. I'd tell you exactly how that turned out but the story says I must restrain myself and reserve that peroration for a more appropriate time.

We practiced on the stage in the study hall. I rolled down the steps. October rolled into November, and December approached, which would be when we did our first performance of the entire play for the public. We decided to do the play both at the school during the school day—for which a few students would be excused to see it—and for the public at the local community college. We printed some flyers. We ordered tickets for the performance, all of the normal things you'd do to prepare for a play. Along the way, though, a few odd things happened.

First, we got better. I cleaned up my diction (quite) a bit. The rain in Spain falls mainly on the plain. Sally sells sea shells by the sea shore. How much wood could a woodchuck chuck if a woodchuck could chuck wood? Diphthongs, glottal stops, breathing, projecting, adding a little burst of air at the end of word ending in a consonant (*tuh*) to make the ending crisper from a stage distance. That's the same thing our Bible-thumping Baptist preachers did, in dozens of little one-room splintered factional churches up and down the creekside road (*Jesus-HUH is a gonnUH take-UH you to Heaven-UH if you puh-Ray-UH for forgive-en-ess-UH!*).

(Actually, Baptist preachers don't thump bibles; that would be disrespectful of the written Word. They thump pulpits and pews and the floor and inattentive foreheads. Sometimes we're trapped by our own imperfect reflections in the popular media, a phenomenon I call the *Jerry Springer Effect.*) And many of those little roadside buildings have been replaced by more monumental structures of brick and stained glass and porcelain baptistries today.

Our version of punching up the diction was just a little less intense than the preachers'. Lying on my back, attempting to speak while

Miss Caudill put pressure on my diaphragm with an impressive stack of books, helped me learn to project. I learned to roll my r's.

Second, we learned to be *professional*. There was something going on between Ben and Lyn, but I wasn't privy to it; and Charmaine Marshall was passing through teenage boys' lives and leaving wreckage in her wake. Often you'd hear arguing and sniping and such after rehearsal and people would complain about each other to Miss Caudill...but when they stepped on the stage, it was like a switch went off and everyone just *worked*. Worked *hard*. It was as if everyone knew she was our last best hope for excellence and we'd best not squander the opportunity.

Miss Caudill took notes on her long yellow legal pad. Afterwards we'd sit in a circle and have to listen to her tell everyone what you did that was good or bad, mostly bad. There was no arguing, no defensiveness, just quiet nods and pledges to do better. *Don't turn your back to the audience when you speak. Stop looking at me and look to the entire audience. Your timing is off. Check the line, you're saying it wrong. Chin up. Different shirt. Two steps back on entrance. Exit faster. Exit slower. You sound like a mouse. Give it a three-count before responding. Don't step on the laugh. Enunciate! For heaven's sake it'd be better if you had your hands in your pockets than just letting them hang there like dead ham. Look like you're paying attention. Don't face her directly, it hides your face. Just turn your head a little in her direction and it'll look like you're facing her from our perspective. Get a haircut. Don't get a haircut–don't even wash your hair just before we open* (that was to me).

And always, always, every single day: *Project! No one can tell you're doing all those wonderful emotional things with your voice if they can't hear you. Louder! Take a deep breath! Pretend your audience is deaf. Push from the diaphragm, don't choke the sound in your throat, you'll rip out your vocal cords. Project, project, PROJECT!*

Most of us didn't comment on the notes. We just hung our heads down, nodded when appropriate, leaped to our feet to redo a particular scene when commanded, and learned to deal with constructive criticism. What was it, I wondered, that made normally recalcitrant teenagers take such personally directed criticism in stride and not rebel or argue? Whatever she had done or said to them must have preceded my arrival. In fact, it seemed to me as if students were disappointed if they didn't get notes from Miss Caudill; it was as if either there was nothing she could do to help them improve or the effort involved was not worth the payoff.

For me, a straight-A student who rarely drew the attention let alone the criticism of teachers, dealing with criticism of any sort was a hard lesson. The only time I'd been punished in school for *anything* was when the 6th grade teacher had taken it upon himself to paddle everyone in class who had never been in trouble just so the good kids would know what it was like.

Dealing with such constructive criticism served me well later in life, though. *Don't make excuses. Acknowledge the information and move on. Don't gloat when others are criticized, because your turn will come.* Everyone got notes, on every performance. Even Lyn. *Especially* Lyn. I suspect she even got notes in the car on the way home or at home as well. Later I learned she probably got an order of magnitude more criticism, both professional and personal, than any of us ever knew.

Miss Caudill, for her part, felt she had *pampered* Lyn during those years. She loved Lyn with all her heart– I know, because she told me– and felt that Lyn had her aunt wrapped around her little finger and would let her get away with *anything*. Lyn, on the other hand, felt stifled and trapped –and loved as well– at the time, but loved perhaps from a different perspective.

I knew these things because of all the students in the play, Jane and I spent the most time with Miss Caudill and Lyn due to our ongoing transportation issues. Lyn and I discussed the best strategy to record blocking movements in our scripts. XDSR was *Cross Down Stage Right*. F-Pet was *Face Petruchio*. EN-SL was *Enter Stage Left*. We made notations in the tiny margins left to us in our paperback-novel style version of the script, marks that resembled football playbooks, with a rectangle representing the stage in the space above each new scene, and sweeping arcs showing which actors should go around others.

When she concentrated she would bite half of her lower lip, so the remainder would protrude off to one side.

"I think I have my blocking pretty much memorized," I said to her one day as we lay on our stomachs on the carpeted area in the back of Miss Caudill's room, sketching the blocking onto blank sheets of notebook paper. "I don't think I need to refer to the notes any more."

"Oh, the notes aren't for *us,* silly goose," she said, looking at me in some surprise. Why had we spent all this time recording everyone's movements so painstakingly?
Aside from the opportunity to be in close proximity to her, I couldn't think of a reason right away. Was I missing something?

Half of being smart is keeping your mouth shut so you don't reveal your ignorance too often.

"The notes are for *her,*" Lyn noted, tossing her head at Miss Caudill, who was drilling Lucentio and Bianca (played by Benny's sister Penelope) on pronouncing words in Latin. *Hic est sigeria tellus,* I remember hearing over and over. *I trust you not.* "Blocking is complicated. She wants a record of it so she won't have to start over if she ever does this play again." She smiled at me. "Besides, figuring out how everyone is moving, where everyone is supposed to be, is kinda *fun.*" More lip biting. "Check back to see where we had Biondello exit," she said.

I also learned how to emulate a variety of Southern accents. Texans talk louder than us, and with a deliberate pace that assumed that everyone in earshot would naturally want to listen to what they had to say. Georgians *add* vowels everywhere and talk slowwwwwly. You can't eliminate an accent without being able to hear it and emulate it. The need to eliminate our Southern accents was so obvious to Miss Caudill she just assumed we saw the necessity; doing Shakespeare with a Southern accent would destroy the illusion that you were watching a story written by an English Playwright, and while it would be OK for Italian characters from Verona to speak with an English accent in a play, a southern accent destroys the illusion. This becomes more significant later in the tale, but the story is telling me to get back to the point.

Benny and I practically danced around the stage as he pretended to beat me up. Visitors to rehearsal actually gasped when he tossed me down the stairs, convinced I was injured. Benny and Lyn's recital of lines took on depth and reflected what felt like, to me, to be an authentic relationship.

Sometimes after rehearsal we would go to Miss Caudill's house, and she would cook for us as we did our homework and awaited the arrival of our father from whatever far-flung job site he was working at this week, at least when he had a job site to go to and return from.

Miss Caudill was many things, but a housekeeper was definitely not one of them. We moved stacks of papers, boxes of unopened food, bags of dog food for her Saint Bernard, and sometimes her Saint Bernard from chairs to find a place to sit. Sometimes Lyn would be there, sometimes not. Lyn was a cheerleader and a band majorette and often was out doing one thing or another every day of the week. I remember wishing she wasn't quite so busy so she would be home more.

Sometimes Miss Caudill scheduled rehearsals of scenes out of chronological sequence just to give her a little time at one activity or another before she was due back at drama practice. Sometimes though, she was there with us, and I asked her once about her seemingly intense relationship with Benny.

"There's Kate and Petruchio, and then there's Lyn and Benny," she said. "They aren't the same."

"Of course not," I replied. "But surely you must at least like Benny...I mean, after all, there's lots of kissing and hugging and wrassling and fighting in this play..." my voice trailed. "How could you do those things if you didn't *like* him?"

"Oh, I *do* like him," she said. "And he certainly is a *handsome* devil." She sighed, looking off into the distance as if I had just given her a nudge in the *wrong* direction. "He's a sweetheart. All that juvvie stuff he does, acting tough, smoking, that's just for show. He's really just a kindhearted fellow with a hard life." A shadow crossed her eyes as she shook her head and sighed. Miss Caudill arrived with a plate of meat-balls and bread. She didn't cook many things, but she did make some great meatballs.

For once I had little appetite, and fiddled with my food, lost in thought. How could I compete with this charismatic, handsome, athletically fit older *man?* Benny was a junior, three years older than I and nearly Lyn's age. From Lyn's perspective, I must have been nearly *invisible–*

No. From Lyn's perspective, I was not even a term in the romantic equation. I was *just a kid.* I liked Benny– he was something of a mentor to me and I stand in awe of his charisma and skills to this day–but sometimes, *sometimes* I wished he was just a little *less* talented and handsome.

A few days before dress rehearsal, I walked by C.C.'s room and heard her laughing, hooting really, and peeked inside to see her wiping her eyes. "Oh, Lord," she said, nearly wheezing from the laughter.

"What?" I said. If it was funny, I was supposed to be involved.

She didn't answer, but handed a thick yellow piece of paper to Benny, who handed it to me.

It said:

I didn't see it at first. We were going to do the play at the local college which had a real theatre, I was told earlier. So what was wrong with the ticket?

"The Schrew!" She cried. "The SCHREW! Oh, my! Oh, my!"

"What's the problem? It's just a spelling mistake," I asked, not really getting it.

Benny rolled his eyes, and inserted his index finger into a circle he made with his index finger and thumb of his other hand. "Screwed? Get it?"

"No," I said. A moment passed as gears engaged in my freshman brain. "Oh!"

Which only set off Miss Caudill again, as she could not conceive that I was so innocent that I didn't get it right away. I blushed as was my usual habit in those situations (it took me a *long* time to stop doing that at the drop of a hat) but I noted, once again, that not only was Lyn not laughing at the *joke*–she was not laughing at *me*. She was sitting there thoughtfully, and smiling at *me*, I thought, not at my discomfiture.

At least, that's what I *hoped* was happening. As I found out later, I was right.

We got the tickets replaced in time, and moved on to dress rehearsal.

St. Matthews

Lyn had started out with an interest in theatre at an early age. While still in elementary school she wrote a play and performed it in the basement of her house for the neighborhood children. She was a beautiful child, and lived with her father Harvey Lee and mother Edie and sister Teri in a one-story brick home in St. Matthews, a suburb of Louisville. Harvey worked at a tractor manufacturing plant, and her mother stayed home to raise the kids. By all outward appearances, it was a picture-perfect setting: nice home, loving parents, good schools, beautiful children. Like many families–perhaps all families, to some degree– Lyn's home life was more complicated than the picture presented to the outside world.

Lyn's home was in a reasonably modern suburb of the 1970's. Large leafy trees lined the streets, which were orthogonal and smooth, with unbroken pavement and lines painted neatly in maintained intersections. Sidewalks lined the edges of the yards. The interior of the home was dominated by a large living room window, which had blinds that were always open; passers-by could see inside the beautifully decorated home, with leather couches, tastefully decorated fireplace mantle, bookshelf lined with books, some of which were turned outward so you could see the covers.

Lyn's older sister dominated the attention of the family, as older siblings sometimes do, by getting into things her parents wouldn't necessarily approve of. Teri was mature for her age, and Lyn often said she looked 16 when she was 12. She was also startlingly attractive. She had long, straight black hair and an arresting gaze. I only met her once, I think, but I can certainly see what brought all the attention of the opposite sex. She had a presence around men, that commanded their attention, with little or no effort on her part. This brought the (not unwelcome) attention of many boys. Unfortunately, it also brought Teri experiences best left to adults, and she became pregnant just a few years later, when Lyn was only 11 years old.

The pregnancy devastated the family. There was no question, in that time and place, that the pregnancy must be accompanied by a marriage; and in the brief but tumultous period that followed, Teri married, became visibly pregnant, had a child before she was old enough to know how to care for one, divorced, and married again at 19– to a boy who was only 16 at the time. But those events lay in the future. When Lyn was 11, Teri was pregnant with her first child.

When Teri first became pregnant, Cheryl, Edie, and Lyn's grandmother discussed what was to be done with Teri. The family would continue to support her any way it could, of course...that's what families *do*.

These events had a profound effect on Lyn. Not only because it diverted her parents' attention from her just as she entered her teen years, but because it altered their expectations and behavior towards her. And their fears for what might happen to her.

"What about Lyn?" asked Cheryl. "Do you think she'll learn anything from her sister's life?"

"Lyn just *adores* Teri," said Edie. "I'm sure anything Teri does is just fine with Lyn."

"Well then, I think we'd best keep a close eye on Lynnie," said Lyn's grandmother, affectionately referred to as *Mamal*. (Isn't it strange how there are so many terms of endearment for grandparents, somewhat regional in nature? Mamaw, meemaw, granny, grandmother: In my house it was "granny." In particular my grandmother on my mother's side was called "Granny Grunt" by everyone; but that's a story for another day.)

"What do you mean?" asked Cheryl.

"She might get the idea that behaving like her older sister is...acceptable." said the eldest of the three women, who had a habit of being polite, if honest. I know–she was always friendly with me when I met her later, but always told the truth.

"Good point," said Cheryl. "You don't have room for another family here, in any case." Edie glared at her sister. *Of course we won't have to face that,* her face said.

Unknown and unnoticed to the three women, Lyn listened quietly to the conversation, taking it all in and absorbing more than they ever knew. Children *listen* even if they don't respond. I know I did.

"Lynnie's a *good* girl," said Edie. *Unlike her sister* went unspoken, but they all thought it.

"Well of course she is, Edie," said Cheryl. "But mom's right. We need to think about how to protect Lyn. If we don't–"

"Cheryl–" said Edie. Cheryl held her tongue for a moment.

"The way I see it, she's likely to wind up as a nun, a slut or a lesbian. We have to do *something* to keep her from following in her sister's footsteps."

"Cheryl." Edie stood with her hands on her hips. "A person can only love their children. You love them, and do the best you can for them. Sometimes you have to let them stand on their own. You don't have children, so you can't know–"

"Don't start in with me with the when-are-you-going-to-settle-down speech again, Edie," said Cheryl. "I haven't found a man who'd put up with me and I've got bigger fish to fry right now, anyway, so you can–"

"Girls!" snapped Mamal. "I'd like to have you note our conversation has not been entirely *private. Behave."*

Cheryl and Edie looked around the room and saw Lyn, wide-eyed, staring from the edge of a doorway. She gasped as she realized they knew she had heard. Heard *everything.*

"Lyn!" said Edie. Cheryl merely shrugged as if to say *Someone has to come out and tell the truth here. It's about time she heard it from us.*

Lyn struggled briefly to decide what to say–if she should even speak, or could even speak– and finally decided to flee. She escaped to her room and lay down upon the bed, tears slowly crawling down her cheeks to the pillow below. Lyn looked around at the frilly pillows, stuffed animals, posters and pretty furniture. None of it seemed to be of any comfort.

I don't want to be a slut, she thought to herself, eyes squeezing a few more tears out. *I don't want to have a baby that no one in my family wants in the house. I want children. Loads of them. And I want them to be loved by my whole family and to love the family back.* She lay there as the sky darkened and her father returned from work, and the conversation in the farther reaches of the house became more heated, more fraught with pain and anguish. Teri was already known for having an undesirable reputation, and was on her way to establishing notoriety as a poor mother as well. Would that be Lyn's fate as well? Could she avoid it?

I've always been the good *child. I never get in trouble. Why would they say something like that about me? Doesn't all the time I've been good count for* anything?

She lay there staring at the ceiling as the evening light crawled its way up her wall. Eventually, her tears dried. No one, she noticed, had come to her room to check on her. Not while there were Bigger Problems that needed solving.

What if Aunt Cheryl's right, and I am fated to be just like my sister? What will I do then? Can I live with myself?

She lay there in the dark, trying to figure out a way out of her conundrum, but nothing presented itself.

Break a Leg

After rehearsing the play in one way or another almost every night for four weeks, Miss Caudill arranged for us to have a dress rehearsal at the local community college theatre. The stage was a small proscenium arch with a seating capacity of about 200, which felt huge to us. There was a lighting booth with, I think, maybe six rheostats and half a dozen switches. The stage had exits off of stage left and right (although stage right was a dead end– *exit* right, you're required to *enter* right or have to make a run for it under cover of darkness.)

We proceeded forthwith to dress rehearsal, which turned out to be practicing in front of a hand-picked audience. There were a few parents, a few students from speech class who were not in the play, a couple of Miss Caudill's theatre friends (you wouldn't think there would be any in Hazard, Kentucky, but there were some, even back then) and a couple of teachers, including Joanne Williams, who would eventually be my chemistry teacher.

I remember Miss Caudill explaining to us what "downstage" actually meant.

"In Shakespeare's day, the audience sat on a level floor," she explained. "So the people in the back could see the entire set, the stage was built tilted. The part farthest from the stage was higher, or *upstage*. The part towards the audience was *downstage.* "

She gestured at the gentle slope in the theatre's audience seating area.

"Now the stage is flat and the audience is tilted, but we still use the same terminology."

"So the terminology is based on *you* being the center of the coordinate system," I said. "Stage left is your left, stage right is your right, as you face the audience. Up and down is relative to your own position.

Someone in the center of the stage can be upstage of you if you're near the audience."

Benny stared at me as Miss Caudill nodded. "That's it exactly," she said.

I looked at Benny. *What?*

He shook his head, and resumed work without commenting.

In theatre lore, there are a few superstitions that are traditional. You don't say the name "Macbeth" in the theatre unless you speak it during the play; you say "break a leg" when you mean "I hope you do well," and the quality of dress rehearsals are the opposite of the opening night. If the dress rehearsal goes well; opening night will be a disaster. If the dress rehearsal is a disaster....well, let's just say that we anticipated a terrific opening night.

"You're not allowed to call "line!" in dress rehearsal when you forget your lines!" hissed Miss Caudill at Tranio. "You get yourself into a mess, you get yourself out."

It's not easy to paraphrase or improvise Elizabethan iambic pentameter. In my only other theatre experience, I hadn't been allowed to improvise anything.

My very first theatrical experience occurred in the second grade in an elementary school in Ohio. During the school's winter Christmas pageant (which wouldn't be allowed in our culturally neutered times today) everyone in the class was assigned a role as Jesus, a shepherd, a wise man, the proprietor of the inn, and so on...except for me. I got the honored position of "prompter," which meant I sat backstage, unseen, and when someone forgot a line, I was supposed to follow along and read it to them. Even that menial task was taken from me, however, because the teacher stood behind me and hissed *"Promterrr!"* fiercely if I didn't supply the word instantly; and eventually she snatched the script from my hand and did it herself. That sort of gave me a negative perception of the whole theatrical "scene" until years later, when I had more or less forgotten this particular ignominy.

Now I stood upon a stage at Hazard Community College, with lights so bright in my eyes I couldn't see the audience, I suddenly couldn't remember any of my lines. And in high school, Miss Caudill loftily informed me, we didn't *use* prompters; you were expected to do the job right the *first* time.

"But what if I forget my line?" I whined some days after I started trying to rehearse without a script.

"Then you're going to have to invent something to do while we wait for your brain to come back," she said.

"Don't TV people use prompters?" I asked.

"I wouldn't know, Hoss. All I know is—"

"Shuddup and learn your lines," growled Benny.

Miss Caudill paused just long enough to catch Benny's attention, gave him the eyebrow and beamed *don't do my job for me* into his brain, and continued, "All I know is if you have a prompter, you will get lazy and *depend* on the prompter. *No prompters.* All right, Hoss?"

I nodded.

"Knock me here sirrah, and knock me soundly!" bellowed Benny. He beat his chest, confusing me. Was I supposed to hit *him?* Did he think I was *stupid?*

"Uh..." I said, sweat popping out on my forehead. "Uh."

"I said Knock me here soundly, you sirrah, or I shall poundeth your head!" yelled Benny, even louder. I believed him, because the veins

86

were rising out of his forehead and his neck muscles looked like they were ready to do the beating all on their own.

"Knock you, uh, here, sir? Why, has anyone here abused your worship-fulness?" I managed to croak, accompanied by a distinct smack caused by Miss Caudill's hand colliding violently with her forehead.

Other entertaining events occurred during the dress rehearsal. Lyn had a special Velcro-fastened costume because she had to change rapidly from traveling clothes to a wedding dress during a short scene. During her initial confrontation with Petruchio, it fell off, revealing her ordinary non-acting, if skimpy, street clothes she was wearing underneath to preserve her dignity when switching costumes in our mixed-gender dressing room–a temporarily appropriated music room off of stage left dominated by a grand piano with just enough room to walk around it. Deathly silence ensued as she reassembled herself.

Missed cues, bungled entrances, and dropped props ruled the day. My sister, portraying the housekeeper Curtis, dropped a tray with cups and glasses which scattered everywhere. If the wine glasses had been actual glass instead of dime-store plastic that might have brought the show to a literal halt. Biondello was nowhere to be found during one of the few scenes where he has something to say. He had misjudged the time remaining and went to buy a pop. For you folks out in the wider world, we called sodas "pop." I knew older people who would say "Co-Cola" for "Coca-Cola" whereas the younger generation would just say "Coke" like the rest of the country.

Finally, the play ended. Some of the attendees had already departed, and we were sure we knew why. Miss Caudill simply sat there with her head bent over her forearm, which was resting on the back of the seat in front of her. We noted she had moved from second row to the back of the theatre when we weren't looking.

Rehearsal notes followed as always and we practiced fixing whatever was wrong right then and there, usually ten times as least until we met her standard of perfection. Some rehearsals went as late as 9 or 10 PM, and we even crossed the midnight line on occasion. Especially on dress rehearsal night. Not that we had anything to dress up in.

Tonight, however, she had no notepad, and her eyes were red and bleary; it was obvious she had been quietly weeping in the back of the theatre.

"That has to be the most Gawd-awful thing I ever saw in my life," she said, choking back a sob. Sort of like Scotty on *Star Trek*, her accent thickened whenever she was emotional. And she was emotional a *lot,* both in frequency and intensity. "And I have to have my name attached to it." She rolled her eyes so far back in her head, I swear all you could see was the bloodshot whites of her eyes between her eyelids. "Oh Gawd Almighty, *help* me," she wailed.

"We'll get it right tomorrow night, Caudill," rasped Benny. His voice sounded older than it should. I couldn't tell if it was the cigarettes he smoked or the situation we were in.

"I am so sorry, Aunt Cheryl," said Lyn, who must have been saving the "Aunt Cheryl" for when she was in big trouble.

"I didn't mean to forget my line," I stammered, "I wasn't used to the lights and ..."

"Don't make excuses," said Benny. I started to object but snapped my mouth shut when Miss Caudill held up a hand.

"No, It's my fault. You're not ready. You're not. Obviously we're going to have to postpone the opening and return the tickets."

"No way in hell, Caudill," said Benny. "No way in hell." He raked back his straight brown hair and scratched the stubble on his chin. "We'll do it right. We'll do it right *right now.* "

"I'd appreciate it if you'd restrain that language around me, young man," said Miss Caudill. "I don't curse at you and I don't expect it aimed in my direction."

Benny looked like he's suddenly forgot to wipe his shoes before coming in the house. "Yes ma'm. Sorry." It may seem like fairly innocent transgressions on our part, but in those days, in that place, you didn't say *hell* and *damn* to your elders. Of course, I hear worse than that every day in the hallways of my school in California. Someone needs to explain to these young whippersnappers that they've entirely diluted the power of cursing by overuse.

Of course, every generation says that.

Charmaine Marshall, who by some awful twist of fate was extremely attractive and mature-looking to my eyes but for some mysterious reason was assigned the role of Kate's father, said "Sure, we can prove to you we can do it. Who can stay?"

My sister and I wanted to but couldn't. Of course we tried to stay anyway, despite knowing our father would be already sitting in the parking lot and fuming about having to wait to go home for supper the late hour of 8:30 PM because he simply came to rehearsal after work, sat in the car and waited until we were finished. My sister went to the parking lot to talk to him, and when she returned she was in tears. "We have to go," she said. "Dad is *really mad*. He said if we were going to stay that late we might as well just stay with Miss Caudill all night."

Miss Caudill heard this whispered report to me, and tilted her head over as she often did when concentrating. She shook her head from side to side, swishing her hair and gaining her composure simultaneously. Then she *glided* out of the theatre and my sister and I stood there, commiserating.

"He's going to make us quit drama," she said. "I know it."

"Nah, he won't," I said. "Mom will make him let us stay."

"That might be true," she said. "She lets you get away with anything."
I allowed that was probably true; I had my first bike at nearly the same time Jane did although she was three years older; I went on my first overnight sleepover younger than she did; I certainly had an easier time getting driving lessons from Dad than she did. I think that might have been the first time I realized it was hard to be the oldest, always having to talk parents into doing things for the first time, taking care of the younger ones–

Just then Miss Caudill returned.

"You two are staying at my house tonight," she declared. Just like that, no forms, no paperwork, no school board approvals. We didn't know what she said to our father, or what he'd said in return, but we had a pretty good idea what he'd say to *us* – "Then you can just damn well stay there all *week* for all I God-damn care–" Then she waved her hand at the stage like a swordmaster with a rapier. "Places!"

We all *ran* to our places and did the entire two-hour play...again. A little faster than we should have, but we got through it, and it was good. We knew then we could finish what we had begun all those weeks ago.

I even remembered to say "rebused."

If It Itches...

You know that story you mother tells that embarrasses you horribly, yet you can't honestly remember doing it because you were too young?

Miss Caudill tells a story like that about me. I swear I don't remember it. I *swear.*

The play opened successfully, and everything went remarkably well. Lighting cues were on time, everyone remembered their lines, costume changes went without a hitch. As we performed we got a little better. I think we did three or four nights, and the crowds grew larger each night.

One of the odd things about performing on stage is that it isn't as nerve-wracking as you might think. When giving a speech in a board-room, you can see everyone's faces and get feedback on how well you are doing from their body language and attentiveness. The same thing is true for teachers–if you pay attention, you can tell how you're doing.

When performing on stage, for the largest groups of audience members, the opposite is true. The lights blind you to the darkness beyond as if you were performing in front of a darkened window or one-way mirror. They can see you, but you can't see them. The only feedback you get is the occasional laugh or clapping or some other auditory feedback; and in a well behaved audience you might not even get that.

Isolated on stage it becomes more and more like the world you are attempting to portray. Under these conditions I could do more than imagine that I was Grumio...I could *be* Grumio, really attend to and respond to Petruchio's words instead of simply saying my line when it was my turn.

These were all things our teacher taught us to think about explicitly. We talked about thinking. We thought about thinking while acting. I believe she wanted us not to just act with our bodies and voices, but with our *brains*. She said to us once, "One of the hallmarks of great acting is what you are doing when the audience is not supposed to be paying attention to you. Are you listening to the main character speak, or is your mind wandering because you know what she's going to say? If you're not focused, in character, every second on the stage, the audience will know it, and they'll stop paying attention to the story in order to see you slip in and out of character."

After I had been a student of hers for a while, she told me what my internal theory of acting was. I wasn't really conscious of it, but when she told me, it made a lot of sense. "You approach acting scientifically, Jeffery Mason," she said. "You put on a role like layers of clothes. First a voice, then a walk, then mannerisms, then your face, then costuming, then, near the end, you tie it all up and actually become the character. Very methodical."

"There's only so much new information I can...program my brain with at once," I said. "I need to master each thing before moving on."

"If it works, it works," she said. "Every actor is different. You're going to be a great character actor. Not like John Wayne or Charlton Heston who always just acts like themselves in every movie."

I had never really thought of myself pursuing acting *professionally*. I wondered if I could handle the competition in a city big enough to make a living doing it. The competition must be *fierce*.

Miss Caudill went to college in a small town called Berea, Kentucky. At Berea College, you could only be admitted if your parents didn't make too much money. Once admitted, you were not charged tuition, just books and living expenses, which you could partially defer by working part time for the college. One of her professors there, a gentleman who eventually became one of my teachers, was a professor named Paul Power, who taught her – and later me– to act with our butts.

"When you're sitting there on the stage with your back to the audience," he'd say in his mild New England accent, "even yoah butt is acting. Even yoah butt. You sit there and tell us what you're thinking with yoah ahss."

At the time when I heard him say it, everyone else laughed, but I knew he was serious, because I'd heard it before. This is one way teachers sort of gain a bit of immortality, I think... they pass on these little gems of wisdom that have a way of propagating themselves.

Then there are things they'd rather *not* remember.

I'm sure Miss Caudill has had second thoughts about the time she decided I had *ham hands* when portraying Grumio, then gave me a large wooden spoon to use as a prop. At first, it was hanging there like my hammy hands, but soon I brandished it like a sword when Petruchio says that Grumio must defend Kate. I tapped Curtis on the head with it to get her attention. I twirled it around my ear, as if to say, "He's *crazy,*" as Petruchio attempted to befuddle Kate with contradictions and confrontation.

"That's some good business you're developing," Miss Caudill said. "Keep it up."

During the second or third performance there was one scene where we were supposed to be lying on the floor, exhausted from hauling all of Petruchio and Kate's gear, while Petruchio berated Kate for not being obedient. "It is the moon if I say it is the moon!" bellowed Benny.

I tried to imagine what Grumio would do in such a situation. Momentarily deprived of the glare of Petruchio's attention, he would take a nap, I decided. I pulled my hat down over my eyes and waited for the command to get moving again. I must have let my mind wander a bit *too* much, because Benny snatched the hat from my face and began beating me with it, like the Skipper beating Gilligan. I reacted with shock at this unrehearsed piece of business, and noticed Benny grinning at me in full view of half of the audience. What was he doing...? Was he going *out of character?*

Ah. He wants that fraction of the audience to see that Petruchio is pretending to beat on Grumio for Kate's eyes, who could see Petruchio's back and not his face.

Now that's *acting.*

Eventually, the spell was broken, the play ended, and we heard applause from offstage even with the exit doors closed (and they were doors–one led to the music room, and the other led to a storage closet with no other exit, which was a challenge for blocking scenes.)

For the first time, I remember hearing what felt like thunderous applause –although the tiny theatre at the community college could only hold a couple of hundred people. The performance was sold out, and when the cast came out to take their bows, we all got lots of positive reinforcement due to standing ovations.

Miss Caudill got roses from someone, and I stood, heartbroken, as Benny and Lyn stood holding hands and taking bows long after decorum and character would have required it.

After the performance, we were excused from the usual after-practice grilling over our performances and sent home. I started to ask Miss Caudill a question, but she merely looked at me with a twinkle in her eye, and waved me away without saying a word. The next day at school we were debriefed. The debriefing started during the last period of the day (when I was still officially in P.E.) and continued through the afternoon before our next performance.

I was puzzled by the reaction of everyone when I walked into the room after school. Miss Caudill, perched on top of her desk with her legs crossed like a little kid, took one look at me and *howled.* Just howled with laughter. Everyone else started laughing too. I looked down at myself. Were my pants unzipped?

Eyes streaming down her cheeks, she said to me, "Tell me, tell me, did you do that on puh, puh, purpose?"

"Do what?" I asked in all honesty, which sent her back into a gale of laughter.

"You upstaged me, you little turd," said Benny. "*Nobody* upstages me."

"What do you mean upstage?" I asked.

"You stole the scene from him, ripped it right out of his hands," choked Miss Caudill.

"I don't know what you're talking about," I repeated.

"You scratched your ass right on stage, with that stupid wooden spoon, and everyone just lost it," declared Benny.

"I did not!" I indignantly declared.

"Oh, yes you DID," said Miss Caudill, "And it was absolutely the most brilliant, the most hilarious ASS-scratching I have ever seen in my entire life! What a HOOT!"

"I don't remember doing that," I protested, blushing hot enough to feel the heat in my face without looking in a mirror.

"I don't care," she said. "It was during the sun and moon scene when you were all laying around the stage. "

"Yup, he did it all right," confirmed my sister, who had been in the scene nearby during the...event. This, however, was the first I'd heard of it. If it was so shocking and funny, why hadn't she said anything about it last night? "You little dweeb."

"CC," said Lyn, "You told us once that if you were sufficiently well trained, *no one* could upstage us." She looked pointedly at me, eyes wide, shaking her head. "I *used* to believe you."

Of all people to be mortally embarrassed around, *she* had to be there. I started radiating into the near infrared. I blushed so much I think I started sweating from the sheer *heat* of it.

Miss Caudill continued, "That was so completely what Grumio would do! Could you be any more in character? I don't think so!" This brought a surprised glance from Benny *and* from Lyn, but they said nothing and accepted the direction, as we all always did.

"Let's just discuss your *timing,* Hoss," she continued. "There's this one spot involving Biondello that drags a bit and could use a little excitement." Benny and Lyn exchanged a glance which I interpreted as *Better him than us,* and I sat down as Miss Caudill leafed through her copy of the script.

"Yes, ma'am," I managed to croak.

At that time, with those people in that play, we would have stripped naked for Miss Caudill and performed in the nude if she thought it was necessary. And if we had been anywhere but Hazard, Kentucky, I wouldn't have put it past her, given some of the things we eventually did in the name of good theatre. At least we never performed a simulated rape and childbirth like the dance troupe from Paducah–which was performed for the theatre competition.

Miss Caudill was so enamored of this story she never hesitated to tell it to anyone who didn't know me. Such as my future college professor, Paul Power. And my *mother*. The next time she has an occasion to talk about me in public it'll probably be the first thing that comes out of her mouth.

I suppose it could be said that in high school I was an award-winning ass-scratcher.

The Final Collapse of Civilization

When Lyn was nine, she saw a production put on by some early students of Miss Caudill, who were in Louisville for a drama tournament. She thought to herself, *I can do that. Maybe better.*

She asked her aunt if she could read a poem to her.

"Sure, darling," said Cheryl, beaming. One more student led to speech and drama, and a relative to boot? Who wouldn't accept such an offer!

Lyn recited the poem, and took a bow to the applause of her aunt and mother.

I wonder how she'd do with one of the pieces my students are presenting, thought Cheryl. She fished around in the satchel she often carried with copies of rulebooks and scripts and permission forms. *Ah. Here it is.*

Lyn looked at the piece of paper handed to her by Cheryl. It was a mimeographed copy of a story by James Thurber, entitled "The Last Flower."

Lyn read the story, which consisted of a few paragraphs about the end of the world due to nuclear war, and its subsequent rebirth. I won't reproduce the story for you here; you should read it for yourself. Suffice to say that when the final line was read by Lyn for her aunt and mother, both were reduced to tears.

"That was beautiful, Lynnie," said Cheryl, wiping her eyes. "Where did you learn to read stories like that?"

"I've been practicing plays in the basement, Aunt Cheryl," said Lyn. "I wrote a whole play by myself too." With that the young playwright ran to her room to fetch a copy of her play, hoping to impress her Aunt.

Lyn performed plays in her basement, plays she wrote herself. They were fun. She made a big production out of each, improvising elaborate sets, making curtains from blankets and fashioning costumes from her sister's clothes and from the Goodwill store's more esoteric offerings. The stage eventually filled with characters from childhood stories and princesses and more, and neighborhood children and their parents, along with Lyn's relatives, often visited and clapped with delight at her creativity and imagination. It was a golden time in her life and the memories of those happy times undoubtedly formed many of her early motivations to pursue a life of acting and performing.

Unfortunately not all the aspects of her life remained in such idyllic suspension.

At about the same time I was starting elementary school school in Kentucky, Lyn was starting high school in Louisville. She had a relatively normal and uneventful 9th grade year there, and started the next year in Louisville as well.

Teri– Lyn's older sister, if you remember– married at 16, then divorced her first husband quickly to the relief of all. Unfortunately, by the age of 19 she married again, this time to a boy younger than herself. Sixteen year-old Roy was her second husband.

 In the meantime, things deteriorated at home. At this time Lyn was 15. They, being nearly the same age, wound up having time to spend together because Teri was working and Roy was not; both were living at home with Teri and Lyn's parents, and this left the young husband and his sister-in-law together frequently.

Being two teenagers, they hung out together; watching TV, talking about school, talking about mutual friends. At first, everything was cordial and above-board; but then things took a turn.

Roy, apparently bored with the frequent absence of his wife, and relatively uninterested in caring for their newborn baby, turned his attention to Lyn. At first the comments were just uncomfortably familiar, verging on the edge of flirting, jokes perhaps inappropriate for a brother-in-law to a *younger* sister-in-law but definitely not between friends of the same age; but Lyn became uncomfortable nonetheless, and wondered where this was leading.

It didn't take long until she found out.

The Liquor Barfer

One day when I was in the 7th grade, I encountered our neighborhood bully Todd Barfier. His father owned a liquor store. I always found his name, which looked like it ought to be pronounced 'Barfy-er' but was instead pronounced 'Bar-fyer' hilariously funny, but no one else did; probably because Todd would have kicked their asses had he heard the mispronunciation said aloud.

I had only recently been given permission to ride my bicycle out of sight of the house. In Ohio, as a 5th grader, I was constrained between two trees within sight of the kitchen window. After my half-brother's death due to liver disease from drinking, we moved to Kentucky so my mother could keep a watchful eye on Bill, her other son by "that Combs man." She was determined that I would not follow the same path they did, so she kept me on a short leash, even after we moved to Kentucky.

Todd was as juvenile a delinquent as you would ever care to meet. I understand he's spent some time in prison, but I don't know his current whereabouts (and that's a *good* thing, said Billy Mumy's mother in that *Twilight Zone* episode). My encounter with Todd brought me right up face to face with the fact that real life is not like TV.

When we lived in Ohio I owned a small blue bicycle which my mother really did not want to get for me in the first place–it was a fairly expensive bike with fenders and tassles on the handles and a thick gas-tank-like contraption over the center spar–and with 20-inch wheels she knew I would outgrow it before I wore it out. But I persisted, and eventually she relented and got it for me when Dad was having a particularly profitable construction job. In Ohio, at the age of 11 or so, I was forbidden to ride beyond the sight of the house even though there was only one house within a half-mile of our home.

When we moved to Kentucky, and I got a little older, I rode farther–as far as Dora's store down the road. Dora had a pinball machine which I occasionally tried to play, and she sold snacks and pop to people who didn't want to drive all the way to town–the next nearest store was about five miles away and the closest thing to a supermarket was Joe's Lycinda which was a considerable distance over Pratt Mountain, a narrow and winding trip that would sometimes result in tipped over bags and not a few broken jars. I never could play as much as I liked, because of time constraints and a lack of quarters.

One day on the way home from Dora's–which was not more than a couple of miles away from my house–I heard a motorcycle approaching from behind. On board was the sneering Todd Barfier–a teenager who was every little kids' worst nightmare. Word on the street was that he smoked, drank liquor when his father wasn't home–smoked marijuana and who knew what else. He was riding on a little dirt bike of the type a real Hell's Angel would use for a kickstand, but it certainly outclassed my little blue bicycle with no gearshift.

Barfier pulled up beside me, and I pulled over and stopped to see what he wanted.

"Where ya goin, buddy?" he said.

"Home," I said.

"Ain't that nice...how fast you think you can go on that thing?"

"Not as fast as you," I admitted. Maybe honesty would deflate the challenge and he would go away.

"Damn straight," he said, and miraculously, he turned a U-turn in the road and puttered away. I resumed peddling, and had just congratulated myself on my strategy when the sputtering dirt bike noise got louder. I looked over my shoulder, and Barfier had turned around again and was accelerating toward me as fast as his sputtering engine would allow.

102

I began peddling as fast as I could. I knew I had no hope of outrunning him, but it was true that the bicycle could stop and start faster than a motorbike; I had an edge in maneuverability. I doubted it would be enough. Just as Todd came roaring by, I braked to a stop so he wouldn't have the satisfaction of being able to outrun me. As a result, he overshot me by a few dozen yards, and he turned angrily around and came puttering back.

"Why'd you stop, punk?" he leered.

"No point in trying to outrun you," I said.

"I think if you don't shut your damn mouth I'm going to give you a reason to outrun me," he said, and I knew then he was simply looking for a fight with someone he knew he could beat. I couldn't outrun him, so I decided to try to get in range of my house and ignore him. I resumed peddling, but instead of trying to stop me, he sat there considering his options.

As I rounded the curve near my friend Sharlene's house, he decided to play a little rear-ending nudge game. I guess you would call it playing *chicken* but I called it pants-wetting *terror.* He came up behind my bicycle and nudged it with his front tire. The rubbing of the rubber tires emitted a high-pitched Freeep! each time, and each time I got shoved forward a little, almost to the point of losing control of the bicycle.

"Stop it, Todd," I said, not as aggressively as I might have, but to merely put it in the record (of my mind, at least) that I hadn't taken his bullying passively.

"You gonna make me, pussy?" he said, laughing. I turned beet red but didn't respond to the insult. I just kept peddling as fast I could.

"I said, you gonna make me, pussywillow?"

By now I had reached the entryway to our hollow, Beetree Fork. Four or five families lived in the hollow, but there were so many trees you couldn't usually see one house from the next, and certainly no one could see me. I made a sudden right turn down the dirt lane as he overshot the entrance. As I rode down the uneven, rocky lane I peddled faster, hoping to outrun him for a short burst of acceleration on what was (hopefully) an unfamiliar and unsmooth surface. I think I actually did surprise him because I got all of about fifty yards away from the road before he finally caught me. He gave my rear tire a vicious shove, which forced me off the road onto a large rock which might have fit in the back end of a pickup truck. It was tilted at an angle, and launched me into a head over heels flip with the bicycle landing half on top of me and half in the nearby creek. I knew I was hurt from the stinging sensations on the palms of my hands. I heard Todd's motorcycle issue a loud BRAP-AP-AP-RAAAAAP and then he sped away without a word, although he was laughing. I sat up to see him flip me off as he returned to the paved road. The grin on his face was unmistakable.

I dragged myself and my bicycle up the steep hill to my house. The bike wasn't damaged, although the handlebars were skewed, but I knew that could be fixed. The bike was scratched up a bit, but I wasn't obsessive about it or anything–I'd never washed and waxed it like some kids did with their bikes, except to flush out mud from under the fenders or oil the chain once in a while.

I was shaking with shame and rage, and a little bit of injury. Nothing was broken, but my palms were pretty scuffed up. A half inch gash in one palm would take years to completely disappear. There were small tears in my jeans around the knee but I wasn't bleeding profusely or anything.

Of course, my mother was livid. She extracted from me the whole sorry tale, and verified that I hadn't done anything to start the confrontation (unlike that time in the fifth grade when I got in trouble for fighting with a kid, and didn't tell them it was because I was writing "Alan loves Yvonne" in the condensation on the bus window.)

When Dad got home, we all piled in the station wagon and drove over to Barfier's house. Dad got out and went inside for a while, and then he came back out.

"What happened?" I said.

"Just remember he's gonna get it worse than you did," said Dad. He refused to tell me more, although through the grapevine I heard that Todd's dad, who wasn't home at the time (he was off working at the liquor store) gave him holy hell, forty lashes with a belt, and God knows what else.

All I know for sure is all I ever got from Barfier after that was dirty looks, and that was O.K. by me.

They say the best revenge is living well, and seeing as how he eventually drove himself into prison, and one of my best friends from high school now lives in his house, I guess justice does come around and bite the bad guys in the ass every now and then.

That's *karma*, baby.

If life was like TV, I would have been able to outmaneuver Todd. In real life, even if I had, he would have later sought me out because I challenged his dominance, and *really* kicked my ass. I was glad it was over. As far as I can remember he never said another word to me.

Saturn Beckons

The previous summer, before I started high school, I had sold Christmas cards to the neighborhood families. The cards were ordered in June, but were not delivered until November, because each was custom-printed with personalized message. *Greetings from the Caudills,* it might say. All my relatives and some of my neighbors chipped in a few bucks each and I delivered the cards and collected the cash in November. After the incident with Todd I was driven around to collect the money by my parents in the aging station wagon we drove. If I encountered Todd again he might not settle for merely shoving me off the road.

After I collected the payments, I could either keep $1.00 a box, or return all the money and collect a prize from the Columbia Gift Card Company Super Deluxe Prize Catalog.

My parents were surprised and somewhat disappointed when I returned the money and chose a Spitz Moon Scope from the catalog.

"It'll be just a God-damn piece of junk," my Dad said. My mother insisted as I had done the work, I would decide what to do with the profits. Dad grumbled, but as usual he deferred to Mom's judgement regarding anything dealing with the kids. Well, *surrendered* is more like it.

There wasn't a store in Perry County where you could buy a telescope. In Lexington, Sears sold refractors on wooden stands with a collection of lenses. I knew, because my cousin got one for Christmas and he wouldn't sell it to me ("I don't sell presents," he declared) or loan it to me ("You can just come over here and use it.") I couldn't have bought it anyway, because it was listed in the Sears, Roebuck catalog as $119.00 plus shipping. His attitude infuriated me because most of the time, the telescope sat in the family room like a set piece on a Hollywood TV set. The only thing he ever looked at with it, as far as I knew, was the full moon, and sometimes the sun using a dangerous little black-glass filter marked SUN that screwed into the eyepiece. (Public service announcement: if you have one of those little filters, take it out in the back yard and *smash it with a hammer*. If it should crack from he intense heat while you use it, you could be blinded. A dangerous and stupid design.) He didn't *use* it, like a telescope was *meant* to be used–

So I ordered the Moon Scope.

The Spitz Moon Scope, for those of you know about telescopes, was a 3-inch Newtonian reflector, on a ball-and-socket mount–less useful than an alt-azimuth mount, if you can believe that–which swiveled freely in any direction until tightened. The bracket had a little slot in it so you could, with some wiggling, even point the telescope straight up. The lenses were plastic–at least the little cylinders that held them were–and the finder scope was simply an empty tube with no cross-hairs, no lenses, and no way to adjust where it was pointing to align it with the main scope.

For those of you who don't know telescopes, that means that it was pretty much a piece of junk. But it was *mine*, and as I assembled the tripod stand and mount from the directions in the box it came in, I became convinced that the stars were *finally* within my grasp.

One cold, winter night, I crept out into the snow-covered hillside and set up my little telescope. According to the painfully thin booklet that accompanied it, you should be able to see planets with it, if you could find them. No one I knew knew any of the constellations except the Big Dipper. The Christian bookstore had practically kicked me out for asking for a star map. The books in the library were filled with facts, but none of them had a map I could use to tell which thing was which, and what thing was what. One book had a tiny, cramped map inside the front cover, and I had painstakingly copied it onto poster board because the librarian wouldn't let me check it out as it was some sort of reference book. All I knew from the vague reference books and encyclopedias was that planets were *bright*, and they didn't twinkle. So, shivering and clutching a small notebook and flashlight, I set out to look at *every* bright star until I found a planet.

I saw red stars, pale red light flickering as the earth's atmosphere shifted the light to and fro as it worked its way to my eye. I saw double stars. The moon was not up that night, so I couldn't look at the Moon Scope's namesake. Blue stars–Sirius looked like cool water, flowing on a bright winter day into a pool; another star flickered and winked at me, sputtering with an *electric blue* intensity– I didn't know its name, but in hindsight I think it might have been Bellatrix or Rigel–

–and then, magically, there was Saturn.

You can check, if you like; Saturn was relatively near the constellation of Orion in December of 1974, and logic and circumstance tells me that is where it was when I saw it. It was placed to be visible all night, although from our tiny hollow it was only visible for a few hours between the walls of the box we lived in.

Suspended in space, impossibly, was a tiny ball, with a ring that went *around* the outside of the ball. The rings make Saturn look very three-dimensional, and unreal. Human eyes cannot perceive color in dim light, and so the pearlescent cold, white light of Saturn fell on my eyes, after traveling over 800 million miles, my mind informed me, and I stared at it for long minutes, wishing I could go *there*, hoping beyond hope I could gain a chance to work on a telescope big enough to see more.

One of the lenses was a Barlow. The booklet said *Insert the Barlow between the eyepiece and the main focus tube to double the magnification.* I tried, but couldn't get the scope to focus; at higher magnification the slightest touch would ruin the alignment, and I was shivering.

Finally I managed to glimpse Saturn through the combined apparatus, but it just wouldn't focus. I noted how the image got smaller as I cranked the lens out, but it was still fuzzy when the mechanism reached the end of its travel. I finally relented and removed the eyepiece, shaking, outside the focus tube. For a brief instant, I *saw* the planet–the rings, curling behind it, the whisker-thin line dividing the rings in half, called the Cassini Divison after the astronomer who first noticed it–

Then I lost the image as the earth turned and the telescope didn't, and I started over.

Galileo thought the rings were *ears*, unable to see the detail necessary to resolve the image all the way around behind the planet. *It may be junk*, I thought, *But it's better than what Galileo started with.* And my cousin's expensive Sears telescope was never kissed by the light of Saturn, the Great Red Spot of Jupiter, the swarming lights of the Hercules Cluster, or the ghostly roiling of the Orion Nebula.

Karma, baby.

I dragged my mother out at 4 AM to look at Saturn. She was freezing, and bewildered, and probably claimed to see it just so she could go back in the house. I looked after she did, and she had breathed on the lens, her breath condensing into a frost that blocked the view. I dragged the moon scope back inside, and packed it into its box against the rising cacophony of my mother's already restarted snoring, and lay on the bed, thinking hard all the way to dawn. *How could I get access to a BIG telescope, like the one they use at Palomar?*

The next day, I looked up the address of the American Astronomical Society and sent them a letter. *How do I join your organization?* I wrote. A few weeks later, I got a reply.

Dear Jeff, it read. *Thanks for writing. The AAS is an organization for professional astronomers, doing research at universities. We would like to very much encourage you to continue your studies, so you can join us later when you are old enough and have begun your own research. Be sure to take plenty of math and science in high school. Good luck and have a good day.*

Plenty of math and science. From what I could tell, I'd be done with everything the school could offer by my junior year. How would I *ever* learn about the real universe, and not the fiction stories I read from the library bookmobile?

I had no idea.

Riding the Bus

I used to tell people that I lived "a quarter mile past where the pavement ends," and they would laugh, but it was quite literally true. Beetree Hollow, near the head (beginning) of Maces' Creek in Viper, was less than a mile from where the pavement ended. Probably the most famous person from Viper was Edna Ritchie, a folk singer of traditional Appalachian songs, a Fulbright scholar no less, and had performed all over the world. Despite her international reputation in folk music, relatively few people I have ever met know who she is.

Leafy trees extended over the deeply rutted dirt road serving Beetree Hollow from both sides, forming a tube of shadow that looked like it disappeared into murkiness until you actually entered it and allowed your eyes to adjust to the reduced light. The hollow itself was about a mile long. We lived in the first house in, perhaps a quarter of a mile in and up a steep driveway that would require us to make a "run-n-go" at the bottom to make it to the top.

In the winter, we would sometimes not be able to make it to the top at all; so we would park at the bottom of the hill and trudge to the top with our groceries or supplies. Everyone who went to the store would fetch one bag up, and then I would (or my Dad would, if he wanted to stay out of the house a bit longer) make the multiple trips necessary to get the remaining bags. The second and later trips were easier because you could step in your own previous footprints in the snow.

Kentucky is one of those border states–bordering those states that get significant amounts of snow (like Ohio) and those that don't (like much of Tennessee). We didn't get snow every year, and when we got any at all--even a fraction of an inch– *everything* closed, especially schools. We had to make those days up in summer, too, so every snow day was bittersweet because we knew we'd pay for it in the hot humid summers in our sweltering school buildings. We used to joke that Perry County only had one snowplow and it was probably stuck clearing all the judge-executive's relatives' driveways *first*. (The judge-executive was in charge of the county's road maintenance budget, if I remember correctly.)

- Our house was perched on the edge of a precipice about 100 feet tall, built on a small level area scraped off the side of a steep slope on the west side of the hollow. Despite this elevated position we only received 6 or 7 hours of direct sunlight (even in summer) due to the horizon above our heads in every direction. At night, we could see countless stars, twinkling and jinking in the murky air, occasionally cleft by a wayward satellite or aircraft so high you couldn't see any details. You could sometimes only tell which was which because satellites are totally silent and aircraft, even at 30,000 feet, are audible in a quiet place on the ground.

Each day I would walk down to the paved road and its cluster of mismatched mailboxes to wait on the bus. I was the first passenger on the bus going in, and the last passenger off coming home; the bus driver, Bobby John Combs (somehow related to my mother) lived a couple of miles from my house, so it was a convenient way for him to start and end the day.

Bobby John allowed one kid, decided by some unspoken hierarchy, to stand in the steps of the bus entrance well and ride as he drove. This was accomplished by hanging on to the metal handle that was used to open the bus door. There was a yellow line just like today, but we ignored it. He also used the door sentry as a snitch, because they were often facing backward and could identify troublemakers.

As the bus proceeded to school, each student would open the door a few times, until someone older, involved in sports, or related to the driver would board the bus; then the person farther down the totem pole would sit down, and the new person would take over. The process repeated in reverse on the way home.

During my freshman year, I was only allowed to stand in the door opening area when I was the only child on board the bus. Whatever

112

status determined the heirarchy of Bobby John's Door Opener, being the Boy Who Skipped 8th Grade clearly had no bearing upon it. And after I started doing more extracurricular things, there were many days I didn't ride the bus at all. That became more true as the years went by.

We never had disturbances on Bobby John's bus, and the reason was probably the pit stops. Every day, we would stop at one of the mom-and-pop "peanut" stores, which dealt exclusively in snacks, a very few staples, pickled bologna, canned food, and a few other odds and ends; we usually stopped at a little shack on the route where most of the bus population would dutifully file off the bus, swarm the store, buy a few things, then get back on the bus. The only rule was we couldn't leave our trash behind, and when we did, he'd skip a day. Some of the boys bought candy for the girls, who remained behind on the bus. When you had a few extra dollars you bought candy for your friends. I didn't have many friends, and the ones I did have didn't ride my bus, and extra dollars were pretty rare in my family as well so it was either pay my own way or nada for me. My favorite was a sort of a sucker on a stick that had a sweet and sour taste, kind of like a giant Sweet Tart on a stick. It cost a quarter, which didn't break the family budget.

There were peanut stores up and down the creek in those days, where credit was established by signing your name on a long yellow legal pad and payment came due when the government check came in. I suppose it says something that many of the stores had a sort of special-ized form on a metal clipboard that looked like it was designed to track temporary credit like this, as if there was enough demand for such a thing that someone created a product to fill the need. Dora's, Odel's, even my uncle and my half brother owned little stores for a while. One thing I remember from my brother's store was he had a pop machine that sat like a footlocker on the floor. You lifted the lid, deposited the money, and maneuvered the pop you wanted through the maze of metal guides until it popped free. Just fiddling with that was worth al-most as much as the pop.

I remember Odel, an older lady with a (I swear I am not making this up) beehive hairdo, the owner and proprietor of a very tiny store near a cluster of houses a few miles from ours. She had glasses like the bottoms of Coke bottles and she looked like she was zeroed in on whatever she was facing. She cut bologna from a giant red roll with a huge butcher knife, sawing it like a carpenter using a hand saw, big fat slightly uneven slices of bologna that would sizzle and smell delicious in the cast iron frying pan my mom used. None of these tiny stores remain today. Competition from Wal-mart, fifteen miles away, tilted the cost/benefit ratio of having a nearby store with limited selection and high prices away from the mild inconvenience of driving to Hazard on gradually improving roadways.

Maces' Creek has three branches: Left fork (where my elementary school, Viper Elementary, was located), Middle Fork, and Right Fork. Right Fork diverged at the former location of the post office near the mouth (exit) of Maces' Creek into the North Fork of the Kentucky River (we always just called it "the river.") Viper itself consisted of a couple of buildings containing a post office, a gas station, a print shop (where we got our tickets for Shrew printed) and a music store, of all things; a couple dozen houses wedged into bits and pieces of bottom land near an old, rusting railroad which carried coal when the mines were active. Even in 1976 the mines were fading. We lived on Left Fork.

When I started riding the high school bus, he had to drive down each branch of the creek to take us home. Mine was last; and thus I would often have a 45 minute bus ride, one way, for a trip that was perhaps less than 15 miles going directly to home. On days when I had drama and no study hall, I finished all my homework in this interval. Sometimes I stared out the window at the blurry landscape rolling by.

I was becoming aware that I might need to have my vision checked. Unknown to me and undetected by perfunctory vision checks conducted by schools in Ohio, I was somewhat nearsighted. During my freshman year, I mentioned to one of the teachers he should write larger, because I couldn't read what was written on the board.

114

The teacher (I don't remember who it was) told me to get my eyes checked, and I dutifully relayed this message to my mother. We of course did not have insurance, other than emergency insurance required by the school district for all students. It did not cover glasses.

Nevertheless, I made my first trek to the optometrists' office, and suffered the usual litany of "better? or worse?" until they arrived at my prescription.

"I have a question, doctor," I asked the optometrist when they settled on my prescription.

"Yes?"

"Can I get bifocals? How much would they cost?" The doctor gaped at me. "Son, only old people need bifocals. You're far too young."

"Well, listen," I said. "I do a lot of book work. So would it hurt my eyes to look through these glasses while I read a book?"

"It might, if you do it all the time," he answered. "Just take'm off when you need to read."

"I read while I'm in class," I said. "Up and down, back and forth. I'd wind up just leaving them on all the time." I visualized me setting down my expensive glasses and forgetting them one day, and the reaction that would cause at home. "I really want something I could just put on and leave on all the time."

"How will bifocals solve that? You don't need anything for close reading."

"Don't make any correction in the bifocal part," I said. "Just the same curvature on both sides of the lens, like looking through a little window."

"Well," said the doctor, "I could order that. It wouldn't *hurt* to wear bifocals. It might make your glasses a bit heavier. Where'd you come up with this idea?"

"I read a biography of Benjamin Franklin yesterday."

Franklin invented bifocals flitted across his face, then *The whole book?* "Well, what about the weight issue?"

"Not a problem. That's what I want. Does it cost a lot more?"

As it turned out, it didn't. I explained my reasoning to my mother, but I'm not entirely sure she understood. As I had done when seeking my way on a few other occasions, I got a bit technical with her and talked about diopters and refraction, and she relented, making my first pair of glasses my first set of bifocals, with no corrections in the semicircular inset lenses.

Most people didn't notice, so I never brought it up unless asked. Miss Caudill was one of the few people who ever did notice. She was holding my glasses because she insisted Grumio shouldn't wear glasses on stage. Actually, being nearsighted is a tremendous advantage on stage– it helps you stay in character because you can't frickin' *see* the audience. Due to my eyesight and the bright stage lights, it's like a gauzy curtain rested between me and my intended audience.

I explained my reasoning to her, and she said, "Only you would deliberately order bifocals while you're so young, Mason," and shook her head. I allowed as that was true, but demonstrated my ability to read both a book on my desk and her board simultaneously. The bifocals made an odd little shift in position at the line where the inset lens lived, but I soon got used to it.

For the first time in my life, I could see leaves, and rain, and snow as it fell. The tops of distant mountain ridges (which surrounded us in all directions, all the time) fell into sharp, detailed relief as I looked at the tree line, often up at a 20 or 30 degree angle with the horizon. I could always see these things before, but I could see in detail now. I even discovered, as I stood in the door well of Bobby John's bus, that I had neighbors I never knew existed because I couldn't see the houses before. It's a little odd first coming into glasses when you're a nearly-functional adult; you can articulate the things you notice more clearly and remember them better than when you are a little kid.

Whatever the reason, the bifocals did me no harm, and it was nearly 20 years before I had to strengthen my prescription, which to this day is still pretty light. Not exactly a scientific study, but as I've learned, what you believe to be true is often just as important as what you can prove to be true.

Recently, I broke my glasses and because I lived in a new town, I got a new optometrist, to whom I repeated this story.

"Talked him into it, did ya?" the optometrist-from-the-future said to me and myself in the past. "Well, that's interesting. Shouldn't have hurt you...apparently it didn't. You want the new lenses with the invisible line for the bifocals?"

I shook my head. The line had never bothered me before.

"These are a little bigger than what I usually prescribe, but it seems you know what you want in that regard," he said.

"I do." I replied, smiling. So he wrote the prescription.

Here's Yer Shoe

We competed in a lot of theatre competitions. If you weren't into drama in high school you wouldn't know, but it is actually a very competitive activity. You load up a busload of kids and go perform on a stage for judges, who evaluate your work and give you ratings. At the end there is a little award ceremony reminiscent of the Oscars: Best Actor in a Drama, Best Technical, Best Supporting Actor in a Comedy, Best Overall Performance, etc. This was a pretty big deal to us when we did Shrew, because we knew it was our best chance to be successful in multiple competitions. We were good and we knew it. These competitions are then held regionally and then the winners compete at the state level. There are even invitational tournaments just like in sports. We sometimes won the local competition and sometimes we didn't. Knott Central won it the year we did Shrew, and we came in 2nd. That really upset us, primarily because of the event that became known as the Great Hick Diversion.

As we prepared for the regional competition we noted that our rivals were scheduled to rehearse in the theatre the same day we were, but later in the day. We had already started to run through our first on-stage rehearsal of the new, cut-down play, when in the back of the theatre a door opened and the entire Knott Central crowd quietly entered and sat in the back.

Back stage, incredulous looks and quiet whispers spread the word that Knott Central was in the theatre. And then we hear Benny utter a line I will never forget:

"Hit shall be th' MOON er STAWRS er WHUT AH LIST, ayre Ah journey t'yer daddy's house!" There was a gasp–a heartbeat passed in silence, and Lyn blinked.

"Fahr-ward Ah pray, sinch we have done come so far," she said, matching his accent. "And be hit moon, or son, er whut you please;

118

and if'n you please t'call it a rush candle, haince-fourth I ah vows hit shall be so fer me."

We looked at each other incredulously. *What the heck was going on?*

"Ah say hit is the moon," said Benny/Petruchio.

"Ah knows it to be the moon," echoed Lyn/Kate.

"Nay then you LIE like the dog you ARE, hit is the gol-darn blessed SON!"

I gasped. Someone elbowed me after I started to ask what was going on, and I figured out, belatedly, we were getting set to dupe the Knott Central bunch into overconfidence.

Lyn fell to her knees and groveled, just as we had rehearsed. The words she spoke were definitely not as we rehearsed. "Then Gawd be blest, hit is the blest son. But son hit is not whin you say hit is not, and the moon changes even as yer mine. Whut you will have hit name-edd, even that it be. And so hit shall be fer me. Kathy. Kath-er-ine."

The accents and action decayed into some improvised business that included Benny throwing me around the stage in *unrehearsed* falls and counting them as he did so ("That be *once,* sirrah! *Twice,* sirrah! *Thrice!*") and a near-riot as Benny flailed his servants, myself and Curtis and Biondello and the rest, scattering us across the stage like ninepins, to the point where someone lost a shoe.

As far as my part as Grumio went, well, it's a real trick to speak Elizabethan iambic pentameter with a goofy sounding lisp and a thick Eastern Kentucky accent. A couple of times, I thought I would choke.

As the party departed the stage to end one scene, Raynard Smith uttered the one line that set Miss Caudill off into gales of laughter and tears, and completely sealed the deal as far as Knott Central's overconfident students were concerned: finding an abandoned shoe on a play with no sets and no where to hide it, he retrieved it, and holding it out in front of him as he exited, he declared:

"H'yere's yer shoe,"

whereupon everyone backstage completely lost it, laughing with the exhaustion of people who had been stressed, overworked, under-slept, and put upon by people with airs perhaps one time too many.

Afterwards, Miss Caudill demanded to know "just what the... just what you *thought* that was all about, that was perhaps, no, it *was, it WAS* the most God-awful performance in the *history* of all theatre..." when Benny interrupted to explain.

"Knott Central snuck in the back of the room and was watching us."

"It's pretty rude considering we're competitors," said Lyn.

Unknown to me at the time, there was a long history of rivalry between our school and Knott Central. When she had started doing competitions, they were held at Knott Central High School, a venue she felt was biased, especially since Knott Central got to perform on a stage, while we were assigned to perform in a cafeteria. Another year the chief judge tired of Miss Caudill's objections so much, he said, "Miss Caudill, I wonder what it would take to please you,"

"All it would take is a certain amount of fairness and impartiality," she said. "I suppose you won't be able to help me, at that."

Then there was the year the judges were removed at the far end of the theatre when Devitt H. Caudill's turn came. So close to the wall was the judges' table that they had to scoot it out from the wall to fit behind it and sit down. This was, we guessed, to make it harder for the judges to hear. "That backfired," she told me later. "They gave us high marks for projecting."

This history undoubtedly tempered her response to our Great Hick Diversion.

"They—they were in the *back*? Then that..." gasped Miss Caudill, her eyes as wide as saucers, her chest heaving as she gasped and gulped air to launch into a tirade....and then all she said was, "then that...that...that was *brilliant*, children. Just *brilliant*. But never do it again. *Ever*. Or I shall *rip* your hearts out with my bare hands."

"We believe you," said Benny.

Then we all dissolved into jerky, silent laughter, again, as we cleared the stage for Knott Central's turn. Once backstage, we escaped into the hall and the real laughing commenced. It may be, in my 44-odd orbits around the planet, that I have never laughed as hard as I did that night, surrounded by people who knew me, accepted me for what I was, and let me join in a moment of joy.

None of us stayed to watch them practice.

Kickapoo Joy Juice

At regionals, the competition started with local school from other districts in our region. I think there were probably 10 or 12 counties in our region (and that usually means that only one or two districts per county in Kentucky). I don't remember much about the regional competition. It's odd, but I don't remember regionals for any of the competitions; and I don't remember thinking about them or not remembering them until just now, as I write this. It's funny how you can strengthen memories (and reinforce mistaken ones) by going through a process like writing this story. Something about the function of memory is buried in this experience; if I were more inclined towards the biological sciences it would make a great study on something or other.

After a performance for regionals (I'll tell you how it came out later) the entire cast was crammed into C.C.'s little sports car. Well, actually, there was another car, but both of them were crammed to the gills. I think it might have been a Mustang but whatever it was, it was tiny. We had three guys in the back seat with girls sitting on each lap and two in the front. Ben was in the front. Benny, naturally, asked if we could stop and get some beer. C.C. just rolled her eyes at Benny and didn't bother answering his facetious question. We did stop to stretch our legs (even carrying a pretty girl in your lap gets tiresome after a while) and buy snacks.

I remember I bought a chocolate drink called a Yoo-Hoo. The only reason I remember is that Benny bought a local soft drink called Kickapoo-Joy-Juice, named after the moonshine in the Lil' Abner comic strip that still appeared in our local paper. You wouldn't think so, given today's politically correct climate, but Lil' Abner and the Beverly Hillbillies were very popular in Appalachia. (Oh, you should know, I'd never even *heard* the term Appalachia until I went to college. Read into that what you will.) It was only lemon-lime pop, sort of like Mountain Dew but with more caffeine. (How many times has that description been used to launch a soft drink? Here, drink this Zap!

What is it? Well, it's kinda like Mountain Dew with *more caffeine.* Mountain Dew was the caffeine standard for our Generation just like Jolt was in the 90's and Rockstar is now. Liquid caffeine with artificial flavorings added and a little water.)

So aaaanyway, here we are, stuffed tighter than a welfare queen's car going to town to apply for food stamps, worried about running into a cop who would ask us "what the God-damn hell do you think you're doing?" when Ben took it upon himself to *act* drunk since he couldn't get access to beer. Somehow or other he wound up sitting on the door (window down) leaning out of the car screaming "Kick-a-poo JOY JUICE! I LOOOOVE Kick-a-poo JOOOY JUUUICE!!" when C.C. finally pulled off the road. Cackling like a laying hen. Tears streaming from her eyes.

"Sit down, you crazy fool," she said to Benny, when she could finally speak. "You're going to fall out."

Benny sat down – on Charmaine Marshall's lap. He showed no compunction to alter that arrangement despite a glare and a sharp elbow from Charmaine. She was, after all, taller than he was. Miss Caudill began to suspect that Benny was being *deliberately* distracting, I think, because she had to tell him twice to settle down. Miss Caudill wiped her eyes and we resumed our trek. Lyn somehow, miraculously, wound up in my lap. I think perhaps I was the only boy Miss Caudill trusted with the task. I could smell Lyn's perfume, which was nice–but such was our arrangement she couldn't look me in the face, and she spent the rest of the trip looking out the window.

That cinched it for me. Caudill was the greatest teacher of all time.

I didn't know, even with Lyn sitting in my lap, that the same exact event had triggered quite the opposite reaction from her.

The Better Part of Valor

The events in the car carried with them some baggage I was not aware of at the time. Events in Louisville came to a head when I was still in elementary school (Viper Elementary is K-8. We didn't have middle schools or junior highs in Perry County, as far as I knew. Why pay for two principals when one will do?)

One day, Teri's husband Roy called the Anderson home, seeking to locate Teri.

Lyn was home alone and answered the phone.

"I don't know where she is, Roy," she said.

"Well, when will she be back?"

"I don't know that either."

"Why don't you know? You're her sister, after all."

"Well, you're her husband–why don't you know?"

There was an ominous silence on the end of the phone.

"You had better tell," he said.

"I said I don't know, and I don't. I don't have any reason not to tell you."

"I'm coming over," he said.

"She's not here," Lyn insisted. It was, in fact, true. Teri was "out," the baby was home being watched by Lyn, and Teri hadn't bothered to tell her younger sister her destination. It wasn't the first time, either.

Shortly thereafter, Roy appeared. Lyn and Roy had already had some uncomfortable moments recently. Once, Roy emerged from the bathroom wearing only a towel. He stood before Lyn until she looked up from her books, then dropped the towel with a grin. Lyn was shocked–too shocked to speak. *What does he think he's doing?* she thought. *What possible outcome is he looking for here? Does he think I'm just going to pounce on him because he's naked? How gross.* She turned away in shock and disgust, and when she looked back, Roy was gone.

In another recent incident Roy had shown her a little figurine he and Teri kept in their room at the Anderson home. It was a little nondescript smiling man, and Lyn wondered what the significance of it was–until Roy turned it over and revealed an enormous penis on the other side. Lyn flinched and looked at Roy, who was enjoying her shocked reaction.

Then there were the increasingly angry "incidents" where Roy would smash his fist into the wall, sometimes leaving marks and dents and occasionally causing something to crash to the floor; when confronted he apologized and swore that he wouldn't strike Teri, but adults know such behavior has a way of escalating.

The Anderson home became tense even when there wasn't an 'incident in progress'; unspoken stress colored all of their lives. Lyn took to avoiding Roy and going the long way around the central part of the house just to avoid passing by him.

After the towel-dropping incident Lyn did tell her mother, who seemed concerned but did not act. Instead, she merely instructed Lyn to "be careful around Roy," leaving Lyn wondering exactly how she was supposed to do that with someone who lived in the same house as she. And now he was "coming over," from wherever he presumably was, to find Teri.

Roy arrived in a foul mood, convinced that Teri was really home and Lyn was lying to him.

"Tell me where she is!" he shouted. Lyn jumped back, startled, from the front door. He had never yelled at her before that way.

"I told you! I don't know!" she cried. "What's wrong? Why are you so mad?"

"A man ought to be told by his wife where she's going!" he yelled. "Now you tell me where she is, or you'll be sorry!"

"I DON'T KNOW!" screamed Lyn. Convinced she was lying, Roy grabbed Lyn by the shirt and lifted her bodily from the floor and slammed her into the wall.

"LIAR!" He yelled. Lyn screamed, and although no one was there to help her or stop him, he released her and left.

Lyn remained, sobbing, as she fell to the floor. *What the hell was that about?* she thought. *Why did he do that? What did I do to make him grab me like that?* Her hands were shaking, and she could barely stand. Eventually, she made her way to the phone and called her father at work.

"I'll be right home," he said, and in minutes he appeared at the door, accompanied by Lyn's mother. Sobbing, Lyn related the story of Roy's aggressiveness. Both parents looked pained but not shocked, as if the incident were merely another brick that Teri seemed determined to lay in the wall between them.

"Daddy, he *grabbed* me," sobbed Lyn. "It *hurt*. I don't ever want that to happen again."

"I'll talk to him, Lynnie," said her father, as he left the room to get his keys.

Talk to him? TALK to him? That's it? That's all? He should be charged with assault! Lyn thought, wide-eyed. Didn't her father *get* what happened to her? *At the very least, they should kick his ass out of the house!*

The next day, she learned that her father had a "talk" with Roy, and whatever was said, he didn't seem to be overly concerned about it. Her protests were met with weary resignation, and Roy's problems absorbed into the larger issue of What Will We Ever Do With Teri.

I've got to get out of here, Lyn decided. *There's no one here I can convince that he might hurt me next time. He might.* She thought–with sudden clarity: *What if I personally did something to make him angry? I didn't do anything to him today. What if he thinks I was trying to get between him and Teri? What if he lets Teri think that too! If my parents think so little of Teri, what will they think of ME if I am accused of trying to steal her husband? Who knows what he would say? What he might do?*

But where could she go? She could run away–

That's it. I'll run away. Start over somehow, on my own. I can't live here.

During her sophomore year, she did exactly that; ran away and lived at a friend's house for several weeks. She called home to tell her parents where she was, that she was OK, and she wouldn't be coming back. Pleading and blaming and accusations ensued, none of which encouraged her to return and reinforcing her decision to move out. Her parents, increasingly desperate to avoid pushing too hard so as not to create "another Teri," didn't aggressively seek to return her to home.

As the weeks dragged on, Lyn realized she couldn't keep imposing on her friend's good will. She had to strike out on her own, at the age of 15. Where could she go?

And then it occurred to her. *Aunt Cheryl's. I could move to Hazard. It's far away. Roy would never go there. And she's family.*

Cheryl had never married, never raised kids. Would she accept a teen-ager into her home?

Lyn waited until her aunt visited and explained what was happening. She perched herself on Cheryl's lap, legs nearly reaching the floor. Hugged her tight as if she were twelve years old again. "And the best part, Aunt Cheryl," said Lyn, "is that I will get to study drama with you, which makes complete sense because I've always wanted to be an actress," she said. She, thinking carefully, had placed the bait at the end of the request.

"Oh, child." Cheryl thought Lyn's attempt to persuade her was quite transparent, but she had her own agenda. *We've got to get this child out of that house,* she thought. *There's no telling when that boy is going to let loose and hurt someone.* "I'll talk to your mother, Lynnie," she promised. "We'll see."

Edie refused to listen at first. Remove her only *good* child? Tears, arguments, pledges and pleas followed, each objection carefully maneuvered through tacit agreement by Lyn and Cheryl. Yes, there would be a curfew. No, no boys would be allowed to visit overnight at Cheryl's home. Yes, she would make sure chaperones were always keeping an eye on Lyn. Lyn would be too busy to date boys anyway, she'd be working hard at theatre every day.

"Cheryl, how can you *ask* me to give up my daughter?" pleaded Edie.

"Edie, how can *you* ask your daughter to say here in this environment, with that boy marching through the house acting the way he does? He's eventually going to *hurt* her. You *have* to know that." Cheryl hoped that Edie would see the light soon. Roy, in her opinion, was a powder keg waiting to explode, for whatever reason.

Edie didn't answer with her voice, but her eyes revealed that she knew she must agree. The next hurdle to cross was Lyn's father, and for that she knew that two "hysterical" women wouldn't be able to persuade him alone.

128

A psychiatrist was consulted. He advocated, almost immediately, getting Lyn out of the environment, as far away from Roy as possible.

Edie, convinced and emboldened, argued for it. If she couldn't protect *Teri* anymore, then by God, she was going to protect *Lyn*. That was what she told herself, when she wasn't crying. Still, Harvey, Lyn's father, refused to negotiate.

"You listen to me, Harvey Lee Anderson," she said. He turned, startled. She hardly ever spoke to him that way. "You have a choice to make. Either Lynnie goes to live with Cheryl, away from *that boy,*" she said, pointing upstairs, "or Lynnie *and I* go to live with Cheryl. Make your choice."

Cheryl, who was witness to this and told me about it many years later, stood agog. She had *never* seen Edie stand up to Harvey Lee like that, in many years of marriage.

Faced with overwhelming opposition, Harvey finally relented.

"There goes my last reason for living," said Harvey to Edie a few days later, as Lyn and Cheryl drove away.

Teri wasn't present for the departure, and neither was Roy.

So, halfway through her sophomore year and over a month out of school anywhere, Lyn stepped into the hallways of Devitt H. Caudill Memorial High School.

A fresh start, she thought. *I can leave all the conflict behind me, all the low expectations of my parents, and I can escape the destiny that fate has dealt me. Things can be better. I know it.*

Two years later, she got caught doing things best left to private situations with her boyfriend, hidden under a blanket while crammed into the back seat of a Mustang on a school trip, and forced *in front of eve-*

ryone to sit on the lap of the only boy in the car who wouldn't dare lay a hand on her.

She rode home, humiliated, ashamed of being caught, ashamed of finding herself on the same path she had struggled mightily to escape, and stared out the window at the silent hills and blinking fireflies as they closed in on her.

Wrassling for Reputation

It's bad enough being kind of small for your age and a little shorter than average (which I was). I skipped the 8th grade and so arrived in high school at the age of 13, which put me at an even greater size disadvantage. And then I had to go and get myself involved in the theatre...especially the International *Thespian* Society. You can imagine the jokes, which I suppose most ITS members have had to endure since the organization started. The sad part is that most of the time, I think the people who teased us not only thought *thespian* sounded like *lesbian* but that they thought that they were in fact the same word, and were unable to hear the difference when spoken. At my progressive left-coast high school in California, even today, the student announcers regularly make announcements about the "Thesbian" society.

To be a member of ITS you had to put in so many hours of rehearsal. You got points for leading roles, a few less for supports, and one point for doing a walk-on. If you got 10 points you'd get a star. If you exceeded the amount of points possible you could get a "bar" which represented extra credit, sort of. I graduated with four stars and a bar and well over 100 ITS points.

Consequently, I had all the ingredients necessary for teasing: small, "thespian", flatter than average accent (puttin' on airs, boy?) and (you think you're so much better than everyone else) that the obvious conclusion my classmates came to was that I was gay. Plus I had no girlfriend when I got involved in this stuff–though Lord knows I went through several in high school. Not because I was trying to prove I wasn't gay, but because I *really really* liked girls. Now, I barely knew at first what *gay* meant; no one in my high school was openly gay (who was, in 1976 in Eastern Kentucky? Who would be now?) but I knew they were insulting my masculinity and they were trying to put me down. Anyone could see that. And the fact was I wasn't physically strong or particularly well coordinated. Like so many other victims of teasing and bullies, I worked with what I had: my wits. For low-grade morons the usual rejoinder that turned the tables was "...and you promised you'd never tell!" followed by crocodile tears.

For those who had heard that one before the next notch up contained "Maybe you'll explain to all these people exactly how you came by that information. I'm sure they'd be interested in the story," which was great if they weren't brave enough to fight in public – it usually finished them off.

These stories are in every "arteests" biography and are so common they've become clichéd in the ABC Afternoon Special and the Lifetime Channel. The usual plot is that a particularly evil kid with a broken home who gets beaten by his father brings it to a head by picking a fight which Our Suffering Hero either wins through physical training, superior strategy or Moral Imperative (he refuses to fight and gets away with it.)

That never happened with me. Not counting the incident with Todd, which I didn't resolve by myself. It never got to that point because of the Six Million Dollar Man.

See, the novel by Marshall Caidin, *Cyborg*, was turned into a TV series in the 1970's called the Six Million Dollar Man, starring Lee Majors. He had a bionic (biological - electronic) arm, two legs, and an eye. Whenever he used the eye they would use a sound effect like this: "Bah-bah-babababa" as his point of view showed the zooming in needed to show detail. And Lee Majors had this sort of permanent squint anyway, only in his right eye. So middle school boys all over the country were running in slow motion across the playground making "babababa" noises while we squinted with one eye and played at fighting. As I've seen as a high school teacher, sometimes these middle school games spill over to high school. We regularly see 14 and 15 year old boys playing tag, for example.

One day during my freshman year several of us were goofing off in an empty classroom (Can you imagine? Kids allowed in an unlocked classroom with no teacher present?) and playing Bionic, as we called it.

When I was young and slender I had the ability to rise from the floor directly from a cross-legged "Indian-Style" position (forgive my political incorrectness but remember we are talking about the 1970's) directly to a standing position by simply standing and rotating 180 degrees in place. It's been quite a few years since I could do that (I could also put the palms of my hands on the floor behind my heels with knees locked) and while we were playing, I did it particularly quickly, arms swinging out and caught someone–a boy named Willie Fine, I think–right in the diaphragm.

Will promptly sat on the floor and opened his mouth. He couldn't breathe. The other boys started to laugh.

Will turned purple. He started to gasp; I had merely knocked the wind out of him. He'd be fine in a minute. But he continued to wheeze when suddenly he gulped and emitted a squeak and started breathing again.

"You play too rough, man," gasped Will.

"Jeezus, what did you do to him?" said Tim.

"I didn't, I didn't mean to hit him so hard, he was kind of in the way," I stammered, but their stares told me it was no use. I had become Formidable. Will delighted in telling everyone about my "secret Kung-fu moves." And from that day forward, no one ever challenged me to a fight or even looked threateningly at me. Whether it was because of my newfound Kung-fu skills or because my parents were known to be aggressively protective I'm not sure.

Glomawr State Penitentiary

After the incident in the Mustang, Lyn was put on virtual lockdown in Cheryl's home in Glomawr, a little community carved out of the hill-side near the river, down the road from Jeff. The village consists of a few dozen houses, a "peanut" store, a gas station (which today is known as ... wait for it... 'Glowmart.') Our local branch of the Kentucky river winds through it, lined on both sides by dense deciduous forests interspersed by occasional temporary eruptions of tires and appliances and headless dolls.

Cheryl's home was perched on a steep hillside in Glomawr, with just enough room to pull over a car next to the steps leading uphill to the front door. One of the things I remember about it was she had a little study off to the side filled from floor to ceiling with books. I never saw so many books in a private home before. Mostly textbooks, scripts, novels, teaching theory, and stagecraft, they were of course unsorted and filled every shelf, floor to ceiling, spilling into stacks on the floor.

Lyn saw this house more or less like a prison although she wasn't literally ever locked inside of it. Forbidden from seeing her erstwhile boyfriend, watched constantly, prevented from doing anything not school related, Lyn joined everything she could just to get out of the house. She was on the cheerleading squad with Pat Hatford. She did plays. She did all sorts of things.

None of it improved the attitudes of her Aunt, her mother, and her grandmother. Edie visited Cheryl regularly, especially during school holidays when she could spend time with Lyn. Mamal lived with Cheryl (or, since it was Mamal's house, you could say Cheryl lived with her mother).

"You're not going out, and that's final," said Cheryl. "Not with that bunch. I've seen how they are. Fifteen minutes of fun in the back of the car and boom, you've got a bun in the oven."

"I wouldn't do that!" cried Lyn.

"That's as may be," said Mamal. When I first met Mamal, she knew my name because of stories Cheryl had told her, but I didn't know hers; I just responded to her questions without saying her name, until some time later when I found out her name was Adelaide Grace Macintosh Caudill. "You have to admit, dear, that the likelihood is much lower if you never get the opportunity."

"That's not fair! We weren't having *sex* or anything in the Mustang, you know." Anger and shame flashed in Lyn's eyes. Mamal's eyes widened. She wasn't used to such language in her presence.

"Lyn!" gasped Edie.

"Life's not fair, child," said her grandmother. "You just have to learn to adapt."

"Lyn, darling, we're only doing this because we love you," said Cheryl. "Mamal is right. You have to learn to adapt to the rules, because the rules are here to keep you safe."

"Adapt," said Lyn. "I've never gotten in trouble at school, never sent to the office, never done any of the things that you are so angry with Teri about," she complained. "Why are you treating me like I'm just like her? I'm not like her. I'm not her."

"Well of course not," said Cheryl. *Why is everything with teenagers so melodramatic?* She wrung her hands in frustration. "We know you're not her, but we're just trying to keep you safe, keep you from falling into the wrong crowd like she did."

Lyn began pacing in little circles in the living room, bouncing off of unseen walls surrounding the furniture as she marched about the room, trying to get her captors to somehow understand that she wanted to be independent, and prove to herself if no one else that she was capable of making her own decisions. *Why is everything with adults so difficult?*

"Don't you understand that the more you treat me like *her* the less value there is in being like *me*? I might as well *be* like her, for all the good being *me* does."

"You're a beautiful, wonderful child," said Cheryl. "You're *so* talented–I sometimes wonder if you know how talented you are."

"Fat lot of good talent does me," she said. "I can't go out without a chaperone, everything I do is questioned–"

"You're too young to know better, dear," said Mamal. Lyn gaped at her. Didn't her grandmother *remember* what it was like to be a teenager? When you got old, did you *forget* what it was like, being in a limbo between childhood and adulthood, made to work like an adult but thought to have the judgement of a child? "You'll see when you get older," her grandmother continued.

"There's not one person in my life who understands me," wailed Lyn. "I have hopes and dreams and ambitions and every day, *every day* I wake up in Hazard, Kentucky and think, It's not my fault that I am here. *Why am I being punished when I didn't do anything wrong!*"

Cheryl swept back her hair in frustration. She deposited herself on the couch. Lyn's nervous energy was wearing her out. "It was *your* idea to come here, Lyn," she said. "Remember?"

"I just wanted to get away at the time. Don't you think it would have been more fair if *Roy* had left? It was *my* home first, after all!"

"I know, honey, but you have to understand, there are some things you can change, and some things–" began Cheryl.

"Just give it some time," said Mamal. She wriggled her hands, seeking a crochet needle or cross-stitch frame without success, unconsciously seeking a prop to make the tension in the room go away.

"Time," said Lyn. "Time, and time and time. I'm so *sick* of waiting for my life to get better. How long do I have to wait?"

"We love you, sweetie," said Mamal.

"Yes, we do," echoed Cheryl. "Someday you'll see that this was all for the best. I know you're hurting. You just have to trust us and believe that we really do love you."

"You love me." She stated, flatly. "You love me. You don't even *trust* me. How can I trust you about *anything*, when you don't believe in *me* enough to even let *me* out of the *house!*" Lyn shrieked, running up the creaky stairs.

Cheryl and Edie and Mamal listened to the weeping girl until she stopped crying. As the false sunset of an Eastern Kentucky afternoon filtered the sun's light through the trees at the ridge-line above and across the highway, and the cooler breezes of eventide began drifting through the open windows, they sat murmuring about youthful defiance, and pain, and memories of sweetness and light and days gone by.

Dreaming of Teaching

During the interval after we had performed the full-length version of *Shrew* and state competition, an article came out in the local newspaper. The article praised Benny, especially, calling him "A shining supernova in a sky of stars," and had quotations from Miss Caudill about how hard she worked, and how little support she had, and how difficult it was to bring theatre to Hazard.

I had to explain to everyone exactly what a supernova *was*– an exploding star billions of times brighter than a regular star. Being called a supernova was a *good thing* in this context. Supernovas were not exactly something high on the list of textbook publisher priorities in 1976. (Truth be told, we had no textbooks from 1976; my science book was published in 1965 or so, and the history book was so old we jokingly referred to it as American Current Events.)

It was a nice article, except for the staged picture of Lyn kissing Benny with the caption *Debra L. Andersen shares a passionate kiss with Benny Doherty in Devitt H. Caudill's production of Taming of the Shrew.* That part, I didn't enjoy seeing. My classmates wanted to know if they were *really* kissing, or just pretending.

"I haven't the faintest idea," I said. In public, I thought it was a stupid question; in reality, I didn't want to know. I heard some of the cast members discussing it, and got up and left the room so I didn't have to hear. Even though I knew in my mind she was acting, in my heart of hearts, I wished she were kissing *me* in that play and not Benny.

I think the article brought some attention to the program, but the little digs at the administration for its lack of support didn't convert anyone at the school. We continued to have issues. During scheduling our classes would be mysteriously rearranged and we'd have to get them fixed to get drama again. That couldn't be attributed to computer errors. We only had 400 students, and scheduling was done on a large piece of poster board with teacher names and classes listed. You signed your name where you wanted to take classes. There wasn't a computer in the entire school until well into the late 1980's. Our fund raisers were cancelled when half-finished. Buses were reallocated at the last minute, making us all cram into Miss Caudill's Mustang on more than one occasion.

I once asked Miss Caudill *why* the administration didn't appreciate the work she did. We were in her classroom, temporarily alone, waiting for rehearsal to start. I was helping her clean the room. It *always* needed cleaning.

"Well, it's not basketball, first of all."

"It's not like we've ever won anything in the past 20 years, " I said. "The best we've ever done is win the region once and a while. In AAA division." Drama didn't *have* stratified divisions. Everyone competed against everyone, which is as it should be, in my opinion. They did have a junior division for younger students, but that was the only accommodation they made.

"I don't really know, Jeffery," she said. "Could be because I'm a woman, not part of the old boy's network. Probably because whenever he sees me coming, Byron knows I want something. If I ever figure it out, I'll tell you someday."

"It's too bad," I said. "Not everyone is motivated by basketball."

"No," she said. "Not everyone."

"You know," I said, "If someone would stitch the bottoms of those little baskets on the hoops together, the ball would *stay* up there and they wouldn't have to keep putting it back in over and over."

This brought a gale of hooting and laughter from her. "You are a unique young man," she said.

"I hope *u* don't *nique* up behind Mr. Caudill when you ask for stuff."
She knew which Caudill I spoke of, her arch-nemesis, Byron "Bear"
Caudill. She winced and groaned, the greatest reward a punster could
ask for. "You might startle him into having a heart attack."

"Administrators don't like being startled or surprised," she said. "They
want everything to be the *status quo*, always bland and boring and
safe. And *easy*."

"Why don't you want that, Miss Caudill?" I asked. It occurred to me
that I had been wrapped up in my own motivations so long, I had
never asked about hers. She always *was*, from my perspective. Just
there. Driven. Like a force of nature you grew up with, but never questioned. Obviously she had a mission. But I didn't know *why*. "What
makes you work so hard?"

She regarded me for a time, gathering thoughts. I don't think she had
to answer this question often. I think she had some close friends she
discussed it with from time to time.

"When I was younger," she said, wistfully, "I saw a play about impossible dreams. It was a musical, called *The Man of La Mancha*. Do you
know of it?"

I admitted as I did not.

"It's about a knight errant, a sort of adventurer, who called himself
Don Quixote. He and his partner Pancho set out on a quest to conquer
evil. As it happens, he's actually insane; he's really a pathetic old man.
He winds up fighting a windmill, thinking it's a dragon. He also meets
a girl, a ... serving girl, that he calls *Dulcinea*. He thinks she's a prin-
cess, sort of, and needs to be rescued from some thugs."

I nodded.

"Dulcinea won't have anything to do with him. He tries to convince
her that she is beautiful, his dream, his muse, but she won't listen. Fi-

nally he fights an evil knight, in reality his doctor, who uses mirrors to show Quixote as he really is: a pathetic old man that only imagined he was a knight."

"He wasn't really a knight all along?" I already knew what a *muse* was. There was an article about *muses* in my half-brother Bill's encyclopedia set, which he bought for decoration. Every time I stayed overnight, I read another volume in the set.

"No."

"What happened?"

"He gave up on living, defeated. He stopped pursuing his Quest. But Dulcinea has in the meantime become convinced she is a worthy person after all, and she rescues his heart, making him believe in impossible dreams again, just before he dies." Tears welled up in her eyes. "I saw this play in New York, and I thought it was just the most *beautiful* thing I'd ever seen. To Dream an Impossible Dream. It... it changed my life, Jeffery. Changed my life. "

For the first time in my life, I hugged my teacher instead of merely returning a hug. Twenty years later, and she would have shrugged me off and had to fill out paperwork with the associate principal. But she just accepted it for what it was. A hug. From a friend.

"What's your impossible dream, Miss Caudill?" I asked when I sat back down. "Can you tell me?"

"Child, don't you *know?* " I had never felt so unprepared for a conversation. Sometimes, when I talked to her, I was forcibly reminded of the lack of depth of my experiences in the world. I shook my head.

"It's *you*," she said. "You and all the other children. My dream, my, my *mission* is to bring a little theatre, a little bit of the larger world, back home here to Perry County. Anyone can wait tables and work as an actor in New York, or in Los Angeles. I've had my opportunities from time to time. But these children here, right here in Perry County, are capable of amazing and *astounding* things. They don't *have* to settle for hauling junk cars and digging coal and welfare checks. Sometimes, I think I'm the only one who knows."

"*I* know," I said. "I'm just beginning to figure it out."

She looked at me for long moment, dabbing tears from her eyes, attempting to wipe away streaks of mascara.

"I believe you, child." She picked up a wad of English papers she needed to grade. "I believe *in* you."

"I *know,* Miss Caudill,*"* I repeated. "We believe in *you*, too. We *all* do, Miss Caudill. Despite the grumbling and complaining we do offstage. We wouldn't keep showing up if we didn't *believe.* We *all* know you believe in us. We believe in you *too.* We always have."

She waved me away, and as I left her room, I could hear her weeping.

Later, when she had calmed down, she loaned me the phonograph recording of *Man of La Mancha.* I listened to it several times. *The Impossible Dream* made me cry the first time I heard it, and every time since then.

Now I knew why the drama students worked so hard, without complaining.

That was also the day I learned what it meant to be a *real* teacher.

Everyone Out of the Pool

Eventually, Miss Caudill did find out what the problem was with Mr. Caudill, and she related the story to me some years later.

Mr. (Byron) Caudill had always wanted to be a basketball coach, and when the opportunity arose to transfer to Devitt he pounced on it. There he encountered Miss (Cheryl) Caudill, who seemed determined to make his life miserable. The first major such incident occurred as a side effect of a suggestion she made to him one day at lunch.

While sitting at the teacher's table in the lunchroom (teachers accompanied their classes to the lunchroom on a complex staggered schedule because the lunchroom was only large enough to accommodate 3 or 4 classes of students at a time) Miss Caudill participated in a conversation about the fact that some students caused trouble in the lunchroom.

"How in the devil's name are they done eating so fast that they can get up and wander around and cause a ruckus every-single-godforsaken day?" he moaned as he got up to send yet another student back to his seat with his class.

"I don't think all of them eat every day," said Miss Caudill.

"What? They just don't eat?" said Mr. (Byron) Caudill, looking around the room as if he saw the students for the first time as individuals, rather than as a conglomerate herd of hormonal teenagers.

"Some don't," said Miss Caudill. "I suppose they're just bored."

"Well they should still just sit there and not cause trouble," he grumbled.

"Actually I have an idea about that, Mr. Caudill," she said. "Why not send them to room 111, in the back. Set up a table with some board games, checkers, and such, and they can play games and not interfere with the lunch crowd."

Sandra Beckney, another teacher, chimed in. "The study hall teacher can watch them," she said. "Lunchtime is the smallest study hall of the day."

"Why, Miss Caudill," said the principal, "You may have very well just come up with a good idea that solves more problems than it causes." She raised her eyebrows at this backhanded compliment. "For once."

Soon thereafter the plan was set into place and students actually played a few games from time to time in the back of the study hall/gameroom/theatre during lunch time. Volunteers donated a table and a few games. Spare chairs were obtained from a little-used classroom. The students took care of the games and put them away each day because it was such a novelty to get to play *games* at school. One regular trouble-maker actually claimed the games were the only reason he *came* to school.

I even played a few times myself when rehearsal involved things that I was not a part of.

Eventually, though, someone donated a pool table. Instead of placing it with the other gaming equipment "The noise might disturb the students trying to study," said Mr. (Byron) Caudill, surveying the fleet of sleeping students one day. "I expect it might be better to put this out in the hall where it wouldn't bother anyone."

Anyone, that is, but Miss Caudill. The spot the principal chose for the donated pool table was directly across the hall from Miss Caudill's speech and drama classroom.

At first, all was well. The occasional *thwack* and *crack* of the pool balls was not *too* annoying. But one day, C.J. Holt , Dan Carpenter, and Albert Sible, three *teachers*, were playing in the hall, during class time, as Miss Caudill was attempting to administer final exams in speech–which consisted of students actually standing up and giving a five minute speech.

"And, so, when the Constitution was written, not everyone signed it on the same day," said Becky Simmons, a student in Miss Caudill's class. Simmons was shy and timid and had to be nearly dragged in front of the class each time she was required to actually *speak* in speech class.

Crack! echoed the sound through the closed door.

Becky glanced at the door, clutched her notes and moved on. Miss Caudill frowned.

"John Hancock was the first person to sign the Declaration," said Becky. The hesitation was slightly greater in her voice.

Thwock! This time the sound was accompanied by some hearty laughter, clearly audible through the door.

"Pause right there, sweetheart," said Miss Caudill. She stepped over to the door and opened it. The coaches and teacher looked over at her. "Gentlemen, I've got kids in here trying to give speeches for a final," she said. They looked sheepish, and she returned to her seat after closing the door. *That ought to settle it,* she thought.

"Continue, Becky," she said.

Crack. "Two future presidents signed the constitution. Not everyone signed it on the same day," she continued. *Thpock.* Becky closed her eyes. "There were fifty-six –" *CRACK!* A clatter of someone dropping a cue stick was followed by more hearty laughter. Miss Caudill held up a hand and Becky stopped. She looked more and more distressed and her hands were shaking.

Miss Caudill returned to the door. "Boys, listen to me," she began. "These children are trying to give speeches. They get very nervous, even when it's quiet. You. Are. Not. Helping."

"Sorry, Cheryl," said C.J.

"Just be *quiet.* Maybe you can do that during break or after school." Holt nodded, putting his cue on the table.

"All right," he said.

She shut the door with a resounding *thud.*

"Becky, would you like to start over?" asked Miss Caudill.

"Yes, please, Miss Caudill. I'm so scared I'm shaking."

"It's all right, dear. I think they're going to stop. "

Becky shuffled her papers and returned to the first page.

"The U.S. Declaration of Independence Signers," she began. "By Becky Simmons. " More shuffling. A nervous exhale followed by a deep breath, which Miss Caudill advised us to do whenever nerves were a problem. "The United States declared its independence from England on July the fourth, seventeen seventy-six, two hundred years ago this year," she said.

Crack!

Becky closed her eyes. A tear worked its way down her cheek.

Crack! Smack!

"Dagnabit!" a muffled voice growled from out in the hall, followed by the loudest guffaws so far.

Miss Caudill, when angry, radiated heat well into the infrared. She was radiating hotly when she *flung* the door open and yelled with eye closed, teeth gritted and muscles taut:

"BOYS I'VE BEEN POLITE ABOUT THIS TWICE NOW!! AND IF YOU CANNOT FIND IT WITHIN YOURSELVES TO KEEP QUIET OUT HERE, I WILL HAVE TO TAKE IT TO HIGHER AUTHORITY! I HAVE CHILDREN IN TEARS IN HERE BECAUSE THEY CANNOT FINISH GIVING A SPEECH WITHOUT YOU YUKKING IT UP LIKE YOU WERE ON HEE-HAW!"

If her eyes had been opened before she slammed the classroom door, Miss Caudill would have seen the latest offense had been caused by none other than Mr. (Byron) Caudill, principal of the school. One of the witnesses to these events had been Mr. Carpenter, who was a supporter of Miss Caudill in later years, and related this story's conclusion to her, and then still later, she related it to me.

Mr. Caudill now thought she intended to approach the *superintendent* with her complaints, when in fact she was intending to talk to *him* about the coaches who had been witness to this affront to his authority.

"Somebody has to put that woman in her place, boys," muttered Byron. "And I'm just the man who can do it." He marched into the office and barked at the secretary. "Sallie Mae! Where's that godforsaken field trip approval file?"

Shortly thereafter, the pool table disappeared from the hall. No one at school knew where it went, but those of us who could add simple numbers concluded it had been confiscated by persons unknown for pool tournaments in a more, shall we say, *welcoming* atmosphere.

No Bed Of Roses

I was born in Kentucky, but my family, like thousands of others in the 1960's, emigrated elsewhere in search of work. My family wound up in central Ohio. We moved around a bit, usually just far enough to trigger a change in school districts, as we rented first one house, then another. Sometimes the owner wanted the house back for some reason, and sometimes the rent increased beyond our means.

My father was a carpenter. He could build anything from a finished piece of cabinetware to an entire house. Most of the time, he mopped up mistakes other people made, or worked for small construction companies. When we moved to Kentucky he worked more independently, but he was never what you would call ambitious. He dropped out of school in the 7th grade, and mastered his trade through hard experience and on-the-job training.

I accompanied him to job sites a few times, as boys will do with their fathers, to see if I could lend a hand, earn a few dollars, and to find out if I had any knack for the work.

Turns out I didn't.

I remember once he assigned me the task of mixing mortar (concrete mix) in a long trough, where it was eventually going to be used to lay concrete blocks in someone's new basement. I dutifully scraped and pushed the mortar back and forth, occasionally adding water to the mix. Shortly thereafter Dad showed up and pointed at the box.

"What do you think you're doing, boy?" he said, an exasperated look already in his eyes.

"Uh, mixing this mortar," I said. "Just like you said."

"Well, you're doing it wrong," he said. "I had mortar on this end mixed for joints, and mortar on this end for doing posts. They ain't the same and now you've mixed 'em all up."

I had no idea the mortar separated in the trough was for specific purposes. Probably he thought it was so obvious it was not worth mentioning. I couldn't say anything other than I was sorry, so I did. All things considered he wasn't too pissed about it, but it was a while before I was invited back to the job site.

Besides, Dad didn't really want me to follow in his footsteps. I don't know if he knew how impressed I was with his ability to make things that would last, had a purpose, and were functional, but I was. I could only move information around, do math, write, act, and learn about science, but none of those things had yet led to a paycheck or even a permanent product. Theatre is so ...ephemeral to a practical man like my father. You work for months, blow it all in a few evenings, and it's gone forever. In the time we spent producing a play my father could build a house that would last a century.

As we drove around the county he would often point out houses or job sites where he had worked. "I built the gym floor for that school over there," he'd say. "Up on that hill there's this strange house, can you see it?" he asked once. This was before I had my glasses (didn't get them until I was 14) but I was in the habit of saying I could see things that I wasn't 100% sure were there–so I said, "Uh-huh."

"That house is like two trailers stacked one on top of the other like this," he said, crossing his arms like a pair of scissors.

"Why did they build it that way?" I asked.

"There ain't no tellin' what rich people will do to waste their money," he said. "But this feller said he wanted to have a small house with a great big living room and a high ceiling, and that was the only way he could get it done."

"Did you design it?" I asked.

"No, there ain't no way I could have done something like that without plans," he said, referring to architectural plans. At some point he thought, I believe, that I was going to be an architect. That might be a useful end point of all the math and science I took in school. It was my stock answer for the 'what are you gonna do when you graduate' question every kid hears sooner or later. "Strangest house I ever worked on," concluded my father.

"So," he said, "You ought to get into architect school, boy. You may not be too useful on the job site but you could learn enough to draw up a set of plans." He said this as if architecture was a sort of fallback position from a *real* job.

"Well, I understand geometry pretty well, but I won't actually take the course until next year."

"Maybe you could draw up some plans for me for a shed, or some such like that," he said. "I could show you stuff like how to space out the floor joists, and how to put in studs in the walls and the run of the roof." The *run* of the roof referred to what mathematicians call the *slope* and ordinary folks call the *pitch* or the *tilt*.

"Sure," I said. *Anything to keep the peace.* "I'll give it a try."

"There's real money there," he said. "Not like that dramer stuff you keep wastin' your time on."

Sometimes you have to pick your battles. Sometimes you stand your ground, other times you feint.

"That's– just a hobby, Dad," I said. "I want a job that makes real money like architecture. Did you know that the father on the *Brady Bunch* is an architect?"

"I don't see how that fella ever makes a livin'," said Dad. "It seems like he don't work but fifteen minutes a day."

"Must be nice," I said.

"Yup. Mebbe you'll live like that some day. I ain't never gonna. I thought I was smart enough not to need school when I dropped out in the seventh grade. Turns out I was wrong."

"I think you do all right," I replied.
"Sooner or later you're gonna have to drop out of that dramer bidness," he repeated.

I issued a noncommittal grunt and left him to interpret that any way he wanted. *Let it go, Dad. You already won this round.*

There was also the time we dug an entire footer for a house–a footer is a ditch into which you pour a moat of concrete to provide a foundation for a house–and when the owner's wife saw the location of the rooms, she decided that she needed the entire thing moved 4 feet to the left. So we had to dig the whole thing over again. We dug the footer with pick, and shovel and hard work. I couldn't work half as fast as my Dad, but at the end of the day, I was exhausted.

My half-brother Bill was actually more like the kind of son my father seemed to hope I would become. At least, he was while I was young; my father didn't approve of heavy drinking because it interfered with your ability to take care of your family. Before Bill was thoroughly alcoholic and drug-ridden, he was a respectable carpenter in his own right. He was much older than I was, 20 years or so, and he could keep up with whatever Dad wanted him to do on the job. Most of the time he worked independently, but occasionally he'd come over to the house and ask Dad a question, or talk about the difficulties of the current job he was working on, and so on.

Once, when I was a freshman, he asked me a question about geometry–one of the few areas where his and my and Dad's worlds collided.

151

He asked me how to estimate the amount of insulation needed to cover the end of a gable roof house–a house with a triangular area under the roof, usually where the attic is located.

"I always wind up ordering too much," he said. "I can't seem to figure out how to get the amount right for the run."

I looked at Dad. "How do you do it?"

"I don't know how to explain it," he said. He doodled out a triangle on a piece of paper. "I just know if you got a roof *this* tall and *this* wide, you'll need *this here* much square foot of insulation and drywall." He scratched his head. "Hard experience." I looked at his writing. He'd figured out the area needed for a triangle one foot on a side, and multiplied by the size of the house in feet. Without formal training, my father had done an algebraic ratio for similar triangles. That was one of the times I really gained an appreciation for how *smart* he was, intrinsically figuring out things that I could not do without relying on my formal mathematical training.

There *is* something to be said for book learning–if you can apply it to the real world.

"Do you know the formula for the area of a triangle?" I asked them.

"No," said Bill. "And if you tell you the truth, it's unlikely I'd understand it even if you wrote it down." *Formulas aren't gonna help here,* I thought. Bill had dropped out of school before high school, just as my father had, to work and bring income to the family as soon as he was able.

I drew a line bisecting the triangular roof. Then I tore the paper carefully, removing the right half of the roof illustration. I spun it over, and placed it carefully on top of the remaining half of the drawing, forming a rectangle.

"Now it's a rectangle," I said. "The area of a rectangle is–"

"Length times height!" said Bill, poking Dad in the ribs.

"Look at that," he said. "That little trick woulda saved me work I don't know how many times."

"And money," said Dad. He looked at me with raised, bushy eyebrows. His eyebrows (then and now) resembled caterpillars. "Speakin' of money..."

Which was his way of launching into another anti-drama tirade. Waste of time, no money in it, no work like that in all of Perry County, and the kind of people you'd wind up with—cutthroat, no morals, drugs, and worse.

Even though he usually caved in to Mom's demands and transported us to and from rehearsal when we needed to go, he was making an earnest effort to see if he could talk me—actually both Jane and me—into dropping the entire effort in drama.

I really had no idea how I was going to convince him otherwise.

Or *if* I was going to be able to convince him otherwise.

You might ask yourself how a man could build a house without the aid of algebraic equations and formal training in geometry. I know *I* certainly couldn't have attempted it. The fact my father could, using a combination of native wits and experience handed down on the job, was always amazing to me.

I think one of the reasons he took me on these little jobs was because he wanted me to appreciate where the money came from to run our home. He charged a decent wage for himself—I remember for years he quoted $8.00 per hour plus expenses—but in Ohio, and Kentucky, throughout the 1970's and 80's it just was hard to find people who could afford to have significant amounts of work done on an ongoing basis. Sometimes he would drive over an hour to get to a job site. And he was always, always tired. Smoking pack after pack of Pall Malls didn't help.

We lived in a house my father built before I was born. It was a little one-story house (later expanded to two) on a hillside in Beetree Hollow. The house had a kitchen, two bedrooms, an incomplete bathroom with no fixtures (because there was no sewage or water supply to support it) and a living room. The house was heated with coal, which my father still uses in his house –the same one– in Kentucky today. Coal burns *hot*. I've seen stovepipes glow red-hot from the heat of a coal fire. It also creates black soot, and gets on everything. It has a peculiar odor, sort of musty, too. It surprises me how many people have never seen coal, let alone seen coal burn. Students in California don't even know what coal looks like.

Our house didn't have hot water, or indoor plumbing for the longest time. We had a cold water tap from a little well higher up the hill from the house. Occasionally that water would dry out in a dry year and we'd have to haul water up the steep, narrow driveway to our house to drink. The bathroom was an outhouse located about 20 yards from the house. It says something that we lived there so long we had to move the outhouse to a new location and dig a new hole for it–twice.

We didn't have a bathtub; I would clean up in the morning with a pan of hot water boiled on our electric stove. We *did* have electricity. We even had a television...when we first moved to Kentucky, the television we had still used vacuum tubes that you had to exchange for new occasionally, and the antenna was a long wire running far up the side of the mountain.

The startling thing about this is that all of these things were true for us in the 1970's, when the rest of the country was settling into a second generation of Ozzie and Harriet (or Brady Bunch, depending on your generation) style suburban ranch home living with built in pools and microwave ovens and live in maids and what have you. From my perspective, we were a lot more like the *Waltons* than the *Bradys*. And the Waltons were well off, in my opinion.

154

As far as that goes, right up until this year– 2007 A.D.– my father used well water. The only reason he stopped was because voices started coming out of his well.

He was inside the house and heard a large THWAP! and a bang, and when he went outside to see what had happened, the metal lid to the small, 4 foot high pump enclosure was blown off onto the ground. As he approached the well, he heard *voices*.

"Dang, Darrell, there's someone's *pump* down here," said one.

"A pump? You don't reckon they was actually *using* it, do ya?"

"Damn straight I was using it!" shouted my father, amazed that he could hear miner's voices so clearly from a well nearly 300 feet deep. "What the hell is goin' on down there?!"

Silence ensued. A long, drawn out, healthy, guilt-ridden pause.

"Well? I know you're down there, 'cause I heard you talkin'!" bellowed my father.

"Um," said the voice identified as Darrell. "We, uh, found your well pump...throw us a line and you can haul it up."

"I ain't got no 300 foot line!" growled my father. "You get your asses outta there and come bring it to me!"

"Where are you?" asked the other voice, still unidentified.

"Y'all's the miners digging into other people's property," replied my Dad. "You can god-damn well figure it out."

A few days later the now useless pump was returned, accompanied by a ditch digger, some pipe, a water meter, and city water. And twenty years of water bill paid off by the mining company. In Kentucky, back during the Depression, poor people often sold off the mineral rights to the land whose surfaces they inhabited, not realizing that in many cases the abandoned mines would eventually collapse and cause shifts in the surface that have in the present day destroyed untold homes, drained water tables, and contaminated those that remain. A high price to pay for the pennies earned all those years ago when carpetbagging speculators defrauded landowners out of the mineral rights to the land they lived on for generations. The mining companies' latest hobby is scraping off the tops of entire mountains, dumping the fill into the un- inhabited (and in some cases, unauthorized) land between the hills, and claiming the resulting flat surface is an improvement that communities can use to build even larger Wal-Marts than before. The local paper is filled with debates about development and jobs vs. the aftereffects of uncontrolled runoff and out of control erosion. I wonder what they're telling the landowners these days whose land gets swamped with fill dirt, and how many cents per acre they get for it.

Anyway, that was now and this story was then.

We were poor, and we knew it, and occasionally people we encoun- tered would tell us as if we didn't already know. I had my shoes (such as they were) made fun of, and when I played trombone in band in Ohio I was told I couldn't participate in the winter concert unless I got a new trombone to replace the beat up, used, cheap one my parents got for me initially. (I caught a lot of grief over the wasted expense of buying a new trombone I only used for six months because there was no band program at Viper Elementary School. That was the last time I remember *begging* for something expensive.)

We occasionally used food stamps–I remember my mother tearing them from booklets carefully, and complaining of people buying snacks and cigarettes with them. We picked up "mod cheese" (com- modity cheese) from social services. Sometimes my mother worked too; I remember her bringing home plastic wheels from a factory that made wheels for washing machines, which I turned into flying saucers and flew around the universe. She would occasionally take a job as a waitress. For a time she worked in a nursing home. She kept her

156

money separate from Dad's; everything he made was community property, but everything she made was *hers*, saved for Christmas and school and emergencies. After she died, my father and little sister Brenda searched the house and found hundreds of dollars stashed away in Mom's extensive collection of glass swans and her *fleet* of antique, restored (by her) sewing machines and in other nooks and crannies; I doubt they've found all of it yet.

On the off chance that one of my Dad's more, shall we say, unsavory neighbors from several miles down the creek (not anyone I *know*, of course) reads this missive and gets any ideas about searching the premises, let me make this clear. That last statement was a *joke*. I'm quite sure they found all the money. Really.

Brenda, if you're reading this, I'm sorry I don't talk about you more in the story. She was 5 years younger than I, and I added a year to that by Skipping. She was never in the same school as I was except for a year and a half at Viper. She was an annoying little sister, and I was a callous big brother, but we got along, I loved her like a sister, and I still do. But unfortunately, she's not central to this story; believe me, I asked the story about it, and it said I had to save stories involving her for another day.

It's something of a cliché to say you grew up poor, but you were happy. Nevertheless, I think we were, most of the time. We had our dysfunctional problems like every family, and some unique to our time and place. My mother was somewhat paranoid and did things like plant hairs from another woman in Dad's truck, and then flamboyantly "discover" them in an attempt to see if he was cheating on her. OK, that's probably beyond "somewhat," but when you live in the middle of such a situation it just seems like normal and routine. Only in retrospect are most families dysfunctional.

When money was especially tight there would be fights—what family hasn't fought over money? Poor people fight over the lack of it, the middle class fights over what to spend it on, and rich people fight over who gets the most of it. I fell asleep to growling and crying and shouting from my parents' open bedroom door more than once. Our home did not have central heat, only floor vents added when the basement was finally constructed, so if you closed your door in the wintertime you froze. Most of the rooms didn't even have a door, anyway.

Nevertheless, despite the threats to walk out and never come back, always made by my father, he never did. He always put the kids first no matter what unbalanced and concocted story was running around in her head that week.

He never understood –at the time– what my fascination with theatre and acting was or where it might lead. His attitude was primarily that it was a time-wasting dead end career, with no acting jobs available in the area, and wanted to know how would I make a living.

"You ought to get in on teaching," he told me once.

"Teaching?"

"Yeah, they make purty good money, you know, and you get your summers off too, so you can take another job just temporary," he said. "And 'round here they're *always* looking to hire teachers."

"You should teach shop," I said. There were few things about building a house my father didn't know.

"They won't take nobody without a college education in that job," he said. "Damn stupid thing is nobody with a college education ever had to build a house just to pay some bills."

"I don't want to teach," I declared. "I'd rather be a scientist. Or maybe an actor."

"That's all well and good, but I don't know how you can make a living doing either one around here," he said. "You should at least get a teaching license so you got something to fall back on. Just in case."

That was the first time I ever discussed any career choice other than architecture with my father. I think he had figured out the subject held little fascination for me. But I listened to him carefully, despite what he thought he knew about my opinions about his advice.

My mother tended to declare her own private little jihads on other family members if they slighted her in any way. She told about how she was treated like the black sheep of the family as a child growing up during the Depression, and the favored older sister received the best clothes, and money, and so on, while she had to do with hand me downs, insults, and worse.

One of her favorite stories involved her toppling over an outhouse with her sister in it and watching it slide and roll down a mountain in revenge for some snide comment my aunt made to her when they were both kids. If you met my mother, who bore an uncanny resemblance in appearance, mannerisms, and temperament to Granny Clampett of the Beverly Hillbillies, you would believe that she would actually do such a thing on a whim, and if you didn't behave yourself, she'd do it to *you.*

Eventually we became estranged from almost all of our relatives over one feud or another, and it got to the point where I didn't know or remember many of them. Oh, I recognized people as being related to me, but I never really memorized how they were related. What was the point when you'd only see your mother's older brother's ex-wife's kids, and your second cousins, and your own grandmother, once in a year, if you were lucky?

A Challenge Before The Whole Human Race

We learned more than just blocking and scene changes and the cadence of iambic pentameter that fall. We all had questions, not the least of which was why what we were doing was worth the enormous effort we put into it. One day as we were drilling on speech exercises, someone (most likely Ben) had the temerity to ask what the point of all the effort was.

"I mean, it's not like any of us will ever act professionally. I mean not really. C'mon, Caudill, give us a break. Why does any of this matter? Isn't this supposed to be *fun?*"

Miss Caudill gave Benny a long, thoughtful look as she composed first her temper, then herself, then her answer.

"Listen to me, young fool," she said. "Let's say you were in a car accident, and ruptured something inside," she said, pointing at Ben's mid-section. Benny, for his part, waited patiently to see where this was going.

"You go to the operating room at the hospital, and there are two surgeons arguing over whose turn it is to cut you up. One of them says, 'I've got years of experience working on cases like this, Buford. Now step aside," and then the other says, 'Ther ain't no way in heck I'ma gonna give up this here patient,' and then they both look at you and ask you to pick. Which one do you pick?"

Benny looked like for a minute he was going to pick the twangy doctor just to be obstinate, but then he changed course. "I get your point, but I'm just as likely to be a doctor as an actor, seriously now. So why should I care?"

Surprising everyone, especially myself, I provided the answer.

"Because no matter *where* you go, or *what* you do, people are going to discriminate against you because of your accent. It's built into the larger culture of America, and *no one will take you seriously even if you complain.*" Everyone looked at me, because especially during my freshman year I had yet to develop the overinflated sense of self-worth that made me jabber incessantly in every conversation. "My mother used to tell us stories about how the factory workers in Ohio claimed they could *smell* her because she was from Kentucky. She sometimes came home crying over it, but usually she was just mad."

"That's true," chimed in my sister. "Dad lost contracts for jobs because they assumed he was too ignorant to do a good job. We got to the point in Ohio that we wouldn't tell anyone we were from Kentucky. Think about the *Beverly Hillbillies.* And *Hee Haw.* There are people that believe those shows are funny because they're *true.*" To much of the country, there isn't much difference between Ohio and Kentucky. They're both flyover states, visited by people primarily at an altitude of 35,000 feet. To the residents of these states in the 1960's and 70's, and to a lesser degree even today, the differences are significant. During the 1960's, President Johnson ran a War on Poverty that targeted Eastern Kentucky as ground zero. Just this summer, John Edwards launched his Poverty Tour in Pikeville, Kentucky, just like John Kennedy did in the 1960's. As I wrote this book, I read an article in the *New York Times* about how the highest proportion of people in the nation with missing teeth are from Kentucky. The more things change, the more they stay the same.

Think about your associations with the Bluegrass State. What comes to mind? Coal mining. *Bad for the environment.* Horse racing. *Gambling is addictive.* Bourbon production. *Drunk driving.* Tobacco farming. *Secondhand smoke and lung cancer.* Hillbilly heroin. Moonshine.

Don't get me wrong; I'm actually a big *fan* of Kentucky as a state. It was one of the first states to initiate the recent wave of "education reform" with a lawsuit that demonstrated property-tax based funding of schools is inequitable. The land is beautiful and most of the people are kind and loving and generous, as much as they are anywhere in America. For the most part, we are victims of outsider's perceptions of us. Sometimes those perceptions creep back into our culture and we start believing them ourselves, much like the fans of Jerry Springer behave as the people do on television as that is all they have for role models of people like themselves. The primary tool for the eradication of a culture is not bombs, or social programs, or ethnic cleansing or anything like that. It's the elimination of *hope*. Without hope people turn away from family and traditions and sever the ties that bind civilization together.

There's still a strong culture unique to our country living in the hills of Kentucky, worth preserving and knowing about. It is fighting a battle right now with drugs and has always fought with poverty. It's survived despite well-meaning social programs that have long targeted Eastern Kentucky and Appalachia as ground zero in the War on Poverty.

I went through a phase where I tried to correct my mom's pronunciation of words to what the schools were teaching me. She would substitute the word "hope" for "help," for example. "I wanted him to hope me with the taters," she'd say. When I attempted to correct her, she would just snap "That's just the way I say it," and "Don't be gettin' too big for your britches, boy." It didn't take more than a few rounds of this before I gave it up as a bad project and disrespectful.

That didn't score any points with Dad, either. In fact, the last time I tried to correct Mom's diction or pronunciation, he declared he had had enough.

"That right there–" he said, bellowing and shaking a finger at me, "that right there is the *last* God-damn time you're gonna get all uppity about that God-damn drama shit with your mother, *boy*," he shouted. "I aim to put an end to this like I should have a long time ago. I ain't taking you to any more of those GOD-DAMN late-night PLAY PRACTICES again–"

"Tad," said Mom.

"If the ONLY thing that DAMN woman is teaching you is how to put on airs and act better than your are like you're DAMN *ASHAMED* of your own *mother, well then...*"

"Tad," said Mom, more sternly.

"I'm *not* ashamed of Mom!" I yelled back.

"LIKE HELL YOU AIN'T! I AIN'T HIT YOU IN SEV'RAL YEARS, BOY, BUT DON'T YOU THINK I WON'T!"

"AMILL!!" shouted my mother. She threw some pots and pans in the sink with a crash, always an indication of fury within her.

She then, almost ritually, retold the story of how she was limited to just a pencil and a single piece of paper a day at school, was never encouraged, never told she could do *anything* by her mother, ridiculed for drawing pictures of birds and trees, unable to go on in school because she married so young she dropped out, and how she *swore* her kids wouldn't be held back *no matter what they wanted to do.*

All the while slamming pots and pans and skillets and baking sheets in drawers and sinks and dishpans, creating such a clatter I was afraid she might hurt herself or break something.

"Well then *you* can just take'm to play-practice an' go fetch 'em, because I'm a god-damn workin' man and my opinion just don't count for nothin' because I ain't got the book learnin' to know any *BETTER!*" he bellowed, punctuating the last word with a door slam so hard it rattled the windows. He stomped off to the other side of the yard, such as it was, and lit up yet another cigarette. The one he'd had when he started his tirade lay half-burned, still smouldering in the ashtray by the kitchen window.

For a while, my mother did go fetch us. But she worked her gradual persuasion upon Dad, claiming she couldn't drive really well after dark (true) and arguing that we were in fact keeping our grades up

(Jane was ranked in the top 10% of her class, and I got straight A's) so what was the *harm* in letting us have our little hobby?

Eventually he started driving us again. Every few months, though, there'd be another flare up, set off by some issue or other, such as needing money for food on the trip to Lexington, and he'd fly off the handle again. *One of these days he's gonna get so mad he'll really make us quit,* I thought.

Suffice to say my attempts at refining my mother's accent ended abruptly.

So adopting a 'flatter' midwestern accent was part of one's ticket to a better life, we learned. Miss Caudill pointed out that while the local newscast and even the feed out of Lexington featured reporters with a local twang, none of the national news readers had much of an identifiable accent. Not only did they not sound like they were from Kentucky, they also didn't sound like they were from Boston, or Texas, either, for that matter.

"In a hundred years, there won't be any accents left," Miss Caudill said, in the classroom. "We'll all talk like we're on TV." That was the closest Miss Caudill ever came to mentioning anything slightly resembling science fiction. When I offered my opinion that what people would be watching almost certainly would be 3-dimensional, fed directly into the brain, she rolled her eyes and said I was missing the point, which in fact I was.

"Where's the harm in everyone losing their accents?" I wanted to know.

"That would be almost as tragic as having to teach you to lose it in the first place," she replied. "Your accent is part of you, and your family. It's as much as part of your home as the walls, the floors and windows. There's history there, variety, and not a little community. Losing it permanently will separate you from them. I don't want that as an outcome," she said. "Learning to drop your accent for a play or a speech doesn't imply you should do it all the time, or at home. They'll think I'm trying to take you away from them." She cast a glance out the window, remembering past altercations with other parents. "It wouldn't be the first time."

I contemplated this for a bit, and quietly nodded.

"I get it, Miss Caudill," I said.

"I expect you do, child," she said.

My Sister Jane

My sister Jane is three years older than I. When we were little, I used to call her "Little Mommy," especially after my little sister Brenda was born. I was a middle child, statistically relegated to the position of least attention, but I was a boy, and unlike my mother's sons by her previous marriage (both of whom gave her much grief and tragedy) I was a *good little boy*, so I never really suffered for attention.

Jane was the pioneer in the family consisting of my father Amill and my mother Bobbie Mae. Every new thing that required permission Jane tried to do first. Having broken the barrier, the parents were much less resistant when I came along and asked later. She thought it would be more fair and symmetrical if I had to wait until I was the same age she was when I was allowed to ride the bike down the street, go out on the first date, join the drama class, go on field trips, etc. I mean, it wasn't *that* big a deal, but it annoyed her, and she brought it up from time to time.

She was heavy in high school, and because she was smart as well, she was by definition Not Popular. She wasn't hated or despised, either, but definitely not the center of attention in her class. She used to help me with my homework, especially when it got to the point that Mom or Dad couldn't answer my questions. Dad helped me learn to multiply and use rulers (as I recall); my Mom insisted that I do any homework assigned.

At one point, they paid us $1.00 for every 'A' we brought home. This worked until the district changed the report cards to break every grade down into ten sub-categories; suddenly they owed us more than $40 – each. "I'll buy you all a swing-set if you just hush up about it," bargained Dad, and so we got our first swing-set not attached to a tree branch.

One time, in high school, I was walking down the hall and someone ran up to me to say, "Your sister fell down the stairs," and I took off at a dead run. It says something about our tiny school and the Speed of Rumormongering that when I arrived, she was still sitting on the floor, surrounded by other students who were checking on her.

"I feel stupid," she said, as I helped her to her feet.

"That's better than looking stupid," I said. "I got no sympathy for you at all." I grinned at her, and she checked to see if she was bruised or cut...apparently not. "Don't worry about it. Everyone falls down sometimes."

"Not in front of the entire school," she said. "I didn't fall *down* the steps, anyway." She pointed at her huge clogs, sandal-like shoes with thick, uneven soles. "I tripped on my shoes and fell *up* the stairs." She shook her head as if to say *What was I thinking when I bought these things?* I imagine it is much the same reaction that some people have today when running from the police and they face the choice of dropping the merchandise or holding up their pants.

"Mom hates these shoes," she said sadly.

"Now you know why," I replied. That earned me a dirty look.

"Don't tell her," warned Jane.

"Tell her what?" I responded. Jane started to reply before realizing I was already pretending not to know anything.

Then she looked at me as if she saw me for the first time. "What are you doing here, anyway?"

"Someone told me you fell." I said. "Word travels fast. Imagine if you'd won some money or something. I'd be trying to talk down the interest rate on the loan you made me already." She laughed. We separated, and returned to class.

She always looked after me. Although she was always aware that I had a "crush" on Lyn, as I recall she never offered her opinion about that, never told me I was too young, or Lyn was from a family too far removed from mine, or anything at all. I think she was kind of neutral about it. I know she appreciated how nice Lyn was to me, and told her so.

Recalling that makes it all the more painful that when Jane finally found someone she loved and who appreciated her, I made the horrible mistake of telling her I didn't like him, didn't think he was right for her, and she shouldn't marry him (she hadn't finished college yet.) It was essentially the same line my parents had used on her, and I thought as unpleasant as it was, I was doing the right thing to try to help her be happy later in her life. In retrospect, she's been married to Will ever since, and they've had their ups and downs and trials and tribulations–but they've always supported each other and stuck together no matter what. If life presented me with the opportunity to go back in the past and take back something I've done or said, I think it very likely that would be the first thing I'd do.

It says a lot about her character that she eventually forgave me, and her husband Will is always a big draw for my kids, who ask specifically to go to his house so he can chase and tickle them. I'm not sure I could be as magnanimous.

In high school, we weren't exactly inseparable, but we did get along pretty well, and we presented a united front to our parents about participating in drama. Jane always resented the fact that she was relegated to technical duties or supporting roles. It would have been difficult for her to carry a lead in most shows, because she was so heavy, but Miss Caudill never made an attempt to pick a show specifically geared towards Jane's talents either, except perhaps for *Charlie Brown*. And given that, her annoying little brother got the title role anyway. Jokes aside, she really did a good job as Lucy. She was funny. She had energy. She had stage presence. You could hear her. She enunciated. She was completely tone-deaf even then (and now) but she sang her heart out and did a good job at that too.

Despite that, by the time she graduated, she felt she had been slighted with all the "drudge" work, stuff that Miss Caudill didn't want to do herself, and even now refers to her as "that woman."

I found out later my sister was upset because traditionally in the program, the senior acting students got to select the spring play, or at least vote on it. When Jane was a senior, so was Benny Doherty. Whatever play Jane had wanted to do, Benny wanted to do the *The Sunshine Boys* by Neil Simon, who was rising to national prominence in the 1970's. Miss Caudill chose Ben's preference over Jane's, for whatever reason (I had a sinking feeling that *I* was the reason– there was a better part for me in *The Sunshine Boys*) but I never said that to my sister. We had enough conflicts arising from our relative status in the theatre group as it was. Anyway, my sister was bitter about this because she felt she'd been waiting patiently for a major role just for her, when it seemed everyone else got one. She wound up playing Nursey in the Simon play, and while she was funny and everyone thought she did well, it's not the same as getting a leading role. Personally I think Lucy was the best thing I ever saw her do.

Miss Caudill often caused people to either love her or hate her. And it's true she worked us like dogs. No, that's not true; she pampered her dogs. She worked us like *interns*.

Essentially, that's what we were. It was many years before I worked at anything quite as difficult and demanding as one of Miss Caudill's plays. Graduate astrophysics was pretty tough. But the professors were nicer about it.

I had no idea I was an unpaid professional acting intern until I went away to work in summer outdoor theatre, and actually got paid real money for doing less work.

My sisters and I remain on good terms, which is surprising considering the tradition of feuding established by my mother. After my mother's death I have gradually begun making contact with my estranged relatives again. My Aunt Aurelia, whom I did not see in person for almost a decade, actually comes up to my dad's house and visits now.

It's astonishing how much of our lives are formed, in both good and bad ways, by the functional and dysfunctional aspects of our families. Lyn told me once that all families are dysfunctional at some level; she thinks that's one of the defining characteristics of a family. Without *dysfunction* you cannot develop an appreciation for and a desire for *function*.

I think she is very probably right about that.

Rocket Science

The Christmas of 1976 was probably about the last time I ever got anything that was actually a toy for Christmas. After that, I got things like board games and clothes and socks and school supplies. All year long everyone had been inundated with Bicentennial-themed things, since the United States was 200 years old that year. But in the Christmas of 1976, when everyone else was getting Bicentennial mittens and Bicentennial mugs and Bicentennial tins of ham and patriotic fruit-cake, I got a present that was perhaps more suitable for my high-flying aspirations. I got a Bicentennial *rocket.*

It was called the *Spirit of America*, and manufactured by Centuri Engineering, Inc.

Now, I was no Homer Hickam; I didn't build my rocket from scratch and I *certainly* didn't manufacture my own rocket fuel (my mother would have had an absolute *heart attack* if I'd tried anything like that) but instead, these were the same kind of kit-based rockets I'd seen the boys flying in the field in Ohio. Small solid-fueled engines were ignited by a thin piece of nichrome wire heated with a battery. The fuel burned for only a second or so, but it moved with sufficient thrust to fling one of the cardboard-and-plastic rockets several hundred feet in the air.

I knew I was getting one for Christmas because I'd asked for it and had to give the order form to Mom to ensure I got the one I wanted. Flying model rocket kits with pre-filled solid fuel engines was another of those things you couldn't buy locally in Hazard.

This was a *big* rocket. It was about two feet long, with lots of extra attachments (all for show) on the wings. Assembled it resembled a jet aircraft more than a classic rocket. *The Spirit of America represents what the future of space travel will look like,* claimed the package. *Taking off from an airport and landing like a plane, the scramjet-based engine technology will push us into the future.* The reality of how the model turned out was a bit more like a space shuttle flies in the real world. It blasted off vertically, and when the fuel ran out, an ejection charge popped the parachute open.

Theoretically.

In reality, I had built the model in a hurry, anxious to fly it and see what it would do. I knew I could never launch a rocket from home, because it would almost certainly drift as it returned to earth and land in the top of some inaccessible tree.

So I built it, using Elmer's glue as recommended to attach the balsa wood fins to the cardboard body tube. A small can of white glossy spray paint provided the finish. Extra "ion rockets" and "guidance fins" adorned the rocket.

I built it all in one night, instead of taking the two or three days for gradual assembly described in the foldout instruction leaflet. I wanted to have it completely ready when school started, when Mr. Monroe and Miss Campbell had agreed to let me fly it *during school* so the other students could see it. They even allowed me to teach a short lesson on trigonometry to the classes so I could explain how to determine the altitude of the rocket based on how steep an angle it made when flying.

Once school started, I collected my rocket kit which included the launch controller (*Never attach the igniter leads unless the safety key is removed*) and some engines, a couple of old rockets I'd made the previous summer, and the *Spirit of America,* and took them to school. Most of my supplies I dumped into a little red tacklebox sort of thing that was part of an old construction set I had from years ago, relabeled *Rocket Supplies* in black magic marker.

At school, the rocket kit was spotted by Wilbo, who immediately saw the comic potential of harassing me over the brand name stamped on the side.

"*Erector* set?" he said incredulously. What kid didn't know what an Erector Set was? In those days when you graduated from sticks and friction TinkerToys, you went to nuts and bolts Erector sets. Of course, it occurred to me after the fact, I'd never seen an Erector set for sale anywhere in Perry County. *"Lookee here, boys!"* he cried. "The Perfesser here needs an *Erector* set."

I looked at him, blushing and shaking my head.

"This one just contains the spare parts I loan out to my *desperate friends,"* I responded, "Just in case you need a *spare* because yours has gone *flat."* I made a drooping motion with my hand. This sent Wilbo into a paryoxsm of giggles and guffaws, and we hauled the gear out and up the hill to the baseball field. Cheryl Ann Barnett, who was also in this class, just rolled her eyes in disgust.

Perhaps a hundred feet up a steep hill, the school owned a large empty field used for baseball, and of all things, golf (probably because one of the coaches was an avid golfer.) It was big enough for low-altitude flights, in my judgement. As long as it wasn't windy.

The day was breezy, but not windy by any means, so I set up the launcher and tested the controller on a spare igniter, which *fizzzed* and popped.

"Plenty of juice," I said to myself.

I removed the launch key and handed it to Miss Carpenter.

"Hold this, please," I said. "And whatever you do, don't give it to Wilbo."

Miss Carpenter nodded, smiling. The launch key prevents the circuit from launching prematurely.

I loaded the engine, igniter, recovery wadding and parachute; then placed the *Spirit of America* rocket on the launch pad. As I slid it down the launch lug, I noted the wings weren't quite level; they tilted over to one side, like a V. This made the launch rod, which guides the rocket until it has built up enough speed to use its fins for guidance, bend slightly over in one direction. *Oh well,* I thought, *Should be ok.*

"Ten, nine, eight..." I started counting, checking off items from the *Official National Association of Rocketry's Countdown Safety Checklist* as I went.

"Seven*." Launch pad area clear of crew.*

"Six." *Safety key inserted. Green light is GO.*

"Five." *Recovery crew ready.* Wilbo stared at me. *What the heck's taking so long?* was the expression on his face.

"Four." *Wind direction noted. Breeze is slow, so no problems there.*

"Three." *No aircraft overhead.*

"Two." *Doublecheck no one is near the pad.*

"One." I looked at the teachers, who nodded and waved.

"Zero. Ignition!" I shouted, and pressed the button.

The igniter *fizzed*, and with a *whoosh,* flames erupted from the end of the rocket. The audience gasped. It seemed to take forever to get off the guidance rod, and fly free, but actually less than a whole second passed before the rocket cleared the pad.

And then, instead of soaring into the sky for a couple of hundred feet, it leaned over and flew *horizontally.*

Directly *toward* the crowd of students observing.

But first, it had to get past *me.*

"Hit the deck!" I cried, falling to the ground. The other students were slower to respond, but having a two foot long *missile* approach you at *eye level* is something of a motivator.

Students cried out, several hit the ground. Cheryl Ann stood in transfixed astonishment as the rocket roared by her head.

It's flying pretty well for an airplane, I thought stupidly as the crowd parted to let it fly past.

Just after it cleared the crowd the parachute ejection charge *phooped*, and the chute ejected. The chute opened just in time to set the rocket gently on the ground.

There was a short intermission filled with screaming and yelling and shouting.

"That didn't quite go like you expected," said Miss Carpenter after the excitement was over. Everyone was laughing and I felt like my over-blown expectations of myself–and everyone else–had finally caught up with me and bitten me on the ass.

"No, it didn't." I said, in full blush. "I have another rocket if you think it'd be ok to try it."

She smiled. "Well, I'm sure this crowd wouldn't mind having an excuse to stay outside a bit longer," she said. "What happened?"

"Not sure," I said. "I did a safety inspection like the manual says. The center of pressure for the rocket is well below the center of gravity when it is fully loaded, so even if there was wind it should fly stably," I said. I looked at the rocket from the end, noting the V-shaped droop of the wings I'd assembled in a hurry over break. "I'd say it was caused by a lack of symmetry around the vertical axis–it's heavier on the bottom than the top when you hold it level like an airplane. It's my fault for building it in a hurry," I admitted.

She pointed to the rocket lying on the ground, ready to fly. "Will that one have the same problem?"

"No," I said. "It's pretty symmetrical trilaterally."

"Go on then," she said. "Time's short. Get moving."

I loaded up another rocket, and she moved the class out to the edge of the field–just in case. This one was smaller, but it would go higher because of the reduced mass. "One of the interpretations of Newton's Second Law," I told the class, paraphrasing my encounters with Asimov, "is that lighter things will go faster if you push them the same way as you push heavier ones." I didn't think the distinction between acceleration and speed was something I could communicate in a pre-launch briefing.

"This is the same engine as the big rocket, except the rocket is smaller, so it'll go faster and higher." I said, running through the checklist again.

"It'd be hard to see how it could go *lower*," commented Cheryl Ann.

I blushed *again*, pushed the button, and this time the rocket *whooshed* into the sky in seconds. Less than five seconds after ignition the rocket had climbed, I estimated, over 400 feet in the air. The parachute popped open, and I walked over to catch the rocket in midair as it landed mere feet away from the launch pad.

The bell rang, barely audible in the quiet cold air, and everyone streamed down the hill, chatting and laughing about the experience.

"Don't feel bad, Jeff," said Miss Carpenter.

"It's OK," I said. "At least one of them worked right."

I handed Miss Carpenter my page of calculations to show how high the rocket goes using the scale drawings of the launch site and a protractor sighting of the maximum altitude.

"Maybe you could use this as the basis for a problem or lesson," I said.

"Maybe," she said. "I'll take a look at it."

I never flew the *Spirit of America* again, but it did make me stick to my guns with safety issues as I flew other rockets later in my high school and teaching career. Such as the time I built a flying scale model of the space shuttle, filled it with baby powder to make the ejection easier to see (unbalancing it *again*) and watched in dismay as it curled over, crashed into the only sidewalk in a hundred yards, and ended its brief career in a little mushroom cloud of baby powder.

That time, everyone was at least a hundred feet away during the disaster.

I think I had some awareness, even then, that my interests in science fiction, theatre, and science itself were all forms of escapism for me, either metaphorically lifting me out of Beetree Hollow or literally opening doors. In the case of the *Spirit of America* I hoped the real life events were not going to go as flat as that particular flight.

The Universe and Everything

After *Shrew* closed in mid-December, we began parallel preparations for the One-Act play competitions held in the Spring and the Speech competitions held a little earlier. The Kentucky High School Speech League was, and is, a loose association of high school speech and drama programs over the state of Kentucky. To someone from a larger state, say, Ohio or even California, the KHSSL must seem to be a relatively minor organization, serving only a few schools. I mean, it's *Kentucky*, how much participation could there be? In fact, so many schools participated that the organization split the state into ten regions each which held its own competition just to cut down on the sheer number of participants that would eventually arrive at state.

The first part of our preparation was to reduce the length of our fall play to fit in the competition schedule. Cutting Shakespeare isn't easy–that's because no one teaches how to do it, because you're not *supposed* to do it–but Miss Caudill toiled over a dittoed copy of the script, scratching out lines here, cutting soliloquies down to mere comments, eliminating characters and rearranging entrances and exits. One of the local paper's articles Miss Caudill was proudest of began by saying "You don't cut Shakespeare. But if you do, it's better to use a scalpel than a hacksaw, and Cheryl Caudill is a master surgeon." By the time school started after winter break, we were collating dozens of dittoed copies in her classroom for the new version of the play.

Among the casualties of the play's reduction was a substantial part of the role of Batista, portrayed by Charmaine Marshall. Whereas Lyn was *in fact* the prettiest girl in the school (in both my opinion and dozens of my other hormonal teenage classmates' opinions) Charmaine was attractive, tall, with long straight black hair and a pleasant face–but, more importantly, she thought that *she* was the most attractive girl in the school, certainly much more so than that blonde city girl who seemed to get all the acting roles from her aunt, the drama teacher.

I actually have independent confirmation of my observations, as Lyn won first runner up in a beauty pageant while in high school. I don't know who won first place, but it sure as heck wasn't Charmaine.

Now Charmaine's part, already small and cast to make her play a *man's* part (an *old* man's part) was further reduced to a few lines in a more or less crowd scene, shared with several suitors of Bianca, Katherine's sister in the play. That, as they say, did not go over well, and had its own role to play in the events that drove Lyn and me together to become friends.

The other kind of preparation we did was for KHSSL events such as extemporaneous speechmaking, poetry recital, storytelling, short scene single and duo acting, debate, and broadcasting. Miss Caudill selected for us most of the pieces we would be preparing, and it was apparent that for the most part, we'd do things she'd used before; "The Last Flower," scenes from "The Sandbox," by Edward Albee, and others.

My storytelling selection was a straight imitation of Hal Holbrook performing *Mark Twain Tonight*. Holbrook was considered by many the master interpreter of the American Bard, and I'd heard that old people who actually had *seen* Twain endorsed Holbrook's interpretation. I did a pretty good old man's voice, and a passable imitation of Holbrook as I told such gems as "One time I rode a train of such limited velocity the passengers removed the cow-catcher from the front of the train and placed it on the rear–to prevent the cattle from climbing on board the caboose." That was the funniest thing to me. I still laugh about it nearly thirty years later.

In the meantime, Lyn planned to enter duo acting, a competition for two performers to present a 10-minute long scene. In her junior year, she had arranged to perform a scene with Jensen Thomas, but he had abandoned her at the last minute to work on a scene with her archnemesis Charmaine Marshall.

This year would be *different*, she thought, because she was going to work with Benny.

Miss Caudill planned for Lyn and Benny to do a scene from *Shrew*– Miss Caudill was nothing if not efficient in her use of already trained students with premade blocking– and the fight scene from *Shrew* was powerful, already self-contained, the right length, and there was obvious chemistry between the two. They had discussed it several times as the new year started, but as March approached and it became time to rehearse the actual scene as it would be performed for competition, Benny became reluctant.

"Benny," asked Lyn one day in class, "when are we going to get together to rehearse this thing? I mean, we've done it, obviously, but we need to practice it so we're not rusty."

"Well," said Benny, facing away from Lyn, "I'm not sure I'm going to be able to do that after all."

"*What?*" gasped Lyn. "Benny, we had all this planned *months* ago. Now there's only three weeks left! Why not?" Lyn could not *believe* that this was happening to her *again. Just great!* she thought.

"Well," Benny repeated, "I, uh, you know, just don't need that kind of pressure. I mean, you know, we might not even win anything..."

"Benny." Lyn took a deep breath and tried to still her shaking hands. "What am I supposed to do here? Why are you having this crisis of confidence? You won best actor, for goodness' sake! We'd be a shoe-in!"

"I don't know," he said. "I've got a lot of things going on in my life, and I just don't need any more pressure right now." In point of fact Benny's mother was ill, and he was having to devote more and more time to running the household. This was something that only a very few people in drama knew about, because it wasn't something that Benny advertised to the school population as a whole because it didn't fit in with his reputation as a rebellious young stallion.

Lyn knew this, and it was the only thing that kept her from pursuing the matter further. "Fine," she said, unable to contain her disappointment. "It's O.K. I'll work with someone else."

None of the other senior actors in drama turned out to be available. Some were already committed to other partners in the competition; others had sports obligations (which of course, always took precedence) or fell under the influence of Charmaine Marshall.

"Aunt Cheryl," said Lyn. "There just isn't *anyone* here I can depend on. I feel so *alone*. I guess I won't be entering."

"Actually, Lyn, there is one person you can probably depend on."

Lyn looked at her. Miss Caudill looked back, and raised her eyebrows.

"Jeff Mason? I don't think he could pull off Petruchio. He's not big enough to look physically intimidating next to me."

"No, he couldn't do Petruchio, yet," said Miss Caudill. "But perhaps there's something else we could try..." Miss Caudill therefore sought a scene for Lyn and me before she even asked me if I was interested. Eventually, she found a role she thought I might be able to pull off opposite Lyn. Miss Caudill talked to me about this role before she actually "pulled the trigger" and had us memorize lines.

"This is a heavy role, Mason," she said. "It's an intense and strange play, and this is the most powerful scene."

"Maybe you should pick someone older, then," I said. It would only be the second part I ever played.

"Well, there're not many people that could do this," she said. "We have maybe two weeks to prepare, and you can memorize the lines quickly."

I nodded.

"What I don't know is if you can handle the intensity of the role. But if you don't do it, then Lyn won't have a scene to perform at state, and frankly, this is her last, best chance to win something in duo acting," said Miss Caudill, leaving the bait until the string had played out.

"So you're saying that if I do this part, I could help Lyn."

"Yes. That is what I am saying."

I was well aware that there was a certain amount of manipulation at play here. I think, given the nature of most of my conversations with her, she knew I knew. Nevertheless, that didn't change the basic facts of the situation. I would have done practically *anything* to help Lyn, and Miss Caudill knew it.

"I'll do it," I said.

Lyn was ecstatic when I told her later in the day that I would do a scene with her. *Any* scene.

"Oh my goodness, you are such a good guy. You are my *hero,* did you know that? Even Benny lets me down–then Jeff Mason steps up to save the day," she said.

Hero echoed. "It should be fun," I managed to say. "No big deal. A ten-minute scene. How hard can it be?"

The scene she picked was part of a play with a strange title: "Oh, Dad, Poor Dad, Momma's Hung You in the Closet and I'm Feelin' So Sad," by Arthur Kopit. We never performed the entire play, but we read it in preparation for the scene. All I remember about it is that Jonathan Rosepettle's mother was overprotective and hovering, controlling every aspect of his life. At some point, she decided that Jonathan needed to be introduced into the graces of female love, and so she hires a prostitute, Rosalie, to teach him about sex. Jonathan was so overwhelmed by the advances of the prostitute he panics and kills her

182

(paralleling the murder of Jonathan's father by his mother, and whose corpse is in the eponymous title.)

Now, I was thirteen years old at the time we started this project. A *mature* thirteen, mind you; with a generally practical mindset, and the ability to see the long-term implications of my actions; but here was a beautiful seventeen year old girl cast as a prostitute whose job it was to overwhelm young Rosepettle until he became unhinged and murdered her. It nearly overwhelmed *me*, let alone Rosepettle. I was directed to adopt a stutter to show how emotionally distraught he was–I remember hours and hours of stuttering at different rates, spitting and not spitting, substituting sound and not substituting sounds for silent breaks, until we got the stutter right. The thing about the stutter was, it was easy because I was scared *spitless*.

Here I was, having never even kissed a girl (other than on the cheek), having this beautiful seventeen year old *goddess* crawl over me, whispering in my ear, kissing my neck, kissing my *lips* (just a light brush, I could barely feel it, but it jolted me like being electrocuted every time anyway), and give me looks that all by themselves just stopped my heart. The stutter got so bad that I could barely control it well enough to be understood. It even stuck with me for months afterward, coming back at inconvenient moments.

What made matters worse was because of the part, I wasn't allowed to even touch her–except when I strangled her in the final moments of the scene. For a good portion of the time my hands were either trapped under my legs or tightly gripping the sides of the chair. *That* took some considerable self control as well. I found out *sweating* was completely involuntary. Freaking out at the end was practically *easy*. Miss Caudill told me later that I was *frightening* there at the end, which was more important than being *funny* at the beginning.

And Lyn collapsed completely when I "strangled" her. She didn't support herself at all, depending on me completely to hang on to her and lower her back into the chair. We even did the classic *trust* exercise a few times where you fall backwards and depend on someone to catch you.

I caught her, every time.

Before we began rehearsing any of this, after we read the script, Miss Caudill had a talk with both of us. She was perched on the ledge where I had first met Lyn some months earlier. It seemed like every time I went in that room for drama, she was located in a different spot, sort of checking out each rehearsed scene from various angles to see how an audience member in that location would percieve the action.

"You children have to know that this is a powerful scene," she started. "I cannot believe that I am casting my own niece as a prostitute, and you–" she said, nodding at me, "are so innocent I just about have doomed you to a life of corruption. But I have to tell you, in all my years, there's never been a casting like this. You're *perfect* together. It's almost typecasting," she said, apparently unaware of the hurt she might be delivering to Lyn with such a characterization. I could see the hurt in her eyes–was her aunt seriously saying that her niece was tan- tamount to a *prostitute*? Surely not–

"I'll be fine, Miss Caudill," I said, hardly believing the words myself. Hardly more believable was the fact she accepted them at face value. It was as if she *wanted* to believe that I could handle the intensity of the scene, and hang the consequences.

"Aunt Cheryl." Lyn was frowning, looking at me carefully. "We need to talk about this." Lyn and Miss Caudill retreated to a corner of the room and held an animated conversation as my ears burned. Was she angry about the typecasting comment? Were they going to reject me because I was too *young*? I *had* to do this part, if for no other reason than to just spend time with and help Lyn. I took a deep breath and struggled to get control of my pounding heart. Lyn's hands flew in animated gestures, and the whispered argument became almost loud enough to hear.

Eventually my heart slowed and they returned.

"Jeffery," Miss Caudill said, which indicated I had better pay attention to what came next. "Lyn requests that I *ask you* if you feel you really want to do this, and can you control yourself while doing it." Lyn winced at this last phrase but said nothing, arms folded, staring at the wall instead of looking at me.

"Miss Caudill," I replied. "I'm inexperienced but not ignorant. I know what you're asking. You can trust me not to... take advantage of your niece in any way. I can do this scene–I *want* to do this scene– and I hope you'll give us a chance at it."

At this declaration they both glanced at me, torn between the nearly ridiculous idea of my taking advantage of a girl five years my senior and the possibility that something untoward might actually occur. Finally Miss Caudill chuckled lightly (a sound that was like a stilletto in my heart, then and there) and said, "All right then, we'll try it."

Lyn, for her part, merely nodded. I noted she hadn't laughed at the thought of my taking advantage of her. As far as that goes, I noticed not for the first time that she had *never* laughed at me, or teased me. She regarded me thoughtfully and said, "Are you sure?"

"Sure," I managed to choke out. "Not a problem."

Lyn turned to her aunt. "C.C., I can't think of anyone else with whom I'd rather attempt this." She seemed determined that if she were going to play a prostitute in this setting, she was going to be the best one *ever*, so convincing that perhaps the audience might think there was really something going on between us because surely *strangers* would never act like that. (As it happens some of my classmates thought exactly that.)

"In fact, there's several in this department I would refuse to work with if asked," she added with frown.

I gave her the slightest raised eyebrow in query, but all I got back was a studied glare that said to me, *not now.* There was also some sort of odd give-and-take going on between her and her aunt/teacher; and it was beyond my limited experience to figure out what it was.

And so we began working on the scene. We never rehearsed the scene anywhere other than in school or at after school rehearsal. Doing such a scene at Miss Caudill's *house* would have exceeded even her liberal definition of propriety.

Now, what we did, by today's standards, would be considered pretty tame. It would certainly pass muster on cable TV, and more than likely would be OK with a prime time movie these days. Maybe not an after school special or Nickelodeon. But this was 1977, the year *Star Wars* came out, in Eastern Kentucky, near the heart of the Bible Belt, in a public school. Pretty risky stuff, and as it turned out, perhaps *too* risky. We had less than two weeks to prepare for regionals, and we worked on it every day.

But the thing was, as we began rehearsing and blocking our move-ments, and I learned a little more subtlety than the role of Grumio had called for, I began to believe that our short 10 minute scene was *good.* On a number of levels. Jonathan Rosepettle's reactions to Rosalie were, at first at least, funny. Even jaded upperclassmen laughed at the contortions I put myself through to show Jonathan's distress. My hands shook; my knees quaked, even my chair legs rattled (during competition we were allowed to use one chair as a set piece; I went on a search for a chair slightly out of balance so it would rattle better.) Unlike Grumio who was sort of like a stereo turned on full blast all the time, Jonathan's distress increased gradually, as Rosalie approached closer and teased Jonathan even more. Even then, I could distinguish between Rosalie teasing Jonathan (it was in the *script*, after all) and Lyn teasing me; they obviously weren't the same. Some of our audi-ence members, especially when we performed the skits we were pre-paring for some general education English students, thought there was more going on there than was immediately visible to the eye. "What was it like working so close to her?" was the tamest of these questions.

I tried to field the whispered questions from my classmates in as professional a manner as possible. I can't tell you how far down her blouse I can see. No, we weren't dating. No, my mother hadn't seen it–and wasn't likely to get a chance to, if I had anything to say about it. Of *course* I enjoyed doing the scene with her. There was no way in *hell* I could get that close to a pretty girl if it *wasn't* for a scene. No, really, I can't tell you that. If I tried that she'd most likely slap me and most definitely would stop being my friend, so no, that wasn't likely going to happen. I guess she likes me, or she wouldn't do the scene with me, but it wasn't like we were a couple, or anything. I have no idea what her boyfriend thinks. I don't even know if she *has* a boyfriend right now. That's not something we talk about.

There weren't a lot of people asking a huge number of questions, but what there was indicated that their lack of experience with things theatrical had, to me, an astonishing level of confusion between the actors and the roles they played. I mean, even a kid knew that Lee Majors wasn't really bionic–he only pretended to be. For them to mistake what we were doing for reality must mean that we were doing a good job; they were certainly paying attention to the scene, I can tell you that. I know *I* certainly paid attention. We enjoyed a surge of young men wanting to take speech and drama classes the next year, and I happen to know that one or two were there simply because of the potential to get to do something like I did. It was, however, many years before Miss Caudill attempted to do that scene again.

I gradually became more comfortable with the role and was able to distance myself from the part, so by the time competition rolled around, I felt like I had the stuttering thing under control, and while I still blushed each time we did the scene it was no longer completely involuntary.

Lyn expressed her concern to me on at least one occasion.

"Are you sure you're comfortable doing this?" she asked once, when we were alone when Miss Caudill stepped away to make a phone call. (In those days, there was only one phone in the school–in the office.)

"Sure," I answered, in an effort to be nonchalant about it.

"I would hate for this... *skit* to come between us, or to make you think that something is going on that isn't," she continued. "I'd like to think I'm your friend, and I would never want to hurt you in any way."

"Oh, I know this isn't real." I sighed. "I do enjoy being close to you. You have to know that. I hope you know that. "

"I know," she said quietly.

"I also know the difference between Lyn and Rosalie."

"Good."

"That doesn't mean I'm not attracted to you as Lyn, you know," I said, knowing as I did so my mouth was running a little too much. "Because, I mean, you're really pretty, you know, the prettiest girl I've ever met– and you *listen* to me–"

"You're so sweet." She said that, sadly, with her eyes downcast.

"I'm 14 now," I said. "well, almost."

"And I'm 18," she said. "And far too old for you."

"When you're 24, I'll be 20," I said. "It won't matter so much then."

"We aren't in our 20's yet," she said. "And if your mother ever sees this scene, I may not live to see 20 myself. " She looked thoughtful.

"Oh, she won't," I said quickly. "But you have a point." I said. "If I were older–"

188

"But you're not." Then she looked directly into my eyes. "But if you were, I –"

Then Miss Caudill returned, and I never found out how that sentence ended for a long, long time.

We took our scene to regionals and to state competition. After winning regionals handily we performed again at state. Only there, at state, there were a few changes introduced to the skit that that I never forgot.

Lounging Around

Most schools have a teacher's lounge. In many schools, including my present-day workplace, the term *lounge* is *verboten*; it gives the impression that teachers just sit around all day and wait for classes to happen. Ours is a *teacher workroom.* We even have cubicles at one end for semi-private conversations and to hide from people looking for you in your room. (That was, in fact, *my* idea, but I don't know how much status you can gain by bragging about installing *cubicles.* So I don't mention it often.)

Devitt H. Caudill had a smoke-filled, ratty-couch lined, *lounge.* There was only one table, usually covered in papers, a coffee pot, a couple of couches and two or three easy chairs rescued from an early death at the landfill. And lots of cigarette butts, in ashtrays, on the floors, generally smelling up the place. Miss Caudill didn't spend much time there, as she was too driven for lounging in general, but she would occasionally make an appearance just for social or networking reasons.

I would occasionally have to deliver things to teachers in the lounge, but I never really entered the room. They were picky about that. A sign on the door said *No students,* and being the Good Boy that I was, I never stepped over the threshold but waited patiently at the door to make deliveries when asked.

One time she told us of a conversation she had in the teacher's lounge with some of her friends. This was while she was still deciding to do *Shrew.*

"I've nearly settled on a show for this fall," she said.

"What are you thinking of doing?" rasped Joanne Williams, one of her closer friends. Joanne Williams was tall, blonde, and always well dressed. She taught, among many other things, journalism and science. She had a hoarse, raspy smoker's voice for as long as I knew her. But she was popular with students because she was smart and fair.

"*Taming of the Shrew,*" said Cheryl.

"Shakespeare?" said Sally Draper, another friend.

"That's a big show," commented Raymond Simmons. Raymond taught English and German at the school. He was longtime supporter of Cheryl's work, despite the fact it had cost him a new windshield.

Once, during a drama trip when the school administration had decided it needed one more bus for a pep rally at the gym in Hazard, Cheryl found herself arranging whatever alternate transportation she could. She drove her own car, stuffed to the gills with students. A parent transported the box of hay used as a set piece in the play. Following this caravan was Raymond Simmons with the students who couldn't fit in the lead car. Even with two cars it was crowded.

Despite the crowded conditions, Raymond toughed it out, enduring a virtual snowstorm of blowing hay. The set was for the play *The Sandbox* by Edward Albee. He tried using his wipers, but they just etched lines in his windshield. *I've got to back off,* he thought, as a vague shape revealed itself in the roadway ahead. Standing. Large. Moving.

He began to slow. What could it be?....!

It was a *horse*.

And its sudden appearance startled Raymond. He hit the brakes, *hard.* With a squeal of tires, the car ran into the horse with a resounding *smack!*

Mr. Simmons' brand new windshield exhibited a widening nebula of cracks as the children in the car screamed and the brakes squealed.

The horse, which had appeared from nowhere, staggered off for a bit, shook its head, walked in a tight little circle. Everyone stopped screaming as the horse walked by the smashed window. They looked at the horse. The horse looked at them. It whinned, sniffed the air, then staggered away.

So naturally Raymond had developed a healthy *skepticism* of plans originating from room 111.

"I think we can do it," said Cheryl. "We have several seniors available with experience. Lyn can play Kate, I'm quite sure of it. Benny Doherty will be perfect as Petruchio. And there are plenty of kids available to play the remaining parts. "

"Well, it's hard to keep so many kids on task," said Raymond.

Cheryl gave him a sideways glance. *Not for me,* it said to the people who knew her well.

"What has Byron said about this show?" asked Joanne. "After all, it is a little...bawdy."

Cheryl raised her eyebrows at that. "It's no worse than anything they're likely to see on a soap opera or TV movie," she said. "They see worse than this every single day."

"I suppose," said Joanne. "It's different when it's a live performance."

"Oh pooh," Cheryl waved the smoke from the other teachers away. "It'll be fine. I haven't told Byron yet, but he'll come around."

"I don't know, Cheryl," said Sondra. "Drama is not really his thing."

"Anything that's not 12 inches in diameter and orange isn't his thing," sneered Cheryl. "I'll handle Byron."

There's a theory of acting that all conversations are actually jousting matches for status. You know what I mean if you've ever had an uncle or buddy that can never let you tell a story without telling one about the fish that was bigger, the car that was faster, getting lost for more

192

days than the few hours you did in the woods. You may be sad, but I'm *sadder.* That was funny, but this is *funnier.* Miss Caudill was not above such verbal jousting, and, frankly, she was *good* at it. Better than I ever was. Perhaps that's why she tended to *elaborate* a little much about her troubles to other teachers, or, God help her, reporters.

As a teacher, I'm well aware that you have to be careful of what you say in a teacher's lounge; I'm quite sure Miss Caudill was aware of it too. However, when you talk to your friends in one end of a room and other people are present, sometimes they overhear things. And sometimes those things get repeated, for an audience for which it wasn't intended.

Miss Caudill had several run-ins with administrators. For her part, she always considered Mr. (Byron) Caudill her *arch-nemesis.* She was always finding ways around the various obstructions she found placed in her path. Her view was some of those were undoubtedly deliberate, some due to incompetence, and a substantial fraction, she suspected, were simply unintentional. Drama and speech were just not on his radar, along with any number of other non-sports related subjects. Maybe it wasn't the relatively few *intentional* roadblocks that Mr. Caudill placed in her way that got Miss Caudill so riled up; perhaps it was the sheer ignorance of the importance of her program, the *lack of attention* he paid to her state-level award winning program that really stuck in her throat, constantly irritating, never really going away.

He never attended a play as far as I knew. When announcements were made on the PA about our accomplishments, the assistant principal made them. When the basketball team lost an important tournament game, Mr. Caudill gave the school an uplifting pep talk about it.

Some years later she was unceremoniously moved from her old classroom down the hall from the stage/study hall, to a new classroom upstairs. The upstairs classroom had a sink in it for some reason; it might have originally been designed as an art room, or as a science room. For whatever reason, it had a sink.

She had had to abandon the room with the specially painted door, with the Comedy and Tragedy faces painted by students, and perhaps most importantly, ground-level access. This was no small change for a heavy person to deal with, adding multiple trips up and down the stairs for her each day. In later years, her knees gave out completely, and she still taught her classes, confined to a wheelchair and rolling around the room, barking commands and directing student traffic with sweeps of her arm.

Once upstairs, she tried to use the sink. *If I have a sink, maybe I could use it to clean paintbrushes for sets, and clean makeup sponges,* she thought. She turned on the water, and nothing came out.

She therefore, logically, asked Mr. Caudill to get it fixed.

"What do you need water for, Cheryl? You teach drama," he asked, genuinely puzzled. To Cheryl, the utility of the sink was obvious, but she took the time to carefully explain all the tasks that a sink could be used for. Cleaning, painting sets, washing costumes, just washing hands without sending kids to the restroom, and so on.

"So, can we get the water turned on?" she concluded.

"No," he said, using the Administrator's Tool of Choice. "There's no water up there."

"I *know* there's no water," she said. "I want the water turned *on.*"

"No," he said, detecting the sarcasm in her voice. "I mean, there's no water in the pipes. Hasn't been for *years.* We'd have to tear out the wall to find the valve to turn the water on. Not going to happen, Cheryl, sorry." He folded his arms across his chest, sending *no* with body language.

Cheryl wasn't receiving. "Are you saying there's no water up there at all?" She asked, incredulous.

"Miss Caudill," said the principal. "There's no water up there. There will never be water up there. Getting water to that sink is *impossible*. It–is–not–going–to– happen."

Even Miss Caudill, who seldom surrendered to anything, recognized a brick wall when she saw one, so she dropped the topic. For a few weeks, she dropped ungraded papers in the sink. She put a bucket of flowers in it. One day she accidentally ran into it while maneuvering around some set pieces near her desk, causing her to cry out in pain.

"Are you all right, Miss Caudill?" Larry Feltner, one of her students at the time, asked.

"Yes, child," she said between gritted teeth. "I just wish this *useless* sink were not in the way all the time. "

"I could pull that off the wall for you," said Larry. "I got some tools in my truck."

"*Could* you?" asked Cheryl. "That would be *wonderful.*"

Larry proceeded to disconnect the pipes from the sink, but the cold water tap wouldn't unscrew.

"I'm gonna have to cut the water line," said Larry. "Can't get the nut to loosen. It's corroded."

"Well," said Miss Caudill. "Mr. Caudill said there was absolutely, positively no water up here and never would be, so I don't see why you can't cut the line," she said.

"OK," said Larry, and he went to get a hacksaw from the truck.

I suppose I've telegraphed the ending of this story pretty well. Larry cut the line, and as you might have guessed, it was fully pressurized with water. A few aggressive cuts into the pipe and he began noticing that his leg felt wet; looking down he saw a strong, steady stream of water squirting from the pipe and hitting him in the leg.

"Dang, Miss Caudill, there's *water* in these pipes!" he cried.

"Oh Lord!" shouted Miss Caudill. She dashed into the hall, across the hall from her room was the teacher's lounge. It had a balcony where you could look down to the front office area. In those days, the schools only had one phone. Teachers had to send a runner to the office if the principal was needed.

"Flood!" she cried after catching the secretary's eye. "There's a flood in my room!"

The secretary nodded and snatched up the phone. Miss Caudill returned to her room and noted a pool of water was already forming under the sink, flowing under her desk and into the hall. She wrestled with getting Larry and some others to move books, desks and costumes from the surge of water heading towards the hall. After a few minutes without any sign of assistance, she dashed back into the lounge.

She waved her arms and saw the secretary talking to a student. *Why aren't they coming to help?* She thought. She waved her arms again, and when the secretary looked, she yelled, "THERE'S A FLOOD IN MY ROOM! A WATER LEAK! SEND SOMEONE UP RIGHT NOW!" and departed before she could see the response.

This cycle of events repeated itself two or three times, until the pool of water flowed down the hall and entered a crack in the floor. The water flowed down, as water is wont to do, until it reached a row of lockers and the trophy case on the first floor. Minutes later, Cheryl heard a cry of anger from the floor below, audible right through the floor and two closed doors.

"WHAT IN TARNATION IS WATER DOING POURING DOWN ON THE BASKETBALL TROPHIES!" boomed Byron Caudill. Most of which were probably on the order of fifteen to twenty years old. Some of which, I suppose, had once been held by Mr. Caudill himself, when he played basketball at our school in the 1950's.

Minutes later, a work crew hastily drafted from the custodial staff (that would be Mr. Smelt and Delmer Back) arrived with a sledgehammer, hacksaw and other tools. They proceeded to pound the wall, ankle deep in water now, to get the valve exposed. Why someone would put a valve *in* a wall, I have no idea. It's equivalent to putting the gas pedal of a car in the trunk. In a thirty-odd year old school, the people who made such decisions are long gone.

Soon plaster and concrete bits filled the floor, and the air, swirling with the water to make a gooey mess, and the water finally was cut off. In the aftermath, while cleaning, a shadow fell across the door.

She told me, "I'd never seen him so mad. He was *apoplectic.* Veins throbbing. The top of his bald head was bright red, he was so flushed."

"What the ... heck *do you think you're doing, Cheryl!"* he snarled.

"Mr. Caudill," Miss Caudill (no relation) replied calmly. "I believe I was removing this useless sink."

"LOOK AT THE MESS YOU'VE MADE! " He screamed. "THE TRO-PHY CASE IS *RUINED!"*

"Mr. Caudill, I tried to get some help half an hour ago," she said calmly. "I told the secretary my room was flooding. Three or four times."

"But you let the water get in the hall!" he growled. Cheryl was flabbergasted. Did he expect her to hold it in her room somehow? With what? Books? "Do you realize what you've *done*?"

"Why, I know exactly what I've done, Mr. Caudill. " Miss Caudill gathered herself together and waved a hand at the growing hole in the wall. "I have extracted water from a wall you yourself told me had no water in it, would never have water in it, and could not possibly have water in it. Therefore, Mr. Caudill, what I have performed here is a *miracle.*"

He gobbled. He gaped. His mouth opened, closed, opened, closed. He marched in a little circle, with his hands in front of him as if he were seeking something. Raised a finger. Lowered his hand. Then he dropped his head, defeated, and trudged out of the room, accompanied by the outrageous, loud, and hooting laughter of a couple of dozen teenagers, and the silent shaking laughter of one teacher.

It was the side effect of events like these, and quotations *in the paper* from Cheryl stating flatly that she did not enjoy the assistance of those in administrative authority, that caused her so much grief in the years that followed my time at Devitt H. Caudill. She never compromised on *anything* that would potentially help her students. Heaven help the administrator who got in her way. For a few years, after Dan Carpenter was in charge, Cheryl mostly got her way. We accomplished amazing and astounding things I can still hardly believe today. Eventually, a change in administration led to Byron's reassignment at Devitt, probably for no other reason than to remove him from the central office.

I carried away many lessons from Miss Caudill. Some of them I wholeheartedly adopted; others had to be taken with a grain of salt. I have been blessed to have been supported by administrators who care about student learning and have done some remarkable things to help me establish my own program at the school where I work now. Miss Caudill, unfortunately, has not had the luck that I have enjoyed. I think it is because she taught me valuable lessons, perhaps unintentionally, about maintaining good relations with administration. When I said this to her later, she wasn't buying it.

"Lord, Jeffery, I tried to work with the administration," she said. "I really did. They just considered it a hobby or something to place obstacles in my path. Especially that *man.*"

That is as may be. However, I do remember two things she said to me that have influenced my dealings with school administrators and made things better for me. The first was: "The primary function of any bureaucracy is to perpetuate itself." The other was: "If your goals are compatible with that mission, you will get all sort of help and assistance. If you take resources from central office to accomplish your goals, you are up the creek and on your own."

I'm not *quite* that pessimistic about such things, but it did make me aware that my goals and the administration goals are not necessarily identical. And the goals of the state, up to and including the Feds, are another separate entity altogether. I've noted on any number of occasions that there is no state or federal standard for *inspiration*, and the concept is foreign to No Child Left Behind.

The other thing she said was, "Administrators hate surprises. No, that's not it. They *despise* surprises. Even good ones."

"Even good ones?" I asked when she said this.

"*Especially* good ones. Bad surprises can be blamed on the messenger. Good surprises are like a gift that's already unwrapped. No chance to spin the message or claim credit if everyone already knows the good news. That's why districts tend to centralize communications with the outside world. They don't like it when you talk to reporters on your own."

Again, my modern perspective is not quite so pessimistic, perhaps because I've enjoyed support and cooperation that she never did. But nevertheless, I have avoided surprising my administrators whenever I can.

Just in case.

Decisions

At the state speech tourney, to save money we drove in on a bus, competed for a day, then drove home. We weren't staying even one whole night.

Miss Caudill had obtained for Lyn a new red dress, short of skirt and deep of neck, which off the bat was more revealing than the ordinary street clothes Lyn had worn before. She had really nice legs that, as the saying goes, went all the way to the floor and back again. Costumes *per se* were not allowed in duo acting; so Lyn had to wear street clothes, more or less. Street makeup was allowed, and Lyn wore bright red lipstick for the first time, in keeping with the "red" theme throughout the play and the scene.

During the scene, she leaned over me to breathe in my ear, and let her long blonde hair fall across my face, as she had done many times before. But this time–*this* time, the view was, shall we say, much improved. And I could testify before a court of law no bra was involved.

The last line of the scene was delivered by me after I had "strangled" Rosalie. I held her close to me, my mouth near her ear, and whispered, barely loud enough for the audience to hear.

"I love you, Rosalie."

No one knew that I was really telling *Lyn* that I loved her.

Jonathan's descent into madness was very nearly matched by my own that day, and the judges must have been convinced, because for the first time, someone from Devitt H. Caudill Memorial High school placed in duo acting.

At the awards ceremony, we received 4th place. Against the entire state, which considering the hundreds of students at the conference, and the tens of thousands of available competitors, this was a pretty big deal. Descending some stadium seating stairs in a physics classroom at the University of Kentucky (some heavy irony *there*, I suppose) to accept our award, there were whistles and claps, shouts and bellowing 'hoo-rahs' as we approached the dias. I was under no illusion that they were for me. Standing there under the glare of the lights, we accepted our brief applause as was our due, and I looked at Lyn's face. She was beaming, obviously pleased with how it turned out. As we were leaving the auditorium later, in the hall, she turned to me, tucked our certificate under her arm, grabbed my face with both her hands and planted a kiss right on the lips–no subtlety there.

Time passed; I'm not sure how much.

Enough to persuade me that the theory of relativity *must* be true; time depends on the point of view of the observer.

When we separated, she whispered in my ear, "That was from Lyn. *Not* Rosalie." That was my first kiss for *me,* and not a character I was playing. And she never knew *that*, either.

From that moment on, I was officially, thoroughly in love with Debra Lyn Anderson. *I love you, Lyn,* I practiced saying in my mind. *I love you more than anyone I've ever met.* My heart pounded, blood rushed in my ears so loud I think I could *hear* it. I'm quite sure I broke out in a cold sweat.

The tragic part is, I thought to myself, as we returned to our bus, is if I tell her, she'll tell me I'm too young. *You're sweet. But you don't know what love is, yet.* I'd read that phrase somewhere. I felt like it was tattooed on my forehead. *DOESN'T KNOW WHAT LOVE IS,* said the sign. *HANDS OFF AND BEWARE. You're only 13. How many people have you loved?*

People clapped me on the back. Miss Caudill gave me a hug. My sister ruffled my hair.

I opened my mouth, then closed it again.

If I told her, she might refuse to ever work with me again. *You don't know what love is yet, sweetie. Pat, pat, pat* on the head. Dismissed. *'Bye now!*

It's funny how they tell you, when you start writing things, to avoid clichés and try to write about original ideas. Clichés, old and tired, too familiar to carry power and deliver meaning, cheap and easy ways out of saying what should really be said, used so often that familiarity has bred contempt. You can toss out a *You're too young, you don't know what love is,* or a *Time heals all wounds* or *A penny saved is a penny earned* or *Let's be friends* or *There's someone else* without a second thought, dismissing someone's pain without consideration or pause.

It's quite different when the cliché is real, and it's happening to *you.*

Perhaps I *was* too young, like everyone said. I didn't *feel* too young. My feelings were *real.* I knew that, and believed it as much as I've ever believed anything. I *still* believe it.

Life sometimes presents you with decisions you'd rather not make. *Tell her* and she might tell me she felt the same. Odds were, though, she'd tell me I was too young for her. I had a practical enough head on my shoulders to acknowledge that most of the *world* would believe I was too young to have a serious relationship with her. Suppose my fondest dream came true, and she proclaimed her love for me, and we began dating, or I moved away to live with her. How would we live? Could I deal with being a dependent, not earning enough money to support myself, or a *family*–a family that would have a father only a baker's dozen years older than the eldest child? Thoughts of statutory limits never even crossed my mind. This was 1977, but it was *Kentucky*, and it seemed like everyone at least knew a friend of a friend or a distant cousin who had married as young as 13, but I didn't even know for a fact if those stories were real, or amplified reflections of what the country thought of us. I think there is a kind of blowback from shows like *Jerry Springer* and *Green Acres* and *The Dukes of Hazzard* and *The Beverly Hillbillies*– people acting like the people they've seen on TV because they don't know any better.
202

If I told Lyn *I love you*, she might be so worried about having to deal with my so-called "puppy love" infatuation that she– or God help me, Miss Caudill– would conveniently arrange things so we would never work together again. *You don't even know what love is.*

If I didn't tell her, she might never know. I would probably never find out if she loved me at all the same way I loved her.

If life was like a TV show, we'd go off into the sunset, happy, together, in love *forever*.

Minutes passed; galaxies twirled. Stars were born, flared briefly, and died. The bus pulled away from the college complex. I clutched my small trophy and noted the nameplate was slightly crooked. Lyn laughed with her (*real*) friends in the seat behind me, and once or twice reached forward to ruffle my hair and say thanks.

I couldn't even decide if I couldn't make up my mind because I was making a mature decision, or merely a coward, or selfish. *Is this moment going to pass you by because you don't have the guts, boy?*

Was this "puppy love?" *You don't know what love is.* It sure felt real to me. And if confirming my feelings had come to the point of making a commitment, I knew I could do it, and make it stick. If nothing else, I was persistent. Loyal. No one really knew how persistent I could be when I put my mind to it. Being smart comes easily and quickly for some people; for people like me, it takes *loads* of front-end work. Over long periods of time. I knew about personal commitments, perseverance, dedication.

I could make it work. I *knew* I could.

But I was 13, and she was 18, and it would be years–*decades*–before the difference between our ages would become insignificant.

I looked out the window, at the city lights and the nice houses, the expensive cars, the stores I'd never set foot in rolling by. I couldn't even drive a car, let alone afford one. Despite my grandiose visions I'd never earned as much as a hundred dollars on any job I'd ever attempted.

The conversations around me ebbed, and flowed. My sister looked at me, concerned, not knowing what was bothering me, carefully deciding not to ask.

The bus pulled up at a Baskin-Robbins. Students began to file out to get some celebratory ice cream. There was no Baskin-Robbins in Hazard. A treat, from our teacher. For a good job, well met.

Lyn stood up and smiled at me as she passed my seat. Touched me on the shoulder.

I didn't tell her.

I *couldn't*.

Not yet.

It was quite possibly the wisest and stupidest decision I've ever made in my entire life. As I exited the bus, Miss Caudill sat near the front, waiting.

"You all right, Hoss?" she said, looking at me intently.

"I'm fine," I said, too quickly. "Just ...tired."

"That's understandable," she said. "Let me introduce you to a friend of mine I like to call Gold Medal Ribbon."

I couldn't risk anyone knowing; a poorly controlled rumor would have the same effect as a face to face admission. I never told *anyone*. What's worse, I denied it when asked later–even if my blushing face

204

gave it away. Even worse than that– despite my reticent agonizing, it was apparently no secret that I had a "crush" on her, even then. *Everyone* knew. Even my sister. Even my *teacher*, for crying out loud. Before long, even my *mother* knew. And each and every one of them, I was sure, would say the same thing to me. *You're too young. You don't even know what love is. Give it some time.* Those words, read in some juvenile teen sci-fi romance I'd read somewhere, echoed through my brain over and over as we made the trek home.

If what I was feeling wasn't real love, then when I got to the real thing, it would pretty likely kill me.

As I said, I'm pretty sure Miss Caudill knew how I doted on Lyn, at the very least. And I think she was aware that my feelings were pretty intense. And, knowing, cast us together one last time in You're a Good Man, Charlie Brown. Even after the events at State One-Act competition, or perhaps because of them.

Nipped in the Bud

Miss Caudill had often complained about the lack of support from school administration, but as the snow began falling intermittently prior to Christmas break, she discovered that not only were they ambivalent towards her program of bringing theatre to Perry County, they sometimes acted overtly to reign her in.

As much as I loved her as a friend and teacher, I could see what the administrators were up against. She did stuff that if I tried it today, I'd get censured, fired, un-certificated, or worse.

One time, we arrived from a dinner at Jerry's to find the entire school had been locked. With new chains, new padlocks, and no way in. The school didn't have a night watchman, so she tried calling Mr. (Byron) Caudill from a pay phone at a nearby gas station.

"You shouldn't be working so late at night anyway, Cheryl," he told her. "Just go on home."

Despite her pleas, and relayed messages from us about trapped homework and school books, he refused to come open the locks. As I recall her report of the conversation, he said something about getting priorities straight, and hung up.

Miss Caudill was furious. Red-faced and with agitation in her hands, she paced back and forth. "Why, that short-sighted, good for nothing, uninspired little *weasel*," was the nicest part of what she said. "If it was the *basketball* team and they forgot a *shoelace*, he would be here." She looked at all of us, ready to surrender. "Doesn't he know I'm just here for *you*? Does he have to take his little power games out on *children?*" She seemed ready to burst into tears, which she did occasionally when confronted with such obtuse behavior, when Benny said:

"Hey Caudill. There's an open window over there."

We looked. Sure enough, there was an open window about seven feet off the ground, leading into Mrs. Williams' room. Someone had opened the cantilevered window, and left it open at the end of the day. "Well, what are you waiting for?" she said to Benny. It wasn't like there was an alarm on the building.

"It's too high," he said. "I can't reach it. I need a boost, or someone to boost."

Slowly, all eyes turned to me.

"No *way,*" I said. "I am *not* breaking and entering."

Turned out my waist fit through the cantilevered section nicely, and with a resounding *thump* I landed on the counter containing Mrs. Williams' old yearbook archive.

I found an unchained exit near Mr. Smelt's so-called "workstation," a wooden chair located right next to the hot water heater.

We not only rehearsed *that* night, we rehearsed *every* night until our turn at using the community college stage came up. Miss Caudill made a great show of complaining to Mr. Caudill about the lack of access. She was quite convincing, and frustrating her clearly met some unmet need of his, so things stabilized for a while. We hung sheets on the windows so the room lights wouldn't give us away.

I think it says something, don't you think, about us, and Miss Caudill, and the school, that we were so desperate to learn we broke *into* the school to get access to our work space?

Each of us was assigned the task of leaving a different window open in a different 1st floor classroom at the end of the day. We used Miss Caudill's room most often, and I wonder if that had some bearing on Mr. Caudill's arbitrary decision to move her to a 2nd floor classroom some years after I graduated. Sometimes we had to sneak in after our "right-after-school" practice to open the window, after the teacher whose room it was had left for the day. Then when we returned after dinner, and the school was locked, we'd slip in again.

This became our regular practice until we learned that someone had seen us breaking in, and after we left, they used a window we forgot to close to break into Mrs. Williams' storage locker and steal a nice camera–the *only* camera– used by the journalism class. I voted for not telling her. Miss Caudill said she would, but I never found out how that conversation went; suffice to say Mrs. Williams kept coming to our shows, and remained a staunch supporter long after I graduated.

The other big conflict between Miss Caudill and the administration that I remember best (there were several) occurred shortly after Lyn and I had done our duo acting scene for state competition. The story says it's not quite time yet to tell about that; you need to know some other things first, so we'll return to this topic when it's time.

A Story in One Act

The regional one-act play competition worked like this:

There were 10 regions in the Commonwealth, each one composed of several counties. At regionals the winners were selected through evaluations by a panel of judges, and some were advanced on to the state-level competition. Awards were also given to individual actors and actresses.

Schools presented their shows throughout the course of the day at regionals, and we all knew the first place winner sent on to state. Each show was scheduled to last not more than 35 minutes and had to be provided in essentially one act, although scene changes were allowed if you could do them in the time alloted. Ten minutes were provided for breakdown at the end. Fifteen minutes were provided for setting up lighting cues with a copy of the script. Most plays didn't use much in the way of lighting cues; too many opportunities for things to go wrong. Thus, you could see one show per hour, approximately. There was also a junior division for grades 7-9, but most schools just used freshmen exclusively as there were not many middle schools, at least in the part of Kentucky where we lived. Freshmen were usually assigned roles in the junior division, where they would be the oldest and most mature students, instead of the youngest students in the Senior division. Miss Caudill paid no attention whatsoever to anyone's age; if you could do the job, you were in, and that was that. At the end, the judges tallied their votes and announced first, second and third place plays, with best actor and actress acknowledged in each division.

Devitt H. Caudill had never managed to win a regional competition before, let alone a state competition. Traditionally we lost out to our perennial rival Knott County Central in neighboring Knott County. Thus, in the early spring of 1977, we set out with high hopes and our relatively large cast in a school bus (funded by candy sales) to see what we could do.

Even though our region consisted of several counties, the year we did *Shrew* there were just two entrants in the senior division. Knott Central and us.

Several things were different about this year's competition. First, it was held in Hazard, at the relatively neutral community college, instead of at an elementary or high school in Knott County, which provided a local bias. Second, the judges were drawn from the community college staff and included representatives from *both* Knott County and Perry County.

These machinations were not lost on Knott Central, and by some means unknown to us they had managed to arrange things such that we had to perform first, always the weaker position in my opinion. Analogous to the concept that there is no such thing as bad publicity, I thought that if you went second the judges would still have your performance in mind as they sat down to vote.

So, we went first. This was the first time we had performed the play in its shortened form in public, and we were understandably nervous. We also were at some risk of running over time, because we had such a long script, many exits and entrances, and even costume changes within the half-hour period. A delay of any kind along the way might mean we'd run a minute over, and none of us suffered any illusions about the likelihood that Knott Central would allow the judges to overlook a rules transgression *just this one time*. Miss Caudill had taken to timing our rehearsals with a stopwatch and had even made last minute cuts to long speeches by some of the characters, hoping we could remember what words to leave out and what things remained.

The performance went well. We were familiar with the theatre, after all, because it was the same place we had made some of our public performances for the full-length play in December. There were occasional, tiny glitches; things like a slight hesitation over what was cut vs. what was not here and there, a moment with a character out of position for a scene, causing everyone to shift slightly to accomodate the change. Such was our training that we forged ahead and provided, I thought, a very competent job.

Miss Caudill was somewhat less sanguine about our chances after seeing our performance.

She spoke to us briefly in the hiatus between shows as Knott Central carted in their sets which included a bed, a desk, partitions and chairs. The tiny stage at the community college seemed crowded with stuff after our sparse set, consisting of four chairs and a small table, were struck.

"That was very workmanlike," she said. "I just hope that Knott Central is not inspired today."

"What do you mean?" asked Lyn. "I thought everyone did a *great* job."

"We've been better," replied Miss Caudill curtly.

"Yeah," said Benny, holding his head with both hands. "We have."

"Well excuse me for being an optimist," said Lyn. "I think we're going to *win* this thing."

"Me too," I chimed in.

Jane gave me a look that said *You're just saying that to agree with Lyn, and it's obvious to everyone your opinion is tainted.* She did not offer her own opinion, however. Just curled up with her feet on the folding theatre chair and pouted.

Knott Central's play was called *Gloria Munde*, and it was about an insane asylum where everyone there, staff included, was insane. A new arrival provides the dramatic conflict, but eventually she, too, succumbs to whatever mysterious effect pervades the hospital, and she ends the play as insane as the rest. Because we had declined to spy on Knott Central after the Great Hick Diversion, the competition was the first time any of us had seen the play.

Knott Central's production was quite competent, and funny enough that I at least was able to forget for a moment or two that we were competitors. I found that enjoyment tempered, following the close of the final scene, with the knowledge that it meant that it was less likely that *we* would win.

There was a hiatus of about an hour when everyone was sitting in the auditorium. I saw Lyn walk over and sit with some of the Knott Central people. I walked over myself.

"Good job," I said to one of the Knott Central kids, who played one of the insane inmates. He still had unkempt hair and streaks of makeup on his face.

"Yeah, thanks," came the reply. No return compliments came my way as the kid studiously avoided looking at me.

"Okaaaay," I said, and stepped over behind Lyn. She stood between the rows of theatre seats with her eyebrows raised, arms akimbo, facing one of the kids who was seated and facing the stage. As I approached, she held out one hand to stop my advance. She waved me away but not before I caught a snippet of a comment from our competitor.

"–did you find that *idiot* with the stupid voice–"

Were they referring to *me?*

Lyn followed me back to our seats in the center section of the theatre. "Did you hear what they were saying?"

"A little," I said. My ears burned. I didn't often fail at things academic, and when I did it was horribly embarrassing. Not that the judgement of a competitor constituted *failure*.

"*They're* idiots," she said, pouting and squinting as she did when she launched daggers at someone who had offended her. "They don't know real talent when they see it. They're just upset because we fooled them so completely with our Great Hick Diversion," she concluded.

212

"You're right," I said. A smile slowly spread across my lips. I stood back up. "I'm going to get a drink of water," I said. Lyn watched me leave, puzzled. I was still smiling. I nudged Benny as I worked my way back to the aisle, giving him a wink that said *Watch this.*

I exited up the stage left aisle, and as I passed the Knott Central contingent I said, "How y'all doin' t'day? Mighty fine weather fer a comp-uh-tishion." Then, without waiting for a response, I breezed into the hall, and got my drink of water.

Moments later Benny joined me. "I reckon I couldn't let you face them varmints alone," he twanged. Followed by Jane. Then Lyn.

We had nearly the entire cast out in the hall, getting a drink of water, before the awards for regional competition began.

When the regional awards were announced, we had a couple of surprises.

I figured Lyn was a shoe-in for best actress, but surprisingly this award went to one of the actresses from Knott Central. The next award was for best actor, and we all assumed that if the judges could judge fairly, Benny should get it.

Then the award was announced, and the astonishing thing was that they called *my* name.

Amazingly, I received the best actor award, over Benny. He mocked shock and dismay, and I was impressed by the fact that he didn't seem to be angry about it. Just determined to beat it next time. I would have pouted about it, at least, and probably whined for a month.

Then the award for best play was made.

"The award for best play for region 10 this year," said the competition director, "Goes to Knott Central for their production of *Gloria Munde.*"

We were flabbergasted when the announcement was made. Even other students from other schools gasped when the award was announced. After our teasing of the Knott Central crowd, the loss burned especially hot.

We applauded politely, and marched out to the bus.

"Does this mean we're not even going to *state* this year, Aunt Cheryl?" asked Lyn, tears brimming in her eyes.

"I already had a bus reserved for the overnight part," choked Miss Caudill. "That's what I get for planning ahead and being arrogant."

One of the judges caught up with Miss Caudill, and drew her aside and held a short conversation.

"Really!?" she exclaimed. We wondered what that meant...good news or bad?

Afterward, Miss Caudill gathered us together in the front of the bus.

"We're going to Lexington," she announced. "We got enough superior ratings they are going to authorize us to go anyway."

Cheers erupted. We were going to Lexington! I'd been driven through the city several times but never stopped there. For those of you not familiar with Kentucky, there are really only two sizeable cities: Louisville and Lexington. Louisville is a full-fledged city with over a million citizens (more than a third of the state lives in Louisville or did at the time) and Lexington had just about a quarter of that. Even the state capital (Frankfort, the most often missed state capital in quizzes from the Olden Days When We Could Ask Kids To Memorize Things) would be considered a suburb of a major city like Atlanta or St. Louis.

"Wish they would have told us when the awards were made," muttered Benny.

Miss Caudill waved these concerns away with a sweep of her hand. "These local judges just can't wrap their heads around the fact that we're *good*. So despite whatever political reason they had for giving first place to Knott Central, they decided they needed to send us along too. "

She hugged all of us–she was *always* hugging all of us– and predicted that despite losing the region, we would do better than Knott Central at State. "We may not win, but by God, they'll know we were there." She always got teary-eyed when she was giving us pep talks. "You children are as good as any I've ever taught," she declared with a sweeping gesture. She had this way of emphasizing what she said with hand gestures, I noted, which probably explained her aversion to "ham hands."

"They'll know little Devitt H. Caudill was there."

She seemed confident, but as for the rest of us, we weren't nearly so sure. If judges at the local level didn't recognize our skills, wouldn't the judges at the *state* level suffer from the same misconceptions?

The Bus and the Bees

Only a short interval of time passed between regionals and state competition. Now that we knew we were going we notified out teachers of the classes we were going to miss, got permission forms signed, and continued rehearsing and tightening the performance.

It was during this time that my father made it clear to me that even winning awards in acting was not, in and of itself, necessary and sufficient cause for me to continue in the program.

"Son, I just want to talk some sense into you," he said one day as we rode home from *God-damn play practice.* "I just don't see how you're plannin' on makin' a living with this."

"Dad, not everyone who studies acting becomes an actor," I said. "Some of 'em become lawyers, and teachers, and politicians–"

"If yer tryin' to make me feel better, talking about bein' a politician ain't a-gonna work," he said. "And I can't say as I'd much care to see you make a lawyer either. Pushing a pencil on paper just to take a man's life savings for some rich asshole, just so you can pocket the leavings, don't seem to me to be a proper way to make a living." He paused. "It shore would be nice to have so much money you wouldn't have to do any real work, though."

"Whatever I do I'm gonna have to stand up and talk to people, Dad," I said. "And because of all this that'll be real easy." Even though both our parents cussed a blue streak, we'd catch holy hell if we started using the same language back at them. It was a double standard, but a double standard enforced with a belt or a switch feels pretty much like a single standard to a kid.

"Well, it means a lot to your mother that you do what you want," he said. "I can't say I understand your figuring on this, but you know how it is with her."

"She don't let up easy, does she?" When I talked to my Dad later in my high school career, I switched off the diction lessons and just talked like one of the boys on the job site. I still do when I pick up the phone to call him. In some ways I consider myself bilingual.

"No," he said. "Just don't waste too much more time on this damn stuff, Jeff," he said.

Just then I had one of perhaps a half-dozen *brilliant* flashes of inspiration in my life.

"One thing at a time, Dad. I will say one thing, though."

"What's that?"

"Some of them girls in drama, they're *awful* pretty."

He turned and looked at me. His eyebrows lifted, slowly. Now *here* was an argument he could understand.

Jackpot.

"There ain't nothing wrong with bein' around purty girls, I reckon," he said. *Is that the real reason you've been doing all this?* crossed his face, and in return I merely smiled.

"Nope, not a thing," I replied, grinning. That right there, that was the complete text of our discussion of the birds and the bees and my relationship to girls.

He nodded. I don't think he ever tried to talk me out of drama seriously again. Unfortunately there were *other* people who thought ending our careers in drama was a good idea.

===

Miss Caudill *thought* she had the bus arranged, but Mr. (Byron) Caudill had other plans.

"I *told* that woman that bus approval was only provisional," he said, grinning, leaning back on a dented metal folding chair against the chalk-dusty brick wall of the school. I was one of the students who would occasionally take chalk-dust laden erasers and pound them against the side of the building to remove the accumulated chalk dust. Caudill was speaking to Dan Carpenter and C.J. Holt as they all smoked. Then he grinned, the thought of frustrating the uppity drama teacher causing his bald head to blush pale red. He brushed the long hairs on his left side over to the right, in an unconscious motion that had become habit in recent years. "We need that bus for basketball, don't we boys?"

"You got that right, Byron," said Holt. He flicked his own butt into the can beside the door. "Never seems to be enough room on the bus for everyone that wants to go."

In those days, students were allowed to smoke as freely as adults, but they had to do it outside the building near a sand filled bucket beside the door. Despite the ready availability of this depository, cigarette butts appeared everywhere on campus—in the grass, beside the road, even on the lunchroom floor once in a while. A person transported from the present day would stare in wonder at the great variety and note patterns of dispersal and discuss second-hand smoke effects with great seriousness. For those of us who lived there the idea of second hand smoke being bad for us was ridiculous. For every person who got cancer from smoking there were just as many anecdotes about grandparents who lived to be 103 and smoked every day since they were seven. Statistics don't stand a chance in such an environment. And besides, even smokers didn't have it as bad as mine workers. People on government welfare actually spoke enviously of mine workers' families who were living on "the disability" when they got their "black lung." This mean they got the black lung *benefit*, not the disease caused by inhaling coal dust itself. It wasn't a huge amount of money, but it was substantial.

People who got the black lung *benefit* still worked hard for their families. It was just that their new, laborious efforts were dedicated to *breathing*.

"So what did you do, exactly, Byron?" said Holt. He squinted through the afternoon sunlight still shining. School was out in a few minutes.

"I'll tell you what I did," he said. "I invited all the parents to ride the bus to the regional tournament down in Chavies," he said.

Holt looked surprised. "How are they supposed to get there? There aren't any more bus drivers available this weekend."

"Oh, there's drivers, for those willing to stand up and make a decision," said Caudill. He lit another cigarette from a breast pocket pack in his shirt. He used a fancy gold-embossed cigarette lighter, inscribed with his name inlaid with gold leaf. Actually it was his *father's* name. He was a Caudill, *Junior*. He made a show of lifting the lighter with the name facing outward even though it required him to use his left hand to light his cigarettes.

"And what decision did you make?" asked Carpenter.

"I reassigned that uppity woman's driver to the basketball trip," he replied calmly, a smile spreading across his face. "It'll be a couple of days from now before she finds out. And *hoo-boy* I'd like to see the expression on her face when she realizes she has a bus with no driver."

"Well how will she get the kids to the drama competition then?" Carpenter asked. *All's fair and all, but this is affecting the kids' work,* he thought.

"I 'spect they'll all have to pile into her little Mustang," he replied, leaning back and closing his eyes. *All thirty of them* went unspoken.

Carpenter looked at the smiling principal, and then glanced at the coach, who shrugged as if to say, *He's the boss, what are you gonna do.*

"Let's say they get down to the state competition somehow, and they win something," said Dan. "She'll have to make a presentation to the school board if they win. They might want to ask her how things are going over here."

"Well, for one thing, they ain't gonna win anything," said Caudill. "They ain't never won a state award in all the years she's been doing all this drama, and I don't see any reason for that to change. And for another–" He stubbed his cigarette butt into the sand bucket beside the door, opened it, and held it open as he spoke further. For someone with no love of the drama program, he was rather fond of dramatic exits.

"For another, if they don't win, I've just about got the board talked into canceling the whole damn program," he said. "It's a waste of time and money that could be better spent on students who might actually make something of themselves."

Carpenter shrugged noncommittally, but his eyes narrowed. The bell rang, and he tossed his own smouldering butt into the can as he went to supervise the afternoon loading of the buses.

Thrust and Parry

The morning we were scheduled to depart for Lexington was a Friday. Competition began on Saturday and continued through the awards ceremony some days later.

Unknown to us, Mr. Caudill carried through on his threat to reassign the bus driver. A fleet of buses arrived at the school, loaded up with students and teachers and parents, and departed for the regional basketball tournament. One bus, ordered by us and stationed at the school, remained empty and without a driver, who had been, we learned later, reassigned to take a second bus to the tournament.

At nine o'clock Miss Caudill glanced out the window and noted all the buses except one were gone. *Where's my bus driver?* she thought. *They usually get here early so they can sit on the clock more.*

She sent a note to the office and the secretary answered in writing.

"Mr. Caudill is not available right now," she said, glancing through the doorway at Caudill's shoes, the soles of which were propped on his desk and aimed in her direction. *I'm not in unless someone's bleeding,* he had told her. *Especially to that Cheryl Caudill woman.*

"Well, when will he be available?" asked Miss Caudill via a second note.

"Try lunchtime," she replied, and was not surprised to see Miss Caudill stomping down the hall. She gave a glance to Mr. Caudill who closed his door quietly before she arrived.

"I want to know where my bus driver is for my trip this afternoon." said Miss Caudill.

"Mr. Caudill said if you were to ask about that he wanted me to give you this here note," said the secretary, handing over a folded piece of paper.

Cheryl, the note began. *The basketball field trip overflowed the buses we had available, so I ordered another one. There were no more drivers available, so I sent the driver we had with the basketball kids. I hope you understand, the good of the many is more important. You can compete again next year if you win regionals. We need to reserve our resources for those who can have a chance at winning.*

Miss Caudill stared at the note for a long time. Her hands began shaking.

"Give me the phone," she said to the secretary.

"Um, Mr. Caudill said...."

"I don't care what he said, give me the phone right now or I'm going to walk down the hill and use the payphone and you can teach my class." This was delivered in a near monotone, quietly so others couldn't hear.

Miss Caudill sent for Jane, who was stage managing, and had her keep tally as she desperately called parents. Benny's parents had no car. Her own tiny car could hold five, as many as seven well-behaved students in a pinch–but she definitely did not want to go that route again if she could avoid it. Six people could fit in Cheryl Ann's mother's car. Meredith's father had a pickup and offered to take some in the back but Miss Caudill said it was too dangerous for a long trip on the interstate. Three more there. Four here, six there... so many parents worked, and those who didn't work, couldn't afford a decent car...

In the end, she could only carry 24 students...six or seven would have to be left behind. By her estimation she could adapt the play overnight and shift lines from one character to another to make it work. After all, she'd done it to make the script short enough for the half hour...

It just wasn't *fair.*

"I just can't do it, Jane," she said, her voice shaking. "There's too many. And no time. There's an empty bus sitting out there, and no one to drive it."

"I bet my brother Bill would drive it if I asked him," she said. "He'd do it just for the hell of it."

"Watch your language, young lady."

She blushed, and was properly chastised. "Sorry."

"Does he have a chauffeur's license?"

"Well, no."

"Can't do it then. He could get arrested for driving a bus without one." She looked toward the closed office door.

"Where is he again?" she asked the secretary.

"Downtown," she said, not looking up.

Miss Caudill gripped the countertop where students stopped to check in at the office so tightly her knuckles turned white. "I swear, if I ever get the chance, one of these days I'm going to give that ....that... *person* a piece of my mind he'll never forget," she growled through clenched teeth. Jane didn't reply, didn't know what to say.

"We could go in on Saturday," she suggested.

"We have to register today before 5 o'clock or we're disqualified," she said. "He *knows* that." She paused, and looked at the door with new understanding. "He *knows....*"

"You think he did this on purpose?" asked Jane.

"The good of the many," she hissed. She was beginning to work up a real head of steam. *"Give someone a chance who can have a chance at winning. Why that good-for-nothing–"* A nudge from Jane reminded her that the secretary was listening.

Psst.

Jane looked down the hall. She saw, off in the distance, a hand waving. Waving at her to come that way.

Miss Caudill and Jane proceeded down the hall and found Dan Carpenter standing in the stairwell.

"I've got to tell you something," he whispered, looking up the stairs to see if anyone was listening.

I Ain't No Plumber, Boy

In the meantime, I was in science class, awaiting lunch. I had no idea any of these events transpired. Miss Caudill had told us to eat lunch prior to getting on the bus, and when the bell rang for lunch, I dutifully went to the lunchroom with my class, leaving my belongings behind.

The science lab room, the only science room in our school equipped with sinks (one), chemicals (some) and tables instead of school-type seats with names carved in the surface of a right-side armrest, was situated directly above the study hall where we practiced our plays, room 111.

In the lunchroom I presented my (burning bright fluorescent orange) free-meal ticket provided by the state for students whose parents were too poor to pay. Each week we got a little strip of tickets with tear-off tabs. We had to present the tear-off tabs to the lady at the end of the line. The only thing that kept the process from being completely em-barrassing was that so many people used the tickets. I remember one class where more than half of us were on free and reduced lunch. On the menu today: spaghetti, which we never ate at home unless it came from a can, included meatballs, and had a picture of a smiling fat Ital-ian guy on the label.

I went upstairs (with permission) to get my stuff so I could get on the bus early. What kid wouldn't want to get on a field trip bus early? I entered the science classroom and noted that there was the sound of water running. I looked around, and spotted the culprit... a sink spout, mounted for some unknown reason to the side of the aquarium, which held a few fish during the school year. And it was running.

And the aquarium was *millimeters* from overflowing.

It was, obviously, up to *me* to save the day.

I had no idea why an aquarium would need a sink spout, but the whole thing had the sort of cribbed-together look that was common to most

of the equipment in the generation-old school. It was probably assembled out of spare parts just to allow an aquarium to exist there in the first place. I glanced at my watch. *Half an hour before I'm supposed to get on the bus,* I thought. *Yeah. I got time.*
I looked for a handle to shut off the water.

It was *missing.* The only thing left in its place was a serrated stem. *Great, just frickin' incredible,* I thought. *Now what?*

My initial attempt of just grabbing the stem and turning it failed, because whomever had done the dirty deed had jammed it tightly open before removing the handle. Just then, water began leaking over the edge of the aquarium and flowing down its sides.

I glanced around the floor. The floor was made of some old slate, and had at one time held many more lab stations in a different configuration. Not even tile protected the bare floor, which sported a number of empty holes that students had been known to drop gum, pencils, and small freshmen through from time to time. Water was beginning to creep, slowly, toward the nearest hole. I grabbed a paper towel and twisted it, jamming it into the nearest hole. That would only be temporary, I thought. *I have got to turn off the water.* There was no shutoff valve under the table. The pipe led directly into the floor. Maybe there would be tools in the supply closet. *A pair of pliers should do the trick,* I thought. If any substantial amount of water drained through the holes, it would ruin the new expensive drop ceiling installed into the classroom below.

Which happened, as I noted, to be room 111.

===

In the meantime, Miss Caudill assembled the cast inside her classroom, after instructing Jane to be quiet about the bus problem.

"Roll call," she said. She read names from the *dramatis personae* to determine who was present. "Petruchio,"
226

"Here," said Benny.

"Kate."

"Present," answered Lyn.

"Bianca."

"Present."

"Biondello."

"President." Eyes rolled at the old joke.

"Curtis."

"Yes."

"Grumio–" she stopped. Looked around.

"Where's Jeff?" she asked Jane.

Jane shrugged and rolled her eyes, the universal sister symbol for *I'm not my brother's keeper nor do I want to be.*

===

I searched through several drawers looking for a pair of pliers to no avail. Now the water was pooling at the bottom of the aquarium, making a sizable pool and advancing on the first empty hole in the floor. I noted the end-of-semester biology notebooks stacked around the room on tables, where people had turned them in. What could I do now?

Just then my buddy Wilbo walked in the door.

"What's goin' on, Jeff?" he said, looking at the puddle. "What did you do?"

"I didn't do *anything.*" I said. "It was like this when I got here."

"Well why don't you turn off the water?" he asked.

"I tried," I said. "The handle's gone. Go get the principal or someone in the office. I'll keep trying to shut it off. And *hurry.*"

Wilbo saluted and sprinted out the door, calling back over his shoulder, "I'm on it."

I grabbed it with all my strength and squeezed the stem of the faucet handle as hard as I could. I was a thirteen year old boy. Adrenaline coursed through me. *Tighter,* I willed my hands. My muscles bulged with effort before I even attempted to turn the stem.

I took a deep breath. *Here goes,* I thought.

I twisted the stem with all my might.

And the entire faucet assembly *broke off in my hand.*

Water, unconstrained by the tiny opening at the end of the conical faucet, used to attach rubber hoses for experiments, gushed out *full force*–straight *up.*

Where it struck the new ceiling in *this* room.

And proceeded to rain down upon five classes of notebooks, ungraded and waiting.

I gasped and looked at the scene of impending destruction in horror.

===

228

"Well *find* him," Miss Caudill said. Jane sighed, and departed. "As for the rest of you, for reasons I cannot explain, we are going to have to change our plans, unfortunately. Did you all tell your teachers where you were going?"

Everyone asserted that they had.

"All right," she said. We're going down to the end of the hall, and exiting near the band room. Then I want you to go *around* the band room to the parking lot, and wait for me there. *Do not wander off.*"

"Why are we doing this roundabout thing instead of just going out the side door to the bus, Aunt Cheryl?" asked Lyn.

"Don't ask questions."

"But–"

"Listen to me carefully," she said. "Mr. Caudill does not want us to go on this trip. He cancelled our bus. I wanted to tell you outside so we could arrange rides–"

Pandemonium erupted.

"Caudill, we worked for *weeks!*" shouted Benny. "Where is that asshole? I'll kick his ass!"

"No you *will not,* young man!" ordered Miss Caudill. "You were expecting an afternoon off from school, weren't you? I intend to see that you get it." She glared at him. "And watch your mouth."

Benny, for his part, subsided. He knew better than to let his foul language draw the attention of Miss Caudill. He was already On Notice.

She pointed to Cheryl Ann Barnett, another student in the class. "I can't trust Benny," she said. "Go find out where Mr. Caudill is. Don't speak to him. Just find him and come back."

229

Cheryl Ann Barnett was a tall, statuesque girl, with a slightly upturned button nose, long legs, and usually seen with a short straight hairdo reminiscent of Dorothy Hamill's hair, popular at the time. She was active in the theatre program the entire time I was in drama. During my freshman year I didn't have a great deal of interaction with her, but what I did was mostly act as a target for her slings and barbs. Part of Cheryl Ann's definition of friendship was to keep me in my place. She was quite good at it. It was practically a hobby with her.

Cheryl Ann nodded and departed.

Miss Caudill began waving her hands as she described her plan.

It just might work, but it absolutely depended on Mr. Caudill not noticing what was going on.

What she was needed was a *distraction*.

===

It was a bit confusing having Cheryl Ann Caudill and Cheryl Ann Barnett be student and teacher, so those people who referred to them by first names referred to the elder as "Cheryl" and the younger as "Cheryl Ann." It was odd, I noted, that people referred to Cheryl Caudill as "Shure-ull" and Cheryl Ann Barnett as "Share-ull Ann." Just one of those things you don't notice at the time, I guess, and can only see with the perspective of time. I even once worked for a woman named Cheryl who pronounced her name "Chair-ell." It's an entirely different approach to naming than people use today, where you take out all the vowels and replace them with the letter 'y' as in "Myryah." What we did was use the same spelling and pronounce it eight different ways.

Cheryl Ann poked her head in the office.

"Where's Mr. Caudill?" she asked.

"Eating lunch."

Cheryl Ann went to see for herself.

"Wait a minute, young lady," said the secretary. "Do you have a hall pass?"

Cheryl Ann dug in her pocket and retrieved her copy of the note we all carried with us, all the time, so we could go do Miss Caudill's bidding. *Hall pass,* it said, undated and untimed. *CC.*

The secretary knew this would be backed up by Miss Caudill, so she waved Cheryl Ann on down the hall. Along the way, Cheryl Ann passed Wilbo, who looked perturbed about something. She started to say hello, but she was on a mission.

She stuck her head in the lunchroom, clutching the pass if needed. She looked at the teacher's table, and didn't see Mr. Caudill. She craned her neck. *Oh–* she thought. *There he is, in line. Or rather, cutting behind the line.*

Wilbo crowded in front of her, glanced around the room, and departed.

She saw the principal take his tray and take up a seat with a clear view of the empty bus in the back parking lot. His back was to the open doorway where she stood.

For some reason, she noted as he turned the corner around the table, he had been grinning.

===

My efforts to stem the water grew more frantic. A brief attempt at returning the faucet to its original place merely drenched me. The thing had been broken before, and as far as I could tell, it was merely *caulked* back in place. *Brilliant.*

The puddle was beginning to drain in the nearest holes. I could hear it dripping, *plishssssssh* as it struck the tiles below. I grabbed a trash can and shoved it under the aquarium. Perhaps a third of the water fell into it. Fish were struggling to control their depth in the turbulent water.

I've got to move the notebooks first, I thought.

I shed my jacket, which was just slowing me down, and began moving stacks of already-dampened notebooks to the ledge on the edge of the room, away from the umbrella of water. Moving the notebooks for hundreds of students took what felt like eternity but probably lasted less than three minutes. *Where the heck is Wilbo,* I thought as I finished. I ran to the doorway, dripping, to see him *walking* down the hall to me.

"I couldn't find Mr. Caudill," he said. "They said he was in the lunchroom, but I looked in there and he wasn't there."

If you want something done right, I thought as I ran down the hall.

"Keep everyone out of there, Wilbo!" I yelled. "I'll be right back!"

"Roger wilbo," he said, and took up guard position at the door. His first name was Roger. He'd been telling that joke for years, after someone had explained to him that *wilco* meant *will comply.* I hope he complied with my orders *this* time.

I dashed down the hall, trailing water.

===

"He's eating lunch, Miss Caudill." reported Cheryl Ann. "But he's looking right out the window at the bus."

"Lyn, go tell Mr. Carpenter it's time," she said. "And if you find Jeff along the way, drag him by the ear and get him down here."

"She won't need to drag him," said Charmaine. "If he sees her, he'll just follow her like a puppy dog."

"Don't pick on him!" snapped Lyn. "He's nice and doesn't deserve that."

Miss Caudill observed this exchange, and filed it away for future reference. *Not now,* she thought. "Can you two snap at each other later? We still need a distraction." Lyn threw a defiant glance at Charmaine and departed.

Just then a hue and cry arose from the direction of the office and lunchroom. Loud voices. Shouting.

A fight! she thought. *Perfect!*

"Now, everyone listen!" she called. "Get ready to go, and when I say go, *move!"*

===

Just moments earlier I screeched to a halt in front of the office and accosted the secretary.

"Where's Mr. Smelt? Where's Mr. Caudill?" I gasped, dripping wet. She looked at me, astonished, and pointed at the janitor's closet across the hall.

He was there, all right. Pot belly protruding underneath his white t-shirt, blue work shirt unbuttoned, he saw in a steel chair with two legs propped up on an empty filing cabinet, ball cap pulled down over his eyes.

"Mr. Smelt!" I cried. I started babbling incoherently. "Water pipe! Flood! broken water! D-d-draining into the floor! Upstairs!" I shook my head so I could speak clearly. *"You've got to come t-t-t-urn off the water in the science lab!"*

One of those moments passed that causes time to slow down, when every moment seems drawn out. He took a deep breath and tilted his head up just enough so that he could see me.

And then he said:

" I ain't no plumber, boy. I don't even know where the cut-off is. You best go fin' Mr. Caw-dell an' tell him 'bout that water pipe. "

I stood there, dumbfounded, for all of five seconds.

He sat there and looked at me with one eye peeking under his ball cap brim, daring me to dispute him.

Time passed.
"Okaaay," I said breaking the spell, and dashed out into the hall. The secretary simply pointed down the hall and said, "Lunchroom," as if she knew what my next question would be.

By now it was nearly time to be on the bus, but I had to try to do something about the leak. So I ran screeching into the cafeteria, and there was Mr. Caudill eating his lunch with his napkin tucked in and everything. Facing the window, his back to the door. I was running fast, and my feet were wet, so I had trouble stopping. I skidded across the cafeteria floor, and *bumped into* my principal from behind, accompanied by the sound of clattering plates and silverware.

He leapt to his feet and turned around, his face turning as red as the spaghetti sauce covering his white shirt.

"What the devil, boy!" he shouted. "Watch where you're going!" He looked at me again before continuing his tirade. "Why're you so *wet?*""

===

Miss Caudill turned to get an update as Jane returned. "I couldn't find Jeff, but there's some kind of flooding problem with the science lab, I heard the secretary say."

Miss Caudill leapt to her feet. The science lab was in the opposite direction from the office compared to her classroom. *One lucky distraction, just in time.* "*Now!*" barked Miss Caudill. Everyone snatched up costumes and props and scripts and dashed for the door.

The secretary, just down the hall from her room, three doors away from the cafeteria, noted the trotting procession as it exited the building, followed by the gliding form of Miss Caudill.

Miss Caudill waved. Smiled sweetly.

The secretary waved back. Smiled, in confusion.

===

"Water pipe!" I cried in response to Mr. Caudill's shouts. "Broken pipe!" My Jonathan Rosepettle induced stutter returned, slowing my efforts further. "Th–th-the science l-l-lab, has a b-b-b-roken *pipe!*" I said. "There's w-w-ater all over, flooding the f-f-f-floor! You've got to sh—sh–"

"YOU!" he shouted, pointing at a big strapping boy at a nearby table. "You, you, you," he continued, pointing at others, and then, finally, me, "and *you,* follow me."

He scraped what spaghetti and sauce he could from his tie as we departed.

"I'm s-sorry about your shirt, Mr. Caudill," I managed to squeak.

"Nevermind," he said. He led us into the hall. Several of the boys exited first and waited.

"I can't believe this is happening," he muttered. Looking at me, he grunted. "Cheryl Caudill is probably mixed up in this somehow. I *know* it. "

===

Miss Caudill saw the boys at the end of the hall exiting the lunchroom. Whatever was happening, it was happening *now.*

"Hurry up!" she hissed. Most of the students were nearly out of the hallway.

Just then Lyn reappeared.

"Mr. Carpenter says, now or never," Lyn reported. "Whatever that is supposed to mean."

"Where's that brother of yours?" Miss Caudill asked Jane again as the last of the students exited the building.

"I have no idea."

"Go look for him again. Come outside in five minutes even if you don't find him," she ordered. Jane went up the stairs at the opposite side of the building from the science lab. *Jeff has science this period,* she thought. *I'll swing by the science lab, check out the damage, and then poke my head in the lunchroom again.*

===

Mr. Caudill led his merry troupe across the hall, out the side of the building opposite the parking lot, looking over the low hills and green forests of Eastern Kentucky Route 7. He began running towards the end of the building where the students had just, unknown to us, exited. He ran, so we boys ran with him.

Then he walked.

So we walked.

Then he ran some more, maybe 10 or fifteen steps.

So we ran with him, pacing him the entire time.

By the time he'd passed four or five classrooms, he arrived near the front right corner of the building, around the corner from the exit where Miss Caudill was shepherding her students toward a wooden staircase built onto the side of the hill, leading to the main road below the school.

===

At the bottom of the staircase, a yellow bus awaited, pulled over on the side of the road. As they approached they saw the door was already standing open. The bus was so far down the hill, it couldn't be seen from the school.

"Get on the bus," she hissed.

"Where's the driver?" asked Lyn.

"Just get *on*," Miss Caudill said.

As they approached, the door opened, and Mr. Carpenter waved from the driver's seat. His blonde hair fluttered in the breeze. He was a handsome fellow, and knew it, and flashed a toothy grin at us as he gestured for us to enter.

"Welcome aboard," he said.

===

Mr. Caudill stopped at a large metal plate on the ground. He reached down and with *one hand* picked up and flung the metal plate aside. Then, using his bare hands on the fiberglass insulation (bound to cause itching later) he tossed out wads of insulation surrounding the giant valve knob which cut off water for the entire school. This was below ground level, and if he leaned over on his knees to reach it, he would have fallen in.

Just then, the *rat* arrived.

It was a *big* rat. Probably not as big as my memory recalls, but big enough that half a dozen strapping high school boys hopped backward en masse, and even the principal jumped as he clambered back to his feet. He spotted the metal plate that had covered the hole, and now hefted it with two hands. I didn't think he could kill the rat with the metal plate, because it wouldn't fit. He didn't even try. Instead, he trapped the rat in one half of the hole with the metal plate. The valve was still free in the other half.

Then he said, with preternatural calmness, as if he'd faced this exact dilemma several times before:

"One of you boys get down in that hole and *turn off the water*."

We all looked at each other to see who was going to be the sacrificial victim. One kid I didn't know standing in the front of the group, next to the hole, turned to leave–and *fell in the hole*. I was standing in the back of the group, attempting to attract less attention to myself. I took another step backward, and noticed a yellow school bus at the bottom of the hill.

"You boys help me out of here!" the boy cried.

"*No!*" boomed Mr. Caudill, gripping the metal plate as if he meant to pick it up and smack the kid with it. "Turn that water off *first*," he commanded.

238

The kid did this, and with a mild hissing sound the water stopped. The kid clambered back out of the hole, and the principal tossed the metal plate over the bare dirt hole again, not bothering with the insulation. I suppose he expected to turn the water back on soon. The rat, no longer the center of attention, retreated to its hole.

Now Mr. Caudill ran one sauce-and-mud-and-insulation stained hand over his balding head and straightened his spaghetti covered tie. He eyed the group, and stopped when he found me. "You other boys go on back to class. *You,"* – pointing at me– *"You* come with me."

===

All of Miss Caudill's latest scouts, dispatched from the bus, returned and reported Mr. Caudill was nowhere to be found. Neither was Jeff, whose role as Grumio could not be shifted or dropped and was so important there was no way to lose it, but not so important that an understudy had been assigned. "I *still* couldn't find him," Jane reported as she boarded the bus.

"Why is Mr. Carpenter driving?" asked Lyn. She didn't care much for him ever since he called her "Miss Popcorn Brain" in typing class, probably due to some prejudice against the intelligence of blondes.

"Dan here has many skills," said Miss Caudill as Mr. Carpenter fished out his wallet.

"Among them he is a licensed school bus driver."

Mr. Carpenter displayed his wallet and driver's license to Lyn, who regarded him guardedly.

"Otherwise we wouldn't be going today, because Mr. Caudill cancelled our bus driver."

"We need to go *now*, Cheryl," said Mr. Carpenter. "If Byron finds out I'm driving he can suddenly assign me some extra duty here on campus. I got C.J. to cover my afternoon typing class but he doesn't know why. "

"Where is that Mason boy?" she asked of no one in particular.

===

That Mason boy was walking back into the building. Mr. Caudill dismissed the others now that the excitement was over. I expected to get the third degree then and there, but instead we walked toward the office.

Not a good sign.

Mr. Smelt was mopping up the water I'd trailed all over the building.

"You'd best look in the study hall, Mr. Caw-dell," he said, and assiduously went back to his mopping. "I tol' that boy I din' know how to shut the water off."

Mr. Caudill ignored him, and proceeded to the study hall, as I tagged along behind.

We stepped into the study hall.

It was *raining*. Everyone was holding notebooks over their heads like umbrellas. Some of the tiles were droopy and half-covered in water drops.

I turned to Mr. (Bryron) Caudill, who looked at me.

"Son, did you cause this?" he asked.

"No *sir*," I replied. "I tried to shut it off."

240

We walked upstairs to the biology room. Wilbo consented to let us enter by scooting away to avoid permanent association with these events. I showed Mr. Caudill the broken faucet, and the bucket I had placed under the aquarium. He noted with some resignation that the faucet had been caulked into place after having been broken in the past. Students began entering and retrieving their things, passing books and jackets along bucket-brigade style to avoid walking through the inch-deep puddle in which Mr. Caudill and I stood.

Mr. Caudill picked up a gasping fish, regarded it briefly, and deposited it back in the aquarium. He then looked around for something to wipe his hands on, saw the condition of his clothes, and wiped his hands on his pants. I picked up my science book and jacket, the original reason I had gone to the room in the first place, and started to ask Mr. Caudill if I could go get on the bus.

"Mr. Caudill, can I go–" I began.

"Just go." he waved at me. "Go on and go."

So I *went*. He thought I went to class; instead I left the campus. In fact, I was about to leave the *county.*

The bus was still at the bottom of the hill, engine already running. Everyone was waving at me as I trudged across the lot. *Am I the last one?* I thought.

I boarded the bus. It began rolling with the customary squeak of the air brakes even before I sat down.

"Where have you *been?*" Miss Caudill demanded. "And... why are you so *wet?"*

"I uhm... I broke a water pipe in the lab and Mr. Caudill had to shut the water off to the whole school."

"You *what?"* We turned a corner by the Stop 'n' Shop, which put us out of sight of the building.

I relayed the tale to her and discovered my unwitting role as the distraction that allowed us to board the bus unnoticed.

"Lord, he doesn't even know we got a bus driver and that we're on a *bus*," said Miss Caudill.

"He is going to be *righteously* p.o.'ed when we get back," said Benny. "I want to be there when he finds out."

"*I* don't," I said. Then I grinned. "He thinks I'm still at school."

"He thinks we're *all* still at school," said Lyn. "And we would be too, if it hadn't been for a very effective distraction."

"Glad to be of service," I said.

Then everyone started laughing.

We laughed all the way to Jackson. Lyn laughed, too; I had helped her laugh out loud for the first time that I knew of since the incident in the Mustang. Suddenly my sodden clothes and wet socks seemed more like a reward than an embarrassment.

I opened the bus window and allowed my hair to dry until someone complained about the cold air and I had to close it again.

Years later after graduating from college, I visited the old school and spotted the stains on the ceiling tile, still there over ten years later. Miss Caudill said it was over 20 years before the ceiling got repaired. It gave me an appreciation for the rate at which improvements are put into schools.

The Continental

We spent the three hour bus ride adjusting some lines and tweaking some specific notes given to us by the regional judges... some people were told to project more, others to enunciate more clearly. We did projection vocal exercises, and a couple of straightforward line-through rehearsals. At a line-through, you don't do the blocking, you just review the lines. It was a common thing for us to do several line-throughs on the bus on the way to a competition. After the broken faucet incident, we did the same thing as we make the long trek to Lexington.

I had only been to Lexington, Kentucky one other time– as a stopover on a trip to Kings Island amusement park near Cincinnati with my Sunday school class, before my mother had severed those ties. The trip to compete with *Shrew* was my first real overnight field trip with a school group, and nearly the first one since we had moved to Kentucky.

We stayed in the Continental Inn. In those days it was one of the largest hotels in the area and served (drunken) conventioneers and (drunken) fraternity brothers and (drunken) friends of the band. It was once a go-to destination in Lexington, and has a book-worth of stories associated with it; one apocryphal tale tells how the future governor of Kentucky, Wallace Wilkinson, was kidnapped for a short time from the parking lot and held for ransom. The indoor Olympic-sized spool area was noted for its near-tropical atmosphere, giant palm trees and steam-room-like humidity. The wear and tear eventually wore it out, and now it looks dilapidated and is abandoned. Given the growth rate in Fayette County, Kentucky, it's only a matter of time before it gets razed and replaced with a strip mall or a Starbucks; but in those days it was actually pretty nice. It was certainly the nicest place I had ever stayed.

In the bus on the way to Lexington, I sat alone and watched Lyn talk to the upperclassmen. I felt pretty lonely all though elementary school in Kentucky; I had few friends since moving from Ohio and my status as the Boy Who Skipped 8th Grade didn't help much. I don't mean to make too much of that; it's likely most of the other students didn't even know, and I'm certain I wasn't the only one who had ever done it. Skipping the 8th grade was the closest thing Perry County Public Schools had to a GATE (Gifted and Talented Education program), so I'm sure there were others, but I had never met one. Well, actually, the closest thing Perry County had to a GATE program was Miss Caudill's drama class, but unfortunately neither Devitt H. Caudill nor county administration ever thought of it that way.

On the bus, I was coming down from the excitement and attention I got for the broken water pipe incident. Lyn and Benny sat together, probably drilling lines from the fight scene, which required rapid-fire and well-timed delivery. My sister sat apart from me talking to some other upperclassmen. Charmaine Marshall sat with her friends arranged around her in order of priority. A few of the other underclassmen clumped together and giggled incessantly. *Even on a bus,* I thought, *cliques happen.*

The miles passed quickly and slowly at the same time for me. I'm not quite sure how to explain that sensation. I would be lost in thought for an hour, participate in an active conversation briefly, then go back to looking out the window. For some reason, as we passed from dry county to wet county (making the sale of liquor become legal and illegal as we crossed county lines) every time we passed a Last Chance/First Chance liquor store on a county border, the sign caught my eye as if I had never seen it before.

Sitting across from me and one row up was Millie Caudill (no relation to any of the other Caudills I knew, as far as I know), a small, long-haired girl with delicate features and long fingernails. Her hair fell halfway down her back. The more I looked at her, the more I noticed how cute she was; I had never noticed how pretty she was, actually, because for the longest time I considered myself ineligible to date anyone due to extreme nerdiness, or I had been obsessed with Lyn.

244

After a time whoever was sitting with her shifted allegiance and joined another clique. Lyn was laughing, enjoying herself. For all I knew she wasn't even rehearsing any more. But that was OK, I told myself. I don't have any particular power over her; she has a lot of friends, some *close* friends, and always had a *real* social life apart from her little talks with me--

I resolved to make an effort to see someone my own age, or at least closer to it. Millie was a sophomore, which placed her 2 to 3 years older than I. But there weren't any other girls in the cast my age– I thought– but hey, what did I have to lose?

I crept out of my seat and stepped up to the empty one beside Millie.

"Do you mind– is it ok, if I uh, sit here with you?" I stammered.

"Sure, OK," said Millie, shrugging.

I sat down. I introduced myself, and she did the same.

It was a pleasant conversation, not emotionally charged, no promises to be made or kept. Just two kids getting to know each other.

We arrived at our destination, and went our separate ways as the rooms were made available. Along the way, I stopped at a little gift shop. In the gift shop were trinkets you find in every motel gift shop: little thimbles with the names of the states on them; calendars with pictures of local bathing beauties, jars of honey from local farms, and giant pencils with your name printed on them.

And a rack of little heart-shaped lockets, which when you opened them revealed the words *I love you.*

I bought one. I wasn't sure who I would give it to, but an idea was forming in the back of my mind. It took half the stash of money I'd brought, but I figured it was worth it.

That evening, we all attended a dance. It was some sort of youth disco, and we were practically the only ones there. The loud music–louder than anything I'd ever heard before–and the pulsing lights made my heart pound. I spotted Millie across the dance floor. She had long, straight black hair, and almond-shaped eyes that were ever so slightly tilted, which gave her an exotic but not quite Oriental appearance.

I don't remember thinking consciously about approaching her, or thinking ahead as was my usual habit as to the consequences of my actions. I only remember that I wanted *someone* to love me, someone closer to my own age perhaps, and Millie was ...just... *there. Available.* But was she willing?

I walked up to her.

"Hi."

"Hi."

"Uhm, wanna dance?"

"Sure."

I couldn't dance much, but I did what I could. The songs were all disco beats, no slow dances. After a couple of dances I drew Millie off to the side.

"I, uh, really like you," I said.

"I like you too," she replied.

"I got you a little gift." I handed her the locket, inside a small white box. She raised her eyebrows. *Already?*

She accepted the box, and opened it. Opened the locket. Read *I love you.* She looked up to see my expectant gaze.

"Listen, Jeff–" *Oh, no.* "I can't accept this." She handed the box back to me.

"I'm sorry– I– Uh–"

246

"You don't love me," she said. "You're ... you're way too young to say something like this. We practically just met. You don't know what love is, yet."

You don't know what love is. The very phrase I'd been terrified of, had tried to talk myself into believing was just a cliché in a book, not a phrase that *real* people used to say to each other in *real life....* was hanging there, in midair between us, like a curtain of lead, blocking my thoughts from forming coherent sentences. *You don't know what love is.*

As she spoke, the sound of the blood running through my head increased until it was a roar. I felt like a meteor had just blasted a hole in my brain. *Idiot. What were you thinking?* I opened my mouth, made some noncommittal noises, pocketed the locket and backed away.

"I'm sorry. I didn't mean–"

"It's O.K." she said. "Really."

I backed further away, nodded, and made my way to the exit and the waiting bus in the parking lot. On the bus, the words echoed through my head repeatedly. I reached a conclusion, realizing finally what had possessed me to put myself through such an emotional wringer. *I can't tell Lyn how I really feel. It'd be a disaster, just like this.*

Millie had been right, in a way. I *didn't* love *her.*

As the years passed, I look back at the events of that night and realize that even Millie was wiser than I that night, and I regret using her in some clumsy experiment my teenage mind had unconsciously concocted to see if I *could* tell a girl I loved her. The only saving grace was the fact that she really had no emotional attachment to me, and thus wasn't hurt. If anything, she was mildly bewildered by the episode. We never spoke of it again, and as far as I recall, never spoke to each other about *anything* again. I hope she forgave me for that evening.

Later on the rest of the cast worked their way out of the disco and back onto the bus. Lyn excused herself from Cheryl and sat down next to me. Her expression looked pained and pitying.

She knows, I thought. *Someone talked. Now everyone's going to know.*

"It's hard growing up, isn't it," she stated, not really making a question out of it.

I looked at her. I nodded.

"I know it is. And it hurts. People will tell you you'll get over it. Grow out of it. But that doesn't make it stop hurting. Believe me, I know."

"Yeah," I managed to croak. "It *hurts.*"

We rode in silence. No one around us bothered us, for a wonder. I wonder to this day if it was intentional on their part, or just dumb luck. I have no idea what I would have said to anyone.

We got off the bus. I started to go to my room, but Lyn took my hand and led me to a quiet corner of the lobby.

"It will be O.K., sweetie," she said. "Just give it some time."

"I feel like such an idiot. So *stupid.* I *hate* feeling stupid."

"Everyone does, now and again. *Everyone.* Even geniuses," she said, winking at me. I wanted to smile at that, but I couldn't. My breath hitched, I gasped, and suddenly she was just hugging me tightly, absorbing my sobs.

I couldn't even tell her the real reason I was crying.

Hitting the Showers

In elementary school in Ohio, all the boys had to take a shower together after P.E. before getting dressed back in street clothes. In Kentucky, there was no locker room, no shower, no gym. The playground was half a dozen jealously guarded swings and a bare dirt patch with a giant rock too big to haul out by hand on a hill. Devitt was worse; you didn't dress out because there was no where to accomplish it. So you returned to class, sweaty and smelly. No one complained because everyone had to do it.

In Ohio at home, we had had a bathtub. In Kentucky, there was no tub. We had cold water coming from a well up the hill, but no hot water heater; no shower, either. Just a sink, and a stove.

Each morning I began my day by brushing my teeth (I was taught to brush my teeth by some public servant wielding those little red tablets to show where the plaque remained even though you tried to brush it off. They taught us about brushing when visiting the school in the first grade and I've brushed religiously every day since). I would put a pan of water on the stove and heat it up nearly to boiling. Then I would pour some in a washpan set into the sink, add some cold water to take off the edge of the heat, and wash, standing, with a washcloth. I got up extra early so I could strip off my underwear and wash "down there," in some degree of privacy. Finally I would lean over the sink and, using an old plastic cup, pour water over my own head and lather up shampoo to get clean. Rinsing and draining the water into the sink, I put the basin under the sink and put on my clothes for the day.

I lived like that for several years. My father didn't install a water heater and shower until long after I had departed for college.

Thus, as we approached the room in the hotel, I viewed the bathroom with some trepidation. Of course, I'd been in nice bathrooms before; my cousins lived in a fairly Bradyesqe ranch home, and I'd stayed overnight with various friends who did, but when I did stay overnight, I'd invariably opted for *baths*.

This bathroom had only a narrow tub and a shower head. I doubted I'd even fit in the tiny tub, let alone be able to be submerged. And there were six of us in the room; I might not have the luxury of a tub bath. So I resolved to use the shower.

Problem was, I couldn't figure out how to turn it *on*.

I tried flipping this lever (drain stop) and twisting this knob (hot wate-cour) and finally yanked on the metal tab on the spout and was rewarded with a face full of blisteringly hot water that nearly took my breath away. I grappled with the knobs and then was pierced by a thousand needles of rock-hard ice. Then my foot slipped, and I had to grab the sides of the tub to keep from falling on my face. Finally I balanced the temperature (*got to do that before I actually get in next time*) and took my first shower in years, and my first shower ever by myself.

My mother had instilled such a fear of drowning in us I had never had my head submerged underwater as far as I could remember. I remember turning my back to the shower spray so I wouldn't get water on my face, which made me panic and gasp for air.

The ironic thing was, in Kentucky, everyone seemed to have a nickname. Mine was "*little bub*," which translates as *little brother.* My father's nickname was *Tad*, short for *Tadpole*, after some incident involving frogs and puddles and brothers pranking each other in his youth. My mother's nickname was *Duck,* again over some obscure event in the distant past. Despite their aquatic nicknames, neither parent could *swim.* When we went fishing, the kids *always* had to sit uphill of the parents and their fishing poles. If we were downhill of Mom and stumbled on a root or rock at the edge of the creek, she would inhale with a sharp *shisssss!* and snatch us with one hand, flinging us away from the water. I don't know why she was so deathly afraid of the water. She certainly passed that on to us, though.

I survived the shower and toweled off and got dressed in my only set of pajamas, then surrendered the bathroom to the next boy waiting in the hotel room.

It certainly was nice having an *indoor* flush toilet, instead of the old two-holer we had twenty yards from the house. Nothing's quite as cold as a frozen outhouse seat in the middle of a January winter night in Kentucky. Not even frozen carbon dioxide.

It was many years before I was comfortable in the water, and I'm not much of a swimmer now. I still don't like getting in pools where the water goes over my head.

The State One-Act Competition

I saw Millie once or twice during the remainder of the trip. She looked at me long enough to see if I was all right; checked to see if I was going to freak out or melt down on her; then she went on her way, saying nothing. Lyn and Miss Caudill and my sister behaved as if nothing had happened, which was *completely* O.K. with me. Maybe Millie had spoken directly to Lyn; I don't know.

After I emerged from the shower, I discovered there was no space left for me to sleep. Benny Doherty and Raynard tossed fitfully in one bed; others occupied the other bed, and a little fold-away cot someone had acquired was filled as well. Hadn't we planned for this?

I looked around to see what I could improvise, and settled on pushing two easy chairs together with a blanket I found in the closet. I stretched between them, covered up with the thin blanket, tried to ignore the AC blowing in my ear, and fell asleep. My last thought was, *If I ever invent a time machine, I'm coming back and erasing this day. I've been such a fool.*

The next morning I awoke to snickers. My sheet had fallen off, and somehow my pajama top was wrapped around my neck. My back felt *cold.* I opened one eye, and there in front of me was a brand-spanking new can of hair removal gel. *Hair removal gel!* I leaped to my feet, the crescendo of laughter already rising, and *ran* to the bathroom and twisted around to see my back. My *hairy* back. Robin Williams has nothing on me, let me tell you.

The hair was still there. The other boys collapsed into hysteria.

"Very funny," I said, pulling down my pajama top.

"Boys, let me introduce you to the missing link. Right here, we found him in this room," said Raynard.

"Jealousy once again rears it's ugly head," I said to Raynard. "At least I have hair where it counts, unlike certain other people." Raynard was notoriously hairless, and what hair he had was fine against his pale skin–practically invisible. My proclamation sent everyone into a new round of giggles, directed at Raynard. I retrieved the gel and stuffed it in my bag, to dispose of it later. Benny told me later that they had nearly carried out the plan to write dirty words on my back, and if I hadn't awakened, they would have really done it.

I believe they would have, too.

I finished the rest of my morning ablutions, keeping an eye peeled for upperclassmen on the prowl. I had recently begun to develop a mono-brow, and dutifully, carefully shaved the hair bursting out between my eyes. Why did I have to have hair *everywhere*?

Thankfully, we were scheduled for the third day of competition–*late* on the third day, we were warned by Miss Caudill, when the judges would be tired of writing and their hands would be cramping and they'd have headaches from writing in the darkened theatre–but the next day after my fiasco with Millie began with a chance for me to attempt to overcome my humiliation, put it behind me, and do my job.

Therefore we spent the day before we performed watching the competitor's plays. One group, from Berea, performed a play with a young scruffy-looking fellow named Harold Owens. Harold and I met while working on a play called *Wilderness Road*, again in college eventually, becoming good friends and doing several shows together.

I don't remember the other plays. I think one school did something from *Our Town*. Knott Central repeated their performance of *Gloria Munde*. There were comedies, and tragedies. Silly stuff. Some of it was pretty good, and it was kind of unnerving to see what kind of competition we would be up against. Some of the Lexington and Lou-isville schools, where all the rich kids lived, had elaborate sets, beauti-ful costumes, sound effects, audio equipment, tech crews. One school from Louisville used *microphones*, earning a sneer from Miss Caudill. Henry Clay. Tates Creek. Calloway County. Jessamine County. St. X.

Louisville Male. Paducah. Kentucky Country Day School. Berea Community School. *Knott Central.* The names were vaguely familiar, the city schools often mentioned by the two Kentucky television stations because they were local to the television stations; the vast majority of schools never noticed, hidden by distance from the range of a local broadcast truck's schedule.

Some teams wore uniforms, all dressed in dark slacks and blazers. Others sported the latest fashions, bell-bottomed jeans and platform shoes and open-collared, button-down shirts with flaring lapels.

One team had a wagon loaded with a cabinet filled with drawer after drawer of makeup.

One play's set consisted of thin frames of wood with stretched canvas across it. Braces and clamps held it tightly in place on stage. It even had functional doors and windows.

Knott Central's extensive set didn't look like it overflowed the stage as it had in the tiny Hazard Community College theatre. In fact, it looked like it fit into the space nicely.

"Good luck," said the Knott County Central director, Mr. Bailey. "I hope *you all* go home with something."

"Why, thank you, Mr. Bailey," said Miss Caudill. "We hope the best for you too. It would be nice if both first *and* second place came from our region." She left unstated the implication that they should take the *second* place award.

They shook hands and parted.

Devitt H. Caudill had a tackle-box full of drugstore makeup, one single milk crate, a small table and a few chairs – our only set pieces, used in a single scene. We had crammed them in the emergency exit door of the bus. Our students were *all* poor, relative to the kids from the city schools.

"Where you folks from?" asked a kid from Louisville. "I'm from St. Xavier." He pronounced it "Eggs-avier," whereas I would have said "Ecks-avier." I thought, *Can't he even pronounce the name of his own school? Sloppy diction.* He had some sort of lapel pin on his blazer he twirled around in circles, as if we were supposed to interpret what it was just because he was twirling it.

"Devitt H. Caudill High School," said Benny. "In Jeff, Kentucky."

"Never heard of it," said the kid, dismissing us as possible competition. "Where is that, exactly?"

"Near Hazard," said Benny.

The kid nodded, closed his eyes and smirked. *Smirked.* He turned and walked away. "Good luck," he said, although his back was already to us.

"You'll know we were here, kid," said Benny quietly. "You *will.*"

Miss Caudill, for her part, took notes on the ubiquitous legal pad during the competitor's performances.

Can't hear leading man.

Set design is distracting, walls are flimsy and wiggle when door is opened.

Actors not facing audience.

These kids are GREAT!! Beautiful Costumes. This performance is excellent. Possible competition?

No stage presence.

Very professional. Good projection. Evenly balanced group.

Sounds like they are reading it from a prompter.

Clumsy blocking. What was director thinking!?

Dropped line.

Good casting.

Ham hands.

Excellent.

Whether to find fault to encourage us or to just get a sense of what sorts of problems *we* might present to other judges, she found reason for hope that we might win something in many of the performances. As far as the others were concerned, she thought there were some serious contenders.

"I think we have a *chance*, children," she told us at dinner. She had insisted we go out to at least one nice restaurant on the trip. The boys were all wearing ties, although Benny was wearing sneakers. The ladies were all in dresses. We ate at a nice "sit-down" restaurant near our hotel. I can't remember which one. "Out of maybe 25 plays in our division, there are maybe five in the same league as us."

"Maybe we'll get fifth then," said Charmaine. "There are still some plays from the city schools tomorrow. There could be more competition."

"Well," said Miss Caudill, "I'm obviously biased. I still think we are better than Knott Central. But there are a couple here that I'm not so sure about. Berea Community School is doing a play written especially for the students in the cast. I know the director, and he is pretty good, if a bit indulgent."

"They *wrote* their own play?" I asked. That sounded impressive to me.

"And that group from Paducah is here," said Charmaine. "The interpretive dance group."

The group from Paducah had performed a dance without words, and even went on tour to show it to schools all over the state. They even stopped by and performed in room 111. Miss Caudill said most of the students in attendance had never seen modern dance performed. It was an interpretive piece obviously meant to tell a story, set to rock music popular at the time, which meant headbanging, loud, screeching with a heavy disco-influenced beat. The performers had essentially acted out a rape and childbirth, followed by a child growing into an adult who continued the cycle of violence. It was pretty graphic for high school and Mr. Caudill had "spoken" to Miss Caudill about screening future performances by visiting schools.

I did remember it was...memorable. If the judges were open to it, it might win something.

"So, I can't say we're guaranteed to win anything," continued Miss Caudill, "But we have a chance. Albeit slim."

"Really?" said Lyn. "It would be nice to win one before I graduate."

"Really," said Miss Caudill. "We just have to keep our heads together and concentrate. By my reckoning there are bout five serious contenders here, counting us," she repeated.

"And does that include Knott Central?" asked Lyn.

"No." she replied. *She's obviously biased,* I thought. *They already beat us once.*

"Remember," she said, "You're here to perform. Don't let the competition rule your thoughts or you won't perform well. You all have to *concentrate.*"

Concentrating was not something I was prepared to do just yet. I scanned the menu. Half of it was incomprehensible to me, consisting of a variety of Italian words with far too many vowels. The rest was seafood and steak.

My only encounter with steak had been an unpleasant affair stuffed with cheese and tomatoes made by one of my aunts, with the consistency and flavor, I thought, of overcooked liver (with which I was, unfortunately, intimately familiar.)

Plus, I *hate* cheese. Always have, once I found out what it really *was*. I tried to imagine the desperate soul, starving to death, who put the first curdled cheese buds in his mouth in a last-ditch attempt to stay alive. No one else would be so reckless, in my opinion. I felt the same way about coffee.

In fact, in those days, I was what you might call *picky.* I would have liked have a hamburger, but it wasn't even on the menu. (Later, when my little sister was in drama, this became a MUCH bigger issue than it had ever been for me...I was downright eclectic in my tastes compared to her. Alas, the rest of that story must await for another time, I'm told.)

I finally settled on rainbow trout, as it was the only thing on the menu that I knew had no cheese, wasn't unpronounceable, or wasn't on my List Of Foods To Be Avoided Unless Truly Starving In The Desert.

They delivered the fish with the head intact.

This provided much entertainment for the boys at the table, as they invited the girls to see. The girls squealed in mock terror and asked how I could be so cruel. That, I thought, was a stupid question from people eating steak and shrimp. The animal's already dead; it doesn't *know* its head was still attached. What difference did it make whether you butchered it, boiled it, or left its head intact? Dead is *dead.* I've never understood how some people think there's some value in killing an animal peacefully and kindly so you can eat it; there's no pussyfooting around the fact that the animal is *DEAD,* and if you wanted to be kind to it, you *shouldn't kill it.* Vegetarianism I could almost understand.

In the meantime, I had never eaten a fish with the head intact; while my parents fished all the time (both for food and for recreation) they did all the cleaning and preparing of the fish, and the heads went into the scrap bucket and were delivered to the dogs, the pigs, or the compost pile.

I began to cut the fish apart, causing a new burst of squeals from the girls nearby.

"Do you want me to move to another table?" I asked Miss Caudill, who, for some reason, was seated right next to me.

"No, child, eat your fish." Miss Caudill stared the looky-loo people into submission. "I'll say this for you, Mason, you're braver than I am. I can't eat food that stares back at me." She was unaware of the fact that the trout was the only thing on the menu I felt brave enough to tackle. "Meat's fine as long as you can pretend you don't know where it comes from."

She taught us which fork to use, to put a napkin on your lap, not to slurp drinks using a straw, and anything else she could think of. For several (definitely not all) of us, myself included, it was the first time we'd ever been served by a waiter. She had to explain the concept of *tipping* to some, but not me; my mother had been a waitress to help ends meet when we lived in Ohio. She always complained bitterly that although she worked harder, the young, pretty and *lazy* waitresses always got bigger tips.

Dessert was apple pie *a la mode* (with ice cream, I learned), and as I dug into it I looked up and discovered that Lyn was suddenly sitting across from me, looking at me calmly.

You're so young, you don't even know what love is, echoed through my head. I still felt ridiculous over the business with Millie, but my *heart* was over it. I blushed, of course, fork frozen in mid-flight between my plate and my mouth. Mouth hanging open. The lump of ice cream and pie fell off the fork with a *plop*.

She smiled. I lowered my fork. Miss Caudill was twisted backwards, beckoning a waiter or something.

You O.K.? mouthed Lyn silently.

I nodded, slowly. *Thanks*, I said, the same way.

Lyn reached across and put her hand on mine. *Let me know if you want to talk.*

I looked at her hand on mine, feeling the warmth, noting the texture of her skin for some reason, and nodded again. Old Ike Newton once said *you cannot touch someone without being touched in return.* She smiled again, starlight fell upon my face, and she stood up to return from whence she came.

But not before Miss Caudill had noted that our hands had been together.

I pushed the half-finished pie away, wiped my mouth with my napkin, discovering a glob of ice cream that had been in my nascent beard, and felt embarrassed all over again. *She didn't even act like she noticed I had food on my face,* I thought.

I sat quietly through the rest of dinner, participating in conversations as necessary. I had been wrong earlier. My heart wasn't over being heartbroken; the entire event would never have happened if I had admitted to myself what I was terrified to admit to Lyn. I never was really in love with Millie. I had sincerely been attracted to her; she wasn't randomly selected or picked from a sense of pity. That brief infatuation *was* puppy love, I was sure. Easily started; difficult to end, but not lasting. The problem was that I was really in love with *Lyn*, and I had no way to act on it, no way to persuade her to see me as anything more than a naive kid.

Last night hadn't helped. It had made things *worse*. Now, she had *evidence* that I was too young. Too immature. Too *impulsive*.

Idiot.

On my way out of the restaurant, I extracted the locket that Millie had returned to me from my pocket, and opened it to read the words again. *Could I risk giving this to Lyn?* I thought. *No. It's been used, and rejected. There's no more love left in it.* I wound it into a little ball and threw the locket and chain in the trash as we left the restaurant.

The Play's the Thing

The day of our performance arrived. The KHSSL sponsored two divisions, junior and senior, and we were in senior. We went nearly last in the rotation.

Before each show, one of the directors of the competition would come out and introduce the play to the audience, which consisted of students and teachers who had already performed or were waiting their turn, local theatre students and even a few members of the press from the Lexington and Louisville papers.

We had reviewed our technical requirements with the stage manager. We had a few lighting cues; no gels, no spotlights. Just lights on, and off. The Guignol Theatre at the University of Kentucky was *much* larger than the stage we performed on in Hazard; several hundred people could sit here. The stage was at least as large as the entire *room* 111 at Devitt, where we practiced initially.

"We're going to have trouble with timing exits and entrances," said my sister, Jane, who was our stage manager and attempted to help us to adapt our blocking to the larger space. "There's like an *acre* of stage."

Lyn was more concerned with a complex costume change, usually accomplished in the music room off of stage left at the Hazard; she used a special velco-based dress to change from her dress from the traveling scene into a wedding dress for the post-wedding scene. Hers was the only real *costume* in the production. The rest of us just wore regular street clothes. Usually, the switch was accomplished when she was stationary; the size of the stage and the location of the next entrance for Katherine meant, Jane insisted, that Lyn would have to change while moving. While *running.*

About an hour before our turn came, we filed out of the theatre, to change into our erstwhile costumes, and apply what makeup we had.

"Where do we go for makeup?" I asked. My sister indicated the ladies room outside the theatre.

"I can't go in *there*," I said. "It's the ladies' room."

"The ladies' room has a lounge in the front," said Jane. *A lounge? Like a bar?*

I entered, hesitantly, only after seeing two other male cast members from our group pop in. It was more like a waiting room at a doctor's office. There were couches– *three of them*– and little end tables and lamps, artwork on the walls, and soft music playing on the background. *No wonder girls spend so much time in the bathroom. Give me a book and I'd stay here too.*

In the lounge, students came and went– girls into the interior door leading to the *real* ladies' room, boys into the hall– and in the center of the maelstrom, Miss Caudill and Lyn and a couple of the other senior girls sat on a coffee table in the center of the room, applying makeup to all who approached them.

I had already worn makeup for the performances we had done in December, but this makeup job was much thicker. (Unlike many of my fellow male performers, this was not traumatic for me and involved no argument. It was just part of the *job* like enunciating.) I was still inexperienced in applying my own makeup–this was a skill we couldn't be trained in until we had enough makeup to *share*.

After we were dressed and made up, we moved to our places back stage to begin the show. Jane donned a headset to stay in contact with the theatre's tech crew. The show ahead of us cleared the stage, and the brief intermission flew by; one of the judges stepped up to a microphone on the side of the stage to announce us.

"Our next play is a *shortened* version of *Taming of the Shrew* by William Shakespeare," he said, almost skeptically, squinting at the information card he held. *No one cuts Shakespeare.* "It will be presented by students from ..." he paused, holding the card closer. "De-Witt Caudill

High School in Hazard, Kentucky. Director and sponsor, Miss Cheryl Caudill."

We were actually located in a small town outside of Hazard called Jeff, Kentucky. (No connection to my name.) Hazard was where regionals were held. The tittering in the audience could have been for the funny name, or the location of our school. We couldn't tell. *Not a good sign,* I thought to myself, but, not for the first or last time, I decided to keep my thoughts to myself.

Then the lights dimmed, Jane hissed "*Places!*" and we prepared to show the world what we could do.

A Shining Supernova

The lights came up and the play began. Benny's stage presence was powerful; almost palpable. In a review of the competition after regionals the local paper had referred to him as a "shining supernova in a constellation filled with stars" and he used his charisma that night like a powerful beacon, leading all of us around wherever he wanted to go. I always thought I would have liked someone to use such an astronomical description about *me*.

I do remember having to explain to Benny what a *supernova* was.

The only person capable of standing up to that intensity was Lyn. She stood toe to toe with him, capturing all of our hearts with her determination to be *herself* for her own sake, not letting Benny (or Petruchio) overwhelm Kate, not completely, not even at the end. The movie version of *Shrew,* unlike the stage play, had Kate walking off without Petruchio, leaving him to follow her at the end of the production, indicating her compliance had merely been a matter of her seeing the advantages of having such a strong husband and accepting that on her own terms. This was how Lyn played Katherine. Benny's power was balanced, delicately and effectively, by her subtlety. I swear, she could act with just her eyelids; a widening of the eye here, a glance there; her stance, her voice, *everything* she did was in character, down to the way she swept her dress along as if it really wasn't torn and she was the most regal person in the universe. The scenes between Benny and me went flawlessly. I said *rebused.* I was loud enough, and obviously clear enough, because the audience *laughed,* sometimes in odd places, because unlike our high school audiences in Perry County, most of this audience *got the jokes.* We didn't step on the laughs. The lights, triggered by Jane, came up, went down on schedule.

The scenes came and went. At one point Benny was supposed to be picking me up and tossing me *down* the steps, for not telling Curtis to have the house ready in time. Our timing, thrown off but not destroyed, left us at the bottom of the steps prior to the moment in question instead of the top. He didn't stop speaking and didn't cause the flow to be disrupted further. With a smooth motion he snatched me off my feet and flung me *on* the stage, where, miraculously, I landed deftly on my feet as if we'd done it that way hundreds of times. I looked startled at this, then fell backwards onto my rear with a thud. The audience *roared* with laughter. I could barely hear it; the bright lights formed a curtain, a shield between my world and theirs. I couldn't pay attention to the audience because Grumio was acting his part of being in mortal terror of Petruchio–all put on for show, for Kate. *Kate* was the audience for our antics. The other people just happened to be in the room.

Moments later, I noticed with horror that Lyn's dress, which was supposed to be Velcroed shut in the back, had come undone– and was in risk of falling off. Her bare back showed through the gap, with a tiny flash of white bra underneath–she wasn't wearing street clothes under the costume this time. The Velcro itself was peeling loose, as if it hadn't been sewn into the fabric. Only a single thread held the loose Velcro to the left side of the seam. What would happen if the dress fell off? Would the play come to a halt? Would we break character? In the speech competition we had seen less well trained students panic and stop in the middle of a scene and *beg* for a chance to start over, tears streaming down their face. But Benny? He would have rather *died* than have shown such panic.

Benny, more focused than anyone ever knew he could be, came to the rescue. He gave Lyn an intense glare and a growl, and dramatically and obviously, in full view of the audience, *ripped* the tenuous connection free in the back while dragging Lyn around. *What the heck–!* I thought, and then I realized, *This fits in perfectly with Petruchio's abuse of Katherine in the play at this point.* Benny was, I decided in that moment, an acting *genius*. I played along and overreacted to his

265

tearing of the dress by pointing and looking as if he must be *really really mad* so that Kate could see that Petruchio was *serious* about making her keep up with him.

Lyn, falling right in with the the strategy, wound one arm around behind herself to clutch the dress shut–and now she had an *excuse* to do so, keeping completely in character all the while. If she had done it on her own, the audience would have been distracted, wondering if the beautiful girl's dress was going to fall off in the middle of the play. Instead, the rip in the dress fit right in, as if it had been intentional. She played her part flawlessly, being angrier than *ever* because of Petruchio's gall. No hesitation, no pause to think; as if we had done it a hundred times. As if she really were Kate, behaving as Kate would have. Benny may have been a genius for solving the problem, but at least he had had a few moments to figure it out. Lyn reacted *instantly*, without the need for metacognitive reflection and discussion; she was *acting* and didn't need to ponder what was the appropriate reaction. That's *true* acting. Anyone can memorize lines and parrot them back. Luckily, the scene ended quickly, and the problem went away with a costume change.

It was an amazing thing to observe. *Someday, I want to be that good,* I remember thinking, then shut down that line of thinking lest I drop my own character.

During the transition between the travel scene and the wedding scene, Lyn had a difficult costume change as Jane had predicted. We drew astonished glances as we *raced* through adjoining rooms, passing other teams preparing for the final performances. Lyn ripped off the damaged dress she had been wearing– I could hear the fabric ripping, and tossed it aside. Two girls chased her and wrapped the wedding dress around her as we ran. For a brief moment, I realized that she wasn't wearing *any* street clothes under her costume; she'd just essentially stripped to her underwear in public and kept on moving.

There was no time to appreciate the view as we continued the race. Benny slipped ahead and shoved chairs and desks from the path and held open the doors. The door to the theatre lay ahead. Benny shrugged, sensing that the transition scene on stage had just ended, and shoved us toward the door. Lyn was not quite reassembled yet. I opened it, scooted in front of her to give an assistant one last chance to Velcro a recalictrant sleeve into place. Then we made our entrance, and *flew* down the hallway to enter on the stage. By that time, Benny had already initiated the dialogue, before he even set foot on the stage.

The play continued. All the actors played their parts. All the world was a stage. *Our* stage. We *owned* that stage that afternoon. No one was hard to hear. No lines dropped. No desperate hisses for a *prompterrrr!* or missed cues. Not a trace of a twang in anyone's voice; no lost shoes, no ham hands, no upstaging.

It was a shining half hour of perfection in the sea of chaos that raged around all of our lives.

Lyn's inner conflicts, and conflicts with her mother and aunt, my struggles to make my achievements match what everyone assumed I could do effortlessly, Benny's somewhat more than mild antisocial tendencies, Charmaine's jealousy, Jane's struggle to define herself and gain independence from home, even Miss Caudill's ongoing battles to fulfill her Mission, all faded away, unimportant, trivial.

It *was* an impossible dream. Nevertheless, it came true before our very eyes.

For that half hour, the audience sat transfixed, not talking, laughing when appropriate, undistracted. It wasn't a competition; we were painting a whole new *world* for them. I could practically *see* the vine-covered courtyards of Padua and smell the rich flavor of the invisible food we had so desperately placed on Petruchio's table, watched the empty water glasses spill upon the table as he banged his fist, quaked in terror at his rage, nearly cried at Katherine's distress, and applauded along with the rest of the audience at the happy ending envisioned by Shakespeare, sexist though it may appear to our modern eyes. Even Charmaine Marshall, shuffling along as the aged Batista, stepped up and convinced the world that somehow, there must have been a dod-dering old man enrolled in our school, for surely there was no one who could have pulled off his aching desperation to rid himself of Katherine but an actual man who had lived through the experience.

We were, each of us and collectively, professional, in character, a team, and *brilliant*. I've never had another moment like that in a long career of teaching and acting. It's unlikely I ever will again.

We knew, as the audience rose to its feet for one of the few "Standing-o's" of the competition, that we had won them over. Regardless of what the judges thought–and they could easily be seen now writing furiously, although I hadn't noticed them during the performance– regardless of what they thought, we had been *good. Really* good. Maybe *great*. It was, probably, the best performance of the play we'd ever given, long or short version, regional or state. For many of us, it was the best thing we'd ever done in our lives. I thought of Miss Caudill, who, as the director, had to surrender all control and *trust us* to carry out the vision, helpless to assist, unable to issue any more notes or edits or changes. It must be hard, being a director, especially of stage plays. Every premiere must be like sending your child away from home, to live alone and make its way without your help.

We joined hands–all of us– and took several bows. Lyn and Benny took separate bows as previously instructed. All of us got another burst of applause, especially Benny. I clapped enthusiastically myself.

When I get older, I hope I'm half as good as he is, I remember think-ing.

Then the lights came up, and we left the stage to clear the way for the final groups of the competition. We gathered our few set pieces and props from backstage–including the remnants of Lyn's dress– and made our way to the green room area where Miss Caudill was already *wailing*, crying, hugging each of us as we came into her view.

"Fantastic!" She cried. "Amazing, and wonderful! Oh, children, let me hug all of you, that was the best thing we've ever done. The *best* thing. Oh my, oh dear, thank you all, thank you all from the bottom of my heart. I'm so happy!" She began wailing, making indecipherable noises and little squeaks.

"Thank you, Miss Caudill," we all said, and hugs and slaps on the back ensued. We made our way to a vacant hallway and collapsed to the floor.

Anytime you come off of an emotional high like that, I've found, there's an inevitable crash. We couldn't bring ourselves to watch the final few performances–we were too drained. As the adrenaline wore off, the doubts and uncertainties returned.

"Did you see that crazy dance thing from Paducah?" said Jane.

"They were disqualified, I heard," said Miss Caudill. "This isn't a dance competition. They had no words in their performance, so it wasn't really a play, the judges said. Too bad. Those children worked *hard*."

"St. X was pretty good, though," said Raynard.

"Couldn't understand that one kid," said Millie.

"Did you *see* what happened to my dress?" wailed Lyn. Jane and a few others nodded.

"Nice cover," said Raynard to Benny. Benny shrugged as if it was the most normal thing in the world to save the production by a literal thread.

"*Someone* pulled out the threads of my Velcro," said Lyn, fire flashing in her eyes. "It worked just *fine* in our last rehearsal." She glared menacingly at Charmaine.

"Well it wasn't *me,* " said Charmaine. "Maybe the dress doesn't *fit* as well as it did."

"Are you calling me f– I can't believe you'd–" stammered Lyn. Further argument was intercepted by Miss Caudill, who held up a hand.

"It all turned out well. Looked like it had been planned, in all honesty, it really did. Your recovery was so smooth I hardly noticed it, and I've been watching you do this play for *months.* Don't worry about it. It looked authentic. Kudos to you, Benny. And everyone else for just moving right along with it."

Benny accepted this as a matter of course, neither basking in the praise nor proclaiming false modesty. He was always like that.

Lyn squinted her eyes, pouting and directing daggers at Charmaine, but held her tongue. *God,* I thought to myself, all thoughts of my humiliation with Millie vanished, all emotional investment drained from the energy we had expended. *She's even cute when she's really pissed off.*

We rested in the hall. Bottles of pop appeared from somewhere. We drank them. Then we settled in for the long wait, the next morning, when awards would be announced and we'd all go home. Lyn had a heated, short argument with Charmaine, Pam, and a couple of others; they moved away and sat on one of the few couches scattered around the lobby. Lyn trudged over and plopped down next to me, still pouting, arms folded.

"You really think she did that on purpose?" I said. "And risk jeopardizing the whole play?"

Lyn nodded. She put her head on her arms. I think she might have been crying, but if she was, it was quiet and not wailing loudly. "I used to think they were my friends," she said. "Now I think...I think they're just jealous, or something. I never said anything to them to make this happen."

270

"I believe you," I said. I'd never seen her say a mean thing to *anyone*. "It hurts, I guess, when you lose friends." Multiple departures from various schools, not too far gone in my past, reminded me of what it was like to walk away from someone and never hear from them again.

"Yes," she said. "It does." She looked at me. "I'm glad you're here. You're my *rock*," she said quietly.

"Always," I said. *Forever*, I thought.

She smiled. "How do you think we did?"

"I don't have a lot of experience to draw upon," I replied. "This is my first play."

"You can still have an opinion," she said.

"I thought we were *great*," I said. "And you– you're absolutely *brilliant*. Amazing. It's sort of like– like you were so good at performing, it didn't matter we were speaking Shakespearean dialog. We could have been using baby talk or gibberish and people would have still gotten what the play was about."

"That might just be," she said, smiling, "the nicest compliment anyone has ever given me."

I shrugged and smiled. "I speak only the truth. It is but for you to accept it."

Lyn realized she wasn't angry about the dress anymore and communicated this to me with a glance, a smile, and a sigh.

"I'm really tired," she said. She looked it, too. No one could act in that part opposite Benny Doherty and not come out looking frazzled. Being frazzled was sort of the point of the role.

I thought about it for a moment, studiously ignoring the pointed stares of some of the other cast members, and put my arm around Lyn, and gave her a one-sided hug. I didn't remove my arm and she didn't ask me to remove it. So I left it there, and hoped it comforted her a bit.

She closed her eyes and put her head on my shoulder.

Benny was up and about stalking pretty girls from other schools; Miss Caudill was chatting with a couple of other directors from other programs, accepting their compliments apparently; my sister Jane and Cheryl Ann were in close discussion about I knew not what, facing away from us. Other cast members looked our way, but made no comment. Jensen Tilden and Raynard looked our way, obviously amused. Tilden had once dated Lyn, sometime in the distant past as far as I was concerned. Of course, when you're 13, last year is the distant past.

Oddly, Tilden never said anything to me about my infatuation with Lyn, not even a *You're out of your league, kid.* I found out from my sister Jane, years later, that Lyn had risen to my defense– more than once. Whatever she did must have been effective, because not one of the upperclassmen ever teased me about Lyn. Not even once. Now that I teach in a high school, that makes a much bigger impression on me than it would have otherwise. I know how teenagers can be.

Because she was my sister, she wasn't privy to the conversations, but whispered arguments usually stopped when she entered the room. My sister Jane was many things, but *stupid* wasn't one of them.

Tilden, as I said, had once been Lyn's boyfriend – before Charmaine interfered and caused a rift between them. Sooner or later, Charmaine caused a rift with *everyone.* The only person I knew she hadn't used up and discarded was *me*, and it was quite obvious it was because I was beneath her notice. I doubt in that entire year she had said twenty words to me not related to our jobs on stage. But as it happened, that was just *fine* as far as I was concerned. The most beautiful girl in the school was my best friend; what need did I have for the runner-up? Smith and Tilden walked away, pursuing Charmaine's retreating back.

The walls of the hallway faded away, like the rows of the seats in the theatre masked by the lights; as far as I was concerned the whole universe was contained in a little bubble consisting of a concrete wall, a snippet of carpet, me, and my friend, who just needed me to return a hug I'd recently borrowed.

To Swim or Not to Swim

Eventually we filed back onto the bus and made our way back to the hotel. Lyn had recovered sufficiently that she became her usual chipper self. We had dinner (I had rainbow trout–again) and some of the students announced that they were going to the pool to swim. Awards for the competition were scheduled for the next morning.

"Come *onnn*, Mason," said Cheryl Ann, standing outside my room in the hall. "Go in. It's just water. People get wet every day." She was embarrassed to swim herself, I think, because of her tall stature; plus I think she wanted someone to walk her down to the pool. Even in those days, we didn't think it was prudent to send teenage girls in bathing suits wandering through a large hotel alone. Not with conventioneers liable to pop out of a smoky room at any moment. I'd heard rumors of a trip from days gone by involving a missing girl, drunken convention-eers, and a forced entry and rescue by a squad of teenage boys. Miss Caudill made us subscribe to the buddy system when wandering the hotel, and recommended at least one boy in every group.

"I don't know how to swim," I replied. "My mother made me drop out of swim class when I was in the fourth grade."

"Well, just sit next to the pool and get your feet wet," she said. "Be-sides, *Lyn* will be there."

I rolled my eyes at this, as if to protest, but she gave me the famed Eyebrow of Skepticism, so I held my tongue. I, fulfilling my role as the Young Chivalrous Lad, agreed to walk Cheryl Ann and some other girls to the pool.

"All this effort to get you to walk to the pool," said Cheryl Ann. "It's not *even* worth it."

I made my way to the pool area, following the girls. Most of the other students were already swimming. I'd never seen so many girls in swimsuits before. I decided that I would have to start looking for op-

274

portunities to take swim classes, if for no other reason than to enjoy the view.

I sat dangling my feet for a while, refusing offers of assistance or loans of cut-offs or trunks, and eventually retired to a poolside chair to read a book I'd brought on the trip. I think I was mostly reluctant to expose the field of hair on my back. The boys were bad enough. Most women, I knew already, thought extensive body hair on a man was *gross*. Millie walked by and looked at me. I lowered my head, embarrassed. When I looked up, she was gone.

Lyn swam a little bit, then wrapped up in a thick towel and left. She touched my shoulder as she left, acknowledging my presence and smiling.

"Thanks," she said.

"No problem," I said. "Do you feel better?"

"Much," she said. "Thanks to you." She looked at me carefully. "How are *you?*"
She must think I'm still all torn up about Millie, I thought.

"I'm not sure," I admitted. "I'm OK, I think." The briefest of pauses. "Thanks to you."

"No problem," she said.

I smiled, and shrugged. She smiled, waved, and left, in the company of a few other of the older girls. I would have escorted them back just to accompany Lyn down the hall, but I had come in with Cheryl Ann and felt like I shouldn't ditch her for my own purposes.

I sat there for a few moments, unsettled in my thoughts, anxious to hear the results of the competition, drained from our energetic performance, embarrassed by my fiasco with Millie, thrilled by my chance to help Lyn with any aspect of her life, as unlikely an event as I could imagine. All these things churned.

Or maybe it was just the fish, which had again stared at me while I dissected it.

I was holding a book, but I found myself reading the same paragraph several times, the words becoming merely a collection of undecipherable symbols. Sometimes, if you read a word too many times, it loses cohesion and simply becomes a mental sound, bereft of meaning, just sitting there waiting for your poor brain to slip back into gear and engage again. I set my book aside and closed my eyes. A few minutes later, Cheryl Ann kicked me (kinda *hard*), and I arose and trudged upstairs with the girls, dropping them off at their room. They entered the room and closed the door without a word of thanks or acknowledgment. I returned to the boys' room and claimed the rollaway cot before the rest of the boys got back from the pool.

Awards

Awards were scheduled the following morning. They would end at noon; we'd pile on the bus, get some lunch, and drive home in the evening.

The morning of the awards at breakfast, Miss Caudill revealed something to us only she and Mr. Carpenter had known until then.

"Children, I didn't want to tell you this, but I heard through the grapevine that Mr. Byron Caudill has been speaking to the school board about our program."

Mr. Carpenter looked at the floor and didn't face us. This couldn't be good.

"Well? What's the bottom line?" asked Benny.

"The bottom line, darling, is that if we don't win an award here at state, Mr. Caudill has asked the school board to shut down our program."

We all shouted and yelled in disbelief. How can that *clueless idiot* call himself an instructional leader? What form of twisted logic could lead him to the conclusion that cutting the drama program make anyone's lives better?

"Well, I don't know if it'll come to that, but it might," she said. "It might. Just cross your fingers and be prepared," she said.

We piled on the bus, possibly for the last time, and Mr. Carpenter drove us to the theatre.

Some bigwigs with the organizing committee of the Kentucky High School Speech League made a couple of speeches, welcoming us. Some special awards for service to the organization were made. I noted the slow progress down the list of items in the program I'd been given. *Man, this is gonna take forever,* I thought.

Eventually the awards actually started. They alternated actress and actor awards, starting with 10th. We all thought that even though Charmaine's part was small, it was well played, and she had a shot. I *knew* Lyn would win something. As Katherine, she was simply *amazing.*

I had entered the theatre later than everyone, a function of my tendency to defer entering a room to my elders and to women. By the time I sat down I noted that Lyn was sitting next to Benny, and in the rear of the theatre the only open seat was next to Millie; my last remaining option was to sit next to my sister Jane, which under normal circumstances I would have done. Perhaps all that time on stage had emboldened me. Instead of sitting next to my sister, I took an empty seat in the same row with Lyn and Benny, but not next to them.

I opened my program to read the list of events, and then felt a light lurch as the seat next to me became occupied.

Lyn had moved from beside Benny to beside *me.*

"Uhm," I said, looking from Lyn to Benny, who was studiously ignoring us.

"I'd rather sit here, if that's all right with you. Do you mind?"

"Uhm, " I said. "Of course not."

Lyn reached over, plucked my hand from where it held the program, and held it tightly as we looked through the list of competing schools.

The awards began. Miss Caudill sat behind all of us. The rest of the cast was scattered around us in the rear of the theatre.

Miss Caudill was obviously nervous about the awards. She had never won any awards at state competition, and clearly she thought *Shrew* was her best chance thus far in her career. I hoped we could bring *something* home for her.

It was beginning to look increasingly unlikely. 10th, 9th, 8th places passed with no awards for Devitt.

"Idiots," muttered Benny.

"Everyone in the cast deserves an award," said Lyn, leaning over to me to quietly add, "Well, *almost* everyone."

I smiled at that and she squeezed my hand. A jolt passed through my body as if I'd been electrocuted. Once, when I was in the fourth grade, I'd crawled under an electric fence and gotten a good jolt on my way to some 4-H club event. This was much more powerful.

7th, 6th, 5th. We all looked at each other. Wouldn't we get *anything?* Then, as from a distance, I heard: "Fourth place for actors; Jeff Mason, from ... DEW-itt Caw-dell High School in Hazard, Kentucky." There was a brief, protracted moment of silence; a few people chuckled at our school's odd name.

Then cheers erupted, all around me. Everyone in reach clapped me on the back. Lyn stood up and tugged on my arm, dragging me to my feet. "Stand up, silly! Stand up! Go get your award!"

"At least *Mason* got something," muttered Benny, but he was smiling. *I got best actor in the region,* I thought. *Does that mean this is the only award we're getting?*

Slowly my brain connected my feet with the fact that *when your name is called, you go up on the stage and get a trophy.*

I ascended the stage, regaining my wits as I went. There was a microphone there, next to the announcer. The trophies had little faces of Comedy and Tragedy on them. He handed me my trophy, shook my hand. Suddenly I leaned over to the microphone – no one else had made a speech, just accepted awards– and I said, so everyone could hear:

"It's *Devitt H. Caudill* High School. " Putting the emphasis on the second syllable in Devitt. Pronouncing *Caudill* like *Coddle*, the way I'd always heard it.

The audience laughed. The Devitt H. Caudill contingent cheered.

3rd place was announced.

"Third place actor. Charley Marshall, *DeVITT H. Caudill* High." *Actor? Charmaine* was a *girl*. A good-looking girl, who had had to wrap *layers* of athletic tape around her... substantial chest to create the illusion she was an old man. She approached the stage. The announcer looked confused; he started to say, "Accepting the award for 3rd place actor is...young lady?"

Charmaine leaned over to the mike as I had. "*I* am *Charmaine* Marshall," she said.

The entire audience gasped. A girl that pretty, playing a man's role? She must be an *amazing* actress! Charmaine accepted the award, and sauntered over to my side of the stage with the other male performers. I mouthed *wow* at her as she walked by, and she smiled at me, possibly for the first time. Probably the only time.

Third place actress was awarded to a girl from Knott Central. Upon the announcement of the school's name, I looked over at them. They were all standing up, and for some odd reason the director was facing them. Most of them had on some variation of purple and white, which must the their school colors. He nodded, and they all clapped twice to the left, twice to the right, and twice in front, in synchronized rythym. Then they all raised their hands straight up in the air and cheered *Knott! Central!* and sat down, except for the award winner, who approached the stage.

The rest of the audience watched this spectacle with a mixture of bewilderment and amusement. *Hey, folks, this here ain't no pep rally.*

It would be a shame, I thought, *if they go home with a higher award than us. Is that it for us? Two of the supporting characters?*

Would that be enough to mollify the school board?

Probably *not*.

Third place actor was awarded, to a school from Western Kentucky I'd never heard of. Benny and I exchanged glances.

Then, I heard as if from a distance:

"Second place actress: Debra Lyn Anderson, from *Devitt H. Caudill* High School." Our cast erupted in even louder cheering than before, enthusiastic and natural and heartfelt. *Second place in the state! The best we'd ever done in a state drama competition!*

Lyn ascended the stage, accepted her award, waved to everyone, and spread starlight around the room. She joined the rest of us in line, looking directly at me. We gave each other a thumbs-up. She even waved at Charmaine, who, miraculously, returned the wave.

Second place actor went to Knott Central. They stood up and did their little coordinated cheer *again*.

First place actress went to some girl from a school in Louisville. We had seen this show, and she *was* good. The sting of not winning is lessened considerably when you can respect the judges' decisions. At least the choice made some kind of sense, although you know how *I* would have voted.

"The last award for acting," the announcer said, "goes for first place actor, and is awarded to... Benny Doherty, of Devitt H. Caudill High School!"

Benny sat frozen for a heartbeat and then leaped to his feet. He paused only to hug Miss Caudill. He hugged her, then shook her hand, as if he thought both were required, both formal and informal reactions. Everyone from Devitt Caudill was standing and cheering and clapping. Benny *ran* down the aisle and joined us on stage, took the steps two at a time and accepted his award and took a sweeping, dramatic bow. The cheering seemed to go on far beyond all human reason. *Four awards!!* We'd never gotten *one* before. We had done something no one else in the history of our school had ever done: we *won* a first place in a statewide competition!

He clapped me on the back as he passed, and we all took a group bow. I realized that of the 20 performers on the stage representing over a dozen schools, our group had managed to capture 20 percent of the awards offered. That wasn't bad at all.

We eventually went back to our seats to await the final awards, for the best play. Miss Caudill's makeup was *ruined*; she was openly weeping. My sister clapped me on the back. Cheryl Ann punched me in the shoulder. *Hard.*

"Great," she said. "Now you're gonna be completely *impossible* to work with."

"I have no idea what you're talking about," I said, grinning. "You want to touch my trophy?"

This earned me a second punch in the arm.

We all let Miss Caudill look at our trophies. We let her *hold* the trophies. They were as much hers as ours, we thought.

Lyn sought me out, and wrapped her arms around me. "Look what we did!" she said.

"I know, I know!" I laughed. "I can barely believe it." She smiled and released me, seeking out her aunt. *I should have tried to kiss her,* I thought, *just a peck on the cheek or something. Maybe it's good I didn't. It probably would have embarrassed her.*

Finally we returned to our seats after a coughed prompt from the moderator. Lyn retrieved our trophies from Miss Caudill and plopped down in the seat beside me, grinning.

The awards for best play began. With so many high-ranking awards for acting, maybe we had a shot at one of the best play awards... we waited as the awards were called. 5th, 4th, and 3rd. Knott Central, we noted, had gotten some awards like we did, and they had *beaten* us in the region. If they were announced next, we might not get *anything.*

Miss Caudill thought they won the regional because some political machination had influenced the judging, but I wasn't so sure. Out of the corner of my eye, I saw a sea of purple and white bobbing up and down – it was Knott Central's contingent, and there were more people there than could possibly be in the cast, I noted suddenly– and their director was inching toward the center aisle seat, as if he expected to be needed soon.

Second, I thought. I was not much for prayer, for a variety of reasons; but I prayed now. *Please, please let us get a second place for Miss Caudill. Please.*

"Second place," said the announcer. "second place goes to St. Xavier High School in Louisville." Cheers from that contingent. Weren't we going to get anything at *all?*

The Knott Central crowd was *writhing.* Their coach was seated on the aisle row now.

"It's all right, babies," said Miss Caudill.

"And the award for best play in 1977," said the announcer.

"If we don't win another thing, I'll still be proud of all of you–"

The director from Knott Central *stood up,* and straightened his tie–

"For their amazing performance ...."

"I've never been so amazed by a group–"

"*Shhh!*" hissed Lyn, smiling.

An interminable pause ensued, and for a brief moment, everyone, even Miss Caudill, was completely silent.

The audio system *tinged.*

The announcer could be heard inhaling to speak.

"First Place for the KHSSL One-Act Play Competition, goes to Devitt H. Caudill High School's production of *Taming of the Shrew*, Cheryl Caudill, Director!"

We all flew our feet, and charged the stage, swamping the other directors, who retreated. Miss Caudill looked as if her eyes might pop right out of her head. She *glided* up the stairs, accepted the award, tears streaming from her face. We leapt to the air, we screamed, we cried; I couldn't stop hopping up and down on my toes, high-fiving everyone I passed. I grabbed Lyn and twirled her around, set her down. Heck, I even grabbed my *sister* and twirled her around.

Benny leaped around the stage like a kangaroo. He nearly leaped *over* Miss Caudill.

I finally looked at the audience, many of whom had seen the performance.

They were *all* standing, and clapping, and cheering. Well, *almost* all of them.

We had done it. We were the *champions.* The Champions from Devitt H. Caudill High School.

I had the sensation of protracted time, of things moving slowly. I remember looking at every single person in the cast. There was hardly a dry eye in the bunch. My sister, Miss Caudill, and even Charmaine, were *weeping.*

There in the lobby, after the awards, we exchanged calmer congratulations. I remember snippets and fragments of conversations: amazement at Charmaine's being mistaken for a man; pride in Benny's first place award, the first major award he had ever won; Lyn, almost relieved with a sense of fulfillment from a long, hard road, well traveled and honor earned forthrightly. I had my head rubbed by everyone, sort of an impromptu lucky mascot. I must have lost a few hundred hairs. (I still have a bald spot there. *Heh.*)

For once, I didn't mind.

For a brief time, there in the Guignol Theatre, our little personal dramas faded away, the stresses of our lives receded into the background, the frustrations evaporated, the barriers to learning dissolved; our past histories no longer mattered, nor did our families' financial status or our reputations, both good and bad.

We could do *anything. Anything.* Everything was possible; and the possibilities were... *inspiring.*

The Knott Central coach sought out Miss Caudill, and congratulated her, and shook her hand.

"Thank you," she said simply, no backhanded compliment or veiled reference to past transgressions crossing her lips.

On the bus, on the way to Baskin Robbins for some celebratory ice cream, we began speaking of what shows we might try for competition *next* year.

Many of us would return the next year. My sister, myself, Benny (a junior, who would wind up purposely failing a year in school just so he could stay in the program another year). Most of the rest, including Charmaine, and a few others, graduating. The only graduate I would be missing, of course, was *Lyn.*

"I cannot *wait* to see Byron's face," said Miss Caudill. "Things are going to be *different* now, just wait and see. The school board is not going to *touch* us."

Devitt H. Caudill was now on the map.

And we would be *back.*

And We'll Keep on Fighting, Till the End

We returned from the state competition, tired but happy.

On the first day of school after we returned, an announcement was made on the P.A.

"Jeff Mason, report to the office. Jeff Mason."

I was puzzled, never having been summoned to the office before.

Along the way, I passed the lunchroom and suddenly it hit me.

The broken water pipe. Oh, no.

I arrived and Mr. Caudill gave me a stern look.

"Son, did you have anything to do with that faucet getting broken up-stairs?"

"Nosir."

Mr. Caudill gave me a long, hard glance. He was well aware of my mother's reputation for confronting school officials about her son, and my own connections to the superintendent, who occasionally asked him how I was doing.

He sighed.

"Son," he said. "Let me ask you something."

I waited patiently.

"Just what do you see in all of this drama business?" he asked. "Surely you can find better ways to spend your time. You have to know this ain't gonna lead anywhere." *Has he been talking to my father?* I thought.

I gaped at him. Was he *seriously* trying to get me to drop out of drama? The first day back after we won the *entire state competition?* And after I myself won fourth place in the entire *state?*

"Mr. Caudill," I said carefully, "I've never fit in anywhere I've ever been in school. I suck at sports. I'm not popular. I'm not in band–" *not anymore, because we didn't have band at Viper–* "and I'm not planning on working in the mines or building houses. What else is there for me here?"

"There's math, and science, and all sorts of things here at the school," he replied.

I'll max out everything you've got in two years, I thought, but didn't speak.

"I'll be entering the science fair this year," I said. "Did you find out who flooded the science lab?"

"Well, we found the handle down the hall," he said. "Next time, don't try to fix it yourself. Just come get help."

"Yessir."

"Good luck on the science fair." He sent me on my way. He was *smirking*, like he usually was... it took a few days for us to find out why.

Later the same week after we won the state drama competition, Miss Caudill arrived in her classroom, ashen faced, with little blotches of bright red visible through her dark red hair. I swear, I think I saw the veins in her neck literally throbbing. I'd never seen her so angry. She was *furious*. Her hands were shaking. She could barely stand.

"Children," she announced, "Come here, we need to talk."

We gathered round. She perched herself on top of her desk, cross legged, as she often did when addressing all of us. She used her arms to pull her legs underneath and tuck them into place. Then she took a deep breath and sat up straight.

"Your principal, Mr. Byron Caudill," she began quietly, "has decided, all on his own, that it is no longer necessary for freshmen and sophomores to participate in the drama program at Devitt H. Caudill High School."

Voices erupted briefly, incredulous, angry, but we were stopped by a hand in the air.

"Henceforth, I am told," she said. "Freshmen and sophomores may no longer receive credit for drama class at DHCMHS. And, because of the decreased enrollment, I will need to teach a couple of sections of remedial reading."

There was more anger, more shouting. Even the upperclassmen, who weren't directly affected by the change, were angry. *We won the state drama competition! How would we compete next year?* Miss Caudill raised her hand again. Just as she did so, my sister managed to squeak in with *"Why,* Miss Caudill? *Why* did he do it?"

Miss Caudill closed her eyes and tilted her head back. "Apparently there have been some complaints," she said. "Apparently, some of our children are *too young* and *too immature* to be able to properly perform their parts."

"That's r-ridiculous," I said, blushing. Was that directed at *me?* "The m-man's a m-m-moron." Apparently the irony of my lingering stutter from performing Jonathan Rosepettle, complaining about the fact that I wasn't mature enough to take drama, was lost on everyone. Lyn glanced at me, but made no comment. I wasn't doing it on purpose. We practiced so much, so long, so *intensely*, and I associated the stutter strongly with being nervous, it just popped out on its own from time to time, like a poorly caged Tasmanian Devil waiting to pounce on me when I let down my guard.

"I'm not in this for stupid *credits*." This from Lyn.

"He's still a m-moron," I said, gritting my teeth to control the stutter. "Miss Caudill, what we need here is *lateral thinking*. Think outside the box. Mr. Caudill doesn't understand that drama is as much a reason to come to school as basketball. His decision is ... irrational."

Miss Caudill looked at me thoughtfully, pushing her hand through her dark red hair, combing it with her fingers as she often did when concentrating. She looked at me, then at Lyn. I listened carefully for the sound of the gears whirring in her head. Finally she spoke.

"No, no, Jeffery, you mustn't speak that way of your elders," Miss Caudill said sweetly. I noticed the flush of anger had drained from her face. What could she possibly be thinking? Wasn't she still *mad*?

Oh. I thought. *She has a plan.*

"I have a plan," she announced. "While Mr. Caudill is completely within his rights as the academic leader of this school to remove any student from any class for whatever arbitrary reason he sees fit, he also failed to mention something. He *failed* to mention that freshmen and sophomores would be prohibited from participating in *extra curricular activities.*"

We looked at each other. Do the plays, but get no academic credit as Lyn had suggested? Not everyone knew they were going into acting professionally, as Lyn clearly did.

I stood up. "I'll do it," I said. I wasn't getting a drama credit *anyway*, so Mr. Caudill's arbitrary decision didn't affect me in any case. "I'll d-do it next year, too."

"Me too," said Cheryl Ann. She glanced at me. "What an idiot." I always wondered if she was talking about me, or Mr. Caudill. I couldn't always tell. Perhaps, in a skillful delivery in the name of efficiency, she was referring to *both* of us. Him for being an idiot, and me for 'pretending' to stutter. (I wasn't pretending.)

We voted. No one dropped out. And thus the Devitt H. Caudill Drama Club was formed.

Miss Caudill dutifully reported that she had enforced his new rule, and freshmen and sophomores would no longer (need to) enroll in drama. Somehow, though, most of us managed to wind up in study hall the same period she taught drama the following year.

I don't think she ever forgave him for that. The sad part was, he thought he had successfully managed to contain Miss Caudill and quell whatever problem had initiated the complaints, and congratulated himself over it. If anything, it made us more determined to succeed than ever before.

For my part, I've always wondered if *Oh, Dad* had something to do with the immaturity issue that surfaced here. But as far as anyone can remember, it was random and arbitrary, done just to show Miss Caudill who was boss. If there was some ulterior motive behind it, we were never told what it was.

If he had known her at all, he would have known it was exactly, precisely, and unequivocally the *wrong* approach.

Dryland Fishing and Poke Salit

My mother loved to walk through the hills, across the ridge tops and down into the hollows, looking for plants and animals, keeping an eye on the strip-mines to see if they were approaching this or that neighbor's property line (or ours, for that matter) and hunting dryland fish.

Dryland fish, for you city folk, is actually a kind of mushroom, referred to in field guides as a *morel*. It has a dark, wrinkly, conical cap, with a white stem. No other mushroom looks like it, and none of them are poisonous. People who live in Eastern Kentucky consider them a delicacy. According to my mother, they sprang spontaneously from decaying tree trunks and leaves (no talk of *spores* and *asexual reproduction of fungi* made any headway with her) and they were not able to be grown in a greenhouse or farm. The only way to find them was trudging through the forest, looking under leaves, poking at decaying tree bark with a found walking-stick, or just having a sixth sense for it.

Many times she would tell me there was one nearby although we were separated by tens of feet. I'd look around, slowly, carefully, trying to get a glimpse of the pale white stem that was the telltale sign of a *fish*, and she, exasperated, would march up to me and show where the mushroom was peeking out of the leaves right between my legs, unseen by me.

We would fill our emptied bread bags with mushrooms. I think the most I ever found was perhaps 40 of them on a single hike. She and my father could gather *hundreds*. Large, small, sturdy, flimsy, dark, light; each one was as different as a snowflake.

She prepared them by dipping them in cornmeal and egg batter and fried in lard, like fish, or chicken, or pork chops, or (it now occurs to me) nearly everything else she fried. The mushrooms seemed squishy and weird to me, and when I lived at home I never ate them. As an adult, I returned in time to develop a taste for them and went so far as to bring a tightly packed bag home to eat and share.

We would often talk on these hikes, pulling ourselves up slopes too steep to walk by grasping young trees and hauling our bodies up. It wasn't as tough as rock climbing, but it wasn't easy at all. Dodging brambles, and low-hanging limbs, keeping an eye out for the occasional snake or wandering dog from some neighbor's house was always necessary.

You can't take such hikes these days through undeveloped, but owned property without stumbling across some erstwhile drug lord's pot farm, complete with booby-traps and motion sensors and vicious pit bulls and worse. One more thing that we've lost, I suppose, to the slowly encroaching tendrils of civilization.

On these hikes she would sometimes stop and take a break, sipping from a thermos or pop bottle she tied to her waist. I'd sit with her; sometimes we'd come as a family (except my little sister, who was an even more addicted book-hound than I); sometimes it was just my parents, and sometimes it was my mother and I. My mother was the only person who *always* went on the hikes. I use the word *hike* advisedly; we never used the word in everyday conversation. We'd call it a *walk* or a *climb* or a *hunt*. Hiking was for folks with custom-made walking-sticks and L.L. Bean knit caps and carefully cuffed blue jeans with the store crease still in them.

One time, as I recall, we were on a *walk* in the spring of my freshman year. We weren't hunting mushrooms (not in season till fall, I think) but we were just out climbing around. We carried empty bread bags. One of mine still had the bunny-foot in it. The last slice of Bunny-brand storebought bread we called the *bunny-foot*, sometimes named the *heel* in the rest of the country. We carried bread bags because you never knew when you might find something interesting.

"Know where you are?" she said. There was no sign of civilization in any direction. The only sounds were birds and crickets and the occasional whisper of a breeze through the mountain trees. No cars, no telephones, no sign of human life except for my mother. The Appalachians may not be tall, but they sure as heck are *steep*. And *quiet*.

As you climb the foothills in Eastern Kentucky, the slope changes in such a way as to make you think you are about to crest the ridge, but upon arriving at the visible destination, suddenly a whole new section of the hillside appeared at a slightly different inclination, not visible until you reached the very spot. Four or five cycles of this shifting perspective later, you arrived at the top of the ridge, where we were now.

That was all I knew. I shook my head. If my mother had had a heart attack right there, I don't know if I could have found help in time to do any good.

"Yer half- brother Bill's house is that way," she pointed. "Down yonder's the old home place, and Eliz-beth's house is over yonder."

"If you say so." I grinned.

"How would you find your way out of here if you had to?" she replied.

"Well, I suppose I'd walk downhill till I found a creek or a road," I said. "Then follow it until I found a house, or someplace I knew."

She nodded. "Better than staying on the ridge," she said. She bent over, and plucked a weed from the ground. "Chew on this."

I looked at it dubiously, but complied because I knew she wouldn't surrender until I did. Nor would she tell me if it was sweet or bitter or what it was called. I bit. *Spearmint*, I thought.

She saw the recognition in my face. "Mint," she said. "Pull up a few and put 'em in your bag. We'll make tea."

I did, and it was good tea, too. She gave me peppermint, and showed me how to find nuts, and I gnawed on some sort of a small yellow-green berry enclosed in a cubical shell (I think she called them *ground cherries.*) They tasted bitter, but they were edible. She also searched for ginseng in later years, when it became part of the health food craze, and made a little money selling dried out roots at flea markets.

We finished filling the bag with *poke salit,* which I eventually figured out was a plant that was used to make boiled greens, which you collected in a *poke*– a sack.

I think those were the times I was closest to my mother, as she related stories of her childhood revolving around the Depression, and how she had had to work so hard all her life to provide for her family; it prematurely aged her, and made her always appear older than she was, all her life. She and my father both fervently hoped for a better life for their kids. Nearly every decision they made was for that purpose. They never went on vacations –- my father's first pleasure trip was when I drove with him to Texas for a workshop when I was an adult– although they were not above going to a state park for fishing or an occasional picnic.

Trudging through the woods was probably her favorite pastime. And I think she really *loved* it when I went with her. She asked me about my plans, and college, and how school was; it was funny how she could ask these things out in the woods, away from home, while at home it was just a continuous grind of work, and cooking, and canning, and cleaning, and washing.

"I need to *ast* you something," she stated abruptly.

"What?"

"You know that if you start fooling around with girls, you're likely to wind up with a baby," she said. *Boom.* There it was. I'd never really had the birds-and-bees talk with either parent. I suppose they figured I learned the facts of life from a book of some sort; I remember during my freshman year they just sort of assumed I knew about girls, and sex. I *was* only 13, and had never had a date.

"Well of course," I said. "I'm not going to get married until I get out of college."

"I'm not talking about marriage," she said bluntly. *Oh. She means sex.*

"Well," I said. "I do like girls, mom. A *lot*. On the other hand," I said, spitting some bitter-tasting bark on the ground, "I'm not stupid."

"I know you're not stupid," she said. "You're book-smart, sure, but do you have common sense? Do you know how to think with your brain, instead of that thing between your legs?"

I was taken aback. My mother hadn't ever spoken to me that way before.

"You're becoming a man," she said. "You might find yourself with a girl and doing things you wouldn't plan for, all of a sudden. You need to *protect* yourself and not throw everything out that you've been working for." She looked pained, as if there were something stuck inside her shoe. I nearly laughed when she reached down, removed her shoe, and shook out a rock. My mind raced as I observed her replace her shoe.

Was she talking about *condoms?* I knew a little about such things through stolen glimpses of my half-brother's Playboys and medical reference books. I just wasn't sure where this was leading.

"OK, Mom," I said. "Let's just be blunt here. I am not going to get some girl pregnant and wind up having to drop out of school and take care of a baby. I'm *not*. Don't worry."

"All right then," she said. "You'd better not," she warned.

"I'm *not*," I repeated.

We began working our way down the hill. Sticks and twigs snapped under our feet as we dodged poison ivy and brambles. The light from the springtime sun was already dimming as the sun set behind the steep hills. We trudged down the hill in silence. Mom held up an ancient wire used as a television antenna that snaked up the hill, serving as the receiving antenna for old UHF transmitters in Hazard. I ducked under, and held the wire for her to follow, not exchanging words because we'd done the same sort of things many times before.

"Why are you asking me about this now?" I said, dropping the wire.

"I know you're sweet on that blonde-headed niece of Cheryl Caudill," she said. *She knows? How the heck did she find that out?* Ice–no, scratch that– *liquid nitrogen* ran through my veins. I suppressed a shudder. *Who told her? Was it Jane? Was it, God help me, Miss Caudill?* If my mother thought I was trying to sleep with Lyn, all hopes of having anything to do with her would be dashed; this was a *disaster,* the worst possible thing—

"You just be careful," she said. "She's a nice girl and all, but teenage boys don't always think with their heads." She grunted as she slid over a large log obstructing the path. "At least the one on top of their shoulders."

"It's not like that, Mom." I said. "She thinks of me... sort of like a little brother. She's really pretty, yeah, and really sweet and my friend. She's... she's the *nicest* person I've ever known. She wouldn't–I– It's not like that," I repeated. I didn't add *but if she asked me, I don't know if I would resist. If I could resist, even if I wanted to resist. But she wouldn't ask. And I can't ask, and risk everything between us. Lyn might be so offended–or worried–that she'd never talk to me again.*

My mother grunted. "Don't matter what she would or wouldn't do. What matters is what *you* do. " We continued our trek down the hill, towards home. "Just be careful," she said. She pronounced it *keerful.*

"I will," I said.

She regarded me for a long minute, balanced between a large rock and a tree, clutching a long vine winding itself around a tree for support. Not *cuzzy vine* (kudzu), which was useless for even that base function. "I reckon you will."

I think, saying it out loud to my mother like that, to my *mother*, for Pete's sake, finally crystallized in my mind that I had to stop constantly wishing for Lyn to fall in love with me. It would eventually strain or ruin my relationship with Lyn, and if it was never going to happen, I had to accept that, or settle for nothing at all.

Making an intellectual judgement and talking your heart into it are two different things, though. My heart wasn't yet ready to concede the argument to my brain.

I realized on the way down the hill that not only was *Mom* was worried about me, and acting to protect me against my own baser impulses; *Lyn* was as well. She never made a pass at me, never encouraged any sexual impulses on my part other than what came my way due to *Oh, Dad*. Not intentionally, anyway. I had always thought it was because she wasn't attracted to me in that way, because I was so much younger, so goofy, maybe...just not really her type romantically. Perhaps it was because she was simply looking after me, keeping me at arm's length for my own good. Never really crossed my mind that she might, in fact, want me in that way. *Impossible. Me?* The best I could possibly hope for was that she merely tolerated my presence. And I sure as *hell* wasn't going to ask her. For a myriad of reasons.

Not the least of which was the risk she might say she didn't want me.

If that's what Mom has to say, I thought suddenly, what about *Dad*?

I worried and fretted all the way down the hill.

We arrived at the front door, and knocked the mud from our shoes. Dad appeared at the door, and Mom handed him the *poke salit* bags. Two large ones filled to the top, one small and half full– mine.

"That boy cain't find bird crap when it falls on top of his head," she announced, and I smiled as Dad laughed with a hearty *Heh,heh,heh* that reminded me for all the world of Fred Flintstone.

Dad, on the other hand, turned out to have nothing at all related to my love life on his mind, so obviously Mom was not discussing these issues with him. I kept my mouth shut (which I seemed to be doing a lot of these days) and my mother didn't bring up the subject again, considering it closed, I guess.

As he got older, Dad laughed more and more. I always attributed it to getting rid of Jane and the stress of having a grumpy teenage daughter. Could be he was anxious to rid himself of me, as well. Jane thought it had to be me moving away to college and not being a drain on his expenses. We used to tease each other about which one of us provided the greatest relief upon departure. My little sister still lives at home with my father, and you can read into that whatever message you like.

It is odd, for me, having lived in that house all my life, how little things like gathering food to eat from the woods made me later feel like a stranger in my own home, as if I hadn't realized we had done the same sort of thing many times in the past. Maybe it was part of my realization that my world was not the same as what most other people experienced.

Mom started cleaning the "*salit*" for supper, and I retreated to my room.

My room, incidentally, was *supposed* to be the bathroom in the original design of the house. We didn't install the fixtures because there wasn't nearly enough water to support a flush toilet, and had no septic tank anyway. I had a single-sized cot, a tiny desk, a short bookcase, and that was it. There was literally just enough room to scoot back a chair and turn around on the floor. I had books stored under the bed, in the windowsill, around my feet in the desk. A tiny desk lamp provided light for schoolwork, when I had any that needed doing at home, and for reading at night. I would often, even as all these events unfolded, read a book each night. I hated putting books down. Still do.

That night after supper, however, there was no reading of books, or homework. I turned off the light, and lay on the bed, fully clothed. Like the other rooms in our house, there were no internal doors–Dad hadn't gotten around to installing them yet. A fact that my little sister took merciless advantage of regularly. *Don't mess with my stuff. Mom, she's sticking her arm in my room again.*

I listened to the birds outside the window, the whispering wind in the leafy trees, the murmur of distant conversations, and the hissing, harsh, whiny yipping of our neighbor's swarm of hounds. (It was a *swarm*, believe me. Not a pack. A *swarm*.) Unidentified insects called out to the world, seeking companionship. Through the window above my head, the cold light of the waxing gibbous moon spread over the hillside and onto my bed.

I didn't find out until after she died, but my mother had married her first husband when *she* was 13. He was an older man, who turned out to be an abusive drunk, and not a fit father. My father, hard worker, nearly a teetotaler, and relatively cheerful (despite occasional bouts of temper accompanied by cussing at everyone in earshot), must have seemed like a breath of fresh air in comparison. No *wonder* she had worried about me.

The moonlight gradually crawled across my face. Mare Tranquillitatis stared at me, balefully. I never could see the "man in the moon." I subscribed to the alternative view that the picture on the moon was a man, carrying a bundle on his back (Oceanus Procellarum) trudging through some frozen expanse of the lunar landscape, seeking something he would never find.

I wondered if I would ever be able to climb to the top of the hollow, and reach out, and touch the moon, and have it carry me away to a distant place, where I could look back at the earth, and remember how it was I came to leave my little room in our little unpainted house on the hill.

A Simple Application

During one of the competition trips, I don't remember which, I had occasion to wander around the campus at the University of Kentucky, and found myself in the college bookstore. I only had a few dollars of discretionary money, and reluctantly leaving the textbook section, I ran across the magazines.

Up in the back, behind some motorcycle rag with scantily clad women on the front, was the top of William Shatner's head.

Now *there's* a sentence I wouldn't mind seeing quoted out of context.

Now, I have to admit the motorcycle mag caught my eye, for, um, a while– but it was the one behind it that captured my *money*.

It turned out to be an early edition of a magazine called *Starlog*, which was a general science fiction magazine, covering books, films, and movies. A dramatic painting of some alien vista was on the cover. The cover announced, across the top, *Starlog interviews Star Trek's Bill Shatner*, and under the painting on the cover, *Spacescapes Demystified: an interview with Don Dixon*.

I spent a few of my hoarded dollars on the magazine, and read it from cover to cover. I was a longtime fan of *Star Trek*. My first book I bought from the scholastic book club, ordered twice a year in elementary school through some school-sponsored program, had been James Blish's adaptation of the TV series episodes into short stories. I read all the adaptations before I ever got to see the episodes on TV, and it was interesting to see where he had "stuck to the script," and where he had diverted in the interests of coherent storytelling.

Also in the magazine was an article about art, written by one of the *Starlog* staffers, and mainly consisting of an interview and several pages of paintings by artist Don Dixon. In the article he explained how he used science to inform his painting, using chemistry to decide the color of the sky on a methane-swaddled world, figuring out the size of the sun for an alien sunrise, or how much of Titan's sky would be spanned by the rings of Saturn, if you could see through the haze. The interviewer asked the artist how he decided how large to paint the planets in the sky. His answer, paraphrased somewhat, went as follows: "Through a simple application of trigonometry, I calculated the angular width of the planet and compared it to the view through a typical single lens reflex camera, which is about 50 degrees."

That was *it*. That was all it said about *how* to do it. *A simple application of trigonometry.* All I knew about trigonometry was that it involved triangles; we were studying triangles in school, and I had studied them in elementary school. I knew a few basic rules such as the interior angles added up to 180, a triangle with a right angle is called a *right triangle*, and so on, but that was the limit of my knowledge.

I consulted Miss Campbell, and she referred me to Mr. Monroe, the geometry teacher.

"Trig?" he said. "Lord, son, I haven't done trig in 20 years," he said. He rooted around his bookshelf and extracted two books. "All I teach are proofs and construction and Euclidean geometry," he said as he handed them over.

One was "Intermediate Algebra and Trigonometry," or some such title. The other consisted entirely of numbers in tables. Its title was "Trigonometric and Logarithmic Tables."

"You take good care of the log book," said Mr. Monroe, indicating the second book. "That got me through college."

"I can borrow these?" I asked.

"Sure, keep 'em," he said. "I don't need 'em anymore."

I pored through the books, especially the chapter on introductory trig. After studying them for a couple of days, I took pen to paper and attempted to figure out the size of Saturn as seen from Titan. Miss

Campbell observed this, and stopped giving me assignments in Algebra class for a short while, so I could figure out what I was doing.

Now, I could pause here and tell you exactly how to do it, if you're interested. I could explain how sight lines are really *tangent* lines, and touch the sphere of the planet at only one point. I could speak of right triangles, and angles of interest, and opposites, and hypotenuses. I could explain how triangles that have the same shape have the same ratio of sides, and that you can exploit any two sides in a right triangle to find the other sides using the Pythagorean theorem, and the memnonic SOHCAHTOA to help find which of the classic trig functions, Sine, Cosine, or Tangent rules a given situation. Yes, I could give you all sorts of hints and explain how I figured it out, but it's better for you if you do it yourself.

A few days–maybe a couple of weeks– of fits and starts, and I came up with the following diagram.

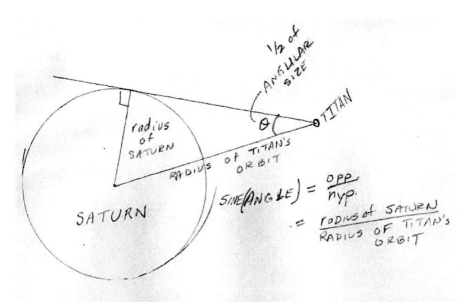

I concluded that the angular size of Saturn seen from Titan is roughly 5.6 degrees. This is about 11 times wider than the full moon appears to us, and doesn't count the rings; Saturn would be *huge* in Titan's sky, if it could be seen through the haze. It would probably look three-dimensional.

I sketched the resulting figure on a canvas board, using 1 centimeter = 1 degree of angle. I even figured out the equatorial diameter was different than the polar diameter; Saturn appears to be flattened due to its rapid rotation, and I sketched the resulting oblate spheroid as best I could when I was sketching the picture I eventually painted. I never could understand why my classmates in graduate school had trouble grasping the concept of plate scale on a CCD; I'd known the same exact concept for years. Then I painted it with my sister's oil set from her art class. *Saturn from Titan*, it said on the back. *By Jeff Mason.*

I showed the resulting painting, when it dried, to Miss Caudill.

"What is it?" she said. "Abstract art?"

I explained what it was, and how I'd done it. The diagrams and calculations were on the back of the canvasboard.

"Mason," she said. "I've never said this to your face, but forgive me child. This painting is pretty interesting. But. You're weird. You really are."

Today, of course, we've *landed* on Titan, and we have *photos* and data and everything. We didn't know then, for example, that Titan has *oceans* of liquid methane, and beaches with ice for sand and dentritic flow channels like the branches of some alien tree cutting through the "soil." In astronomy, as in life, you have to go with what you know. I thought what I did was pretty cool.

A few years later, I related this story to Dr. Powell, my all time favorite astronomy teacher from Berea.

"Let me get this straight. You *taught yourself trig* so you could paint Saturn?"

I nodded. "Just enough, not everything like identities and so on. Just SOHCAHTOA."

"Weird," he said. "But cool. Only you would do that."

Dr. Powell, if you're reading this, I could write another whole book about my adventures at Berea. If this one is successful beyond all reason, perhaps I will. You should know this: Miss Caudill inspired me to be a teacher, but you inspired me to teach *astronomy*.

As it happens, I *am* an astronomy teacher, and just so you know, I have the *best* job in the entire school. And my school has a *lot* of amazing teachers, some of whom are my friends, many of whom earn my admiration. Having had the experiences I have had, as a teacher, a student, and other jobs, it is not an insignificant compliment to say the school where I work now is really and truly a *good* school. I would have sacrificed *several* major body parts to attend it when I was in high school. But I'm glad I didn't. Some things can't be taught in a physics class.

But, the story says, that's a divergence for another day.

The spacescape exercise taught me a few important things. First, math can be *fun*. Second, math, when taught correctly, is not merely a series of rules or patterns or some sort of bizarre game where you shift variables around like the sides of a Rubic's Cube. Math is a *means to an end*. If you have a desired endpoint, and you need math to get there, you do math. If you need to make a speech or paint a painting, or dig a ditch, then do those things. Unlike math majors and math teachers, I never did math just for the joy of math...at least, not much. Instead, I looked at math like a crowbar. You don't need it all the time. But when you do, you *really* need it, so you'd better keep it handy, sharpened, and in your toolbox.

Oh, and I learned to paint a little. I painted a mural of the space shuttle and space station on the wall of my geometry classroom as an assignment for art class. The shuttle hadn't even launched once yet; they were still using the white external tanks in those days, before they figured out there was no point in painting the tanks since they were going to burn up in the atmosphere anyway. Now the tanks are orange, and the shuttle fleet has only has a few more years left before it is retired.

The mural remained there for many years after I graduated, surviving a couple of re-paintings of the room and changes of administration. I don't know if it survived the repurposing of the building into office space. I would be somewhat surprised to find that it had, given the number of years that have passed.

You're a Good Man

After we won the state competition, we came home. There were accolades waiting for us at school, but it's not like we won the state basketball tournament or anything. There would have been a parade (at a minimum) if that had happened. Still, there was an announcement on the P.A. made by the assistant principal, and all of my teachers offered their congratulations, and even my parents' hard line against doing acting as anything more than a hobby eased a little (the trophy didn't hurt.)

Having that level of success emboldened us. Several of the senior high students approached Miss Caudill with the idea of doing a musical. There was a rumor floating around for a few days that we were considering doing "Hair," but considering how everything comes later to Eastern Kentucky culturally, there were still enough anti-hippie elements in local society that Miss Caudill quashed that idea firmly pretty early on. Or maybe it was the whole performing-in-the-nude thing.

She had a recording of "You're a Good Man, Charlie Brown" on a phonograph album, and one day in drama class we all listened to it. (I was more or less officially allowed to be there now, and only visited study hall on occasion when I needed to study for a test or complete some homework—in other words, not often.) I don't recall the exact decision making process but it probably involved something like Miss Caudill announcing she had decided we would do it, and the only questions remaining were who would get which role.

The play was scheduled after Lyn's senior prom, and her date for that event was, I think, Halsey Caudill, son of the basketball coach, star of the team and all-around tall guy. Halsey had hair that surrounded his head like a globular cluster of curls. In fact, he resembled Neville Smith, with whom Lyn had attended her *junior* prom. We called Neville "Poodle" because of *his* large curly Afro-style hair. (Neville was white; there were no black people in our whole school and few in the county at the time. The only Hispanic person I had ever seen, even in Lexington, was Ricky Ricardo on TV.) Neville's hair was easily twice the diameter of his head. Neville was cast as Linus. My sister Jane was cast as Lucy, and took a certain amount of perverse pride in the claims we all made that she had been typecast. The leads in this show, if there are leads, are Charlie Brown and Snoopy, of course, just as in the Peanuts comic strip.

As it turns out, there was a bit of significant high school history going on with the prom choices. Lyn's original plan had been to take Jensen Tilden, Jr., to her *junior* prom, but Cheryl didn't approve of Jensen's, shall we say, less than honorable tendencies. So Cheryl coerced Lyn into taking a hand-picked date, Neville Smith. During her *senior* year, Cheryl and everyone else expected Lyn to take Neville again. After all, they were in *Charlie Brown* together, and despite the fact Neville had graduated and started college, it would probably be O.K. for him to go with Lyn to the prom. However, determined to make her *own* choices, Lyn decided instead to go with Halsey Caudill, son of the coach, no relation to her, just because he *looked like* Neville. Plus, he played *basketball*.

In your face, Aunt Cheryl. I make my own choices, she thought.

Now, this isn't like first year trig or anything. But I think you can see how, as a freshman not with the "in" crowd anywhere, I didn't really know all of this until later.

If it sounds very dramatic, well, it was, but just like all machinations in high school that seem unimportant to others, these events were of utmost importance to Lyn because *they happened to her.*

Lyn had now been involved in Devitt H. Caudill theatre for three years. She worked on a dozen different productions and scenes and skits. She maxed out her obligations for the International Thespian Society. By this time of the year I was nearly eligible for my first star, and we decided to have a short induction ceremony later in the year. Lyn was, in fact, the president of the Thespian Society, and organized the freshmen and kept track of the points for awarding levels of achievement for the students actors and technicians.

Given the long and complex road Lyn had taken to arrive where she was, it seemed inevitable to me that Lyn would be given the part of Snoopy. She could sing, she could dance, and she wouldn't hesitate to play a dog. I remember asking her if she would feel silly playing a dog, when she had just been playing two roles (Katherine and Rosalie) which cast her as beautiful women.

"Acting isn't about trying to make yourself look beautiful all the time," she said. "It's not a pageant. Snoopy looks like a fun part. Lord knows I could use some fun in my life."

"Well, then, I think you should do it," I said. "I think you'd be great."

"You'd think I'd be great doing anything," she said, grinning. "But oh yeah, I'm going to do it. If CC will cast me in the part."

I was surprised to hear her say that. "How could she not?" I asked. "You're her niece."

Lyn looked a little shocked by that. "I wouldn't think *you'd* say that," she said. "I've had to work for everything I've done here–*everything*– and she wouldn't give me a part I wasn't right for. Believe me."

"Sorry," I said. She continued to pout, looking hurt. "It must be hard living with the drama teacher and her being your aunt," I said, by way of further apology.

"You have no idea," she said. "She watches what I'm doing all the time. I'm essentially under guard like a prisoner, 24 hours a day. Going to rehearsal, playing a role is like...escaping that, a little bit."

"I'm held pretty close to the vest, too." I said. "I wasn't allowed to ride my bicycle out of sight of the house until last year."

"Really? *Last year?*"

"Yeah, my mom's really overprotective," I said. "I've never learned to swim because she's afraid I'll drown, for example."

Lyn's eyes widened. She was silent, and as I could think of nothing else to add, I remained silent.

"Why do you think she's like that?" she asked.

"My older half-brother Ida died from drinking too much," I replied, matter-of-factly. "My brother Bill is OK, though." At least, he was at the time.

"I'm so sorry." She touched my arm, and looked like she might cry herself.

"I didn't know him that much," I shrugged. "He was grown up and married while I was still a kid." I explained to her how I wound up in Kentucky.

"Why do you think...Cheryl..is so overprotective of you?" I asked. I'd never referred to Cheryl Caudill as *Cheryl* before, and it felt awkward. Still does, as far as that goes. Lyn looked pained.

"I've done some things...that give her reason to worry. I kind of understand where she's coming from, but I still feel trapped and confined."

"What sort of things?"

"Maybe I'll tell you that someday," she replied. "Let's just say I hurt myself and some other people that I love, and leave it at that."

"I'm here for you if you ever need to talk. You know that, don't you?"

"Yes," she said, looking directly at me, still wearing the pained expression of someone who clearly wanted to change the subject. So, when she did, I let her.

"What do you want to do when you get out of high school, Jeff?" she asked. "Will you stay in Hazard?"

"I used to want to be an astronaut," I said. She smiled. What kid didn't want to be an astronaut in those days? The last moon landing had only been five years ago. "Now I'm thinking either an actor or maybe an astronomer."

"You'd be a *great* actor," she said. "You *are* a great actor. You have more talent without trying than some of these guys have who've been working for *years.*"

I blushed. Then again, I usually did when I was around her.

"You're no slouch yourself," I said. "You have a way of commanding attention on stage. When you're on stage *everyone* pays attention, and it's not just because you're pretty."

"Thanks," she said.

"I mean it."

"I know. I believe you." She became thoughtful again, and I was content for a bit to just sit there with her.

"Lyn," I asked. "Can I ask you something?"

"Of course," she replied.

"Why...um, did you ... sit with me at the awards ceremony for *Shrew?*"

"What?"

"The awards ceremony for *Shrew*, in Lexington," I repeated. "You got up and left Benny, and sat with me. But he was your co-star. And he's...more like your age."

She regarded me carefully. Reached over, and rubbed my head. "Benny's a great actor, with lots of talent," she said. "I liked working with him, and I thought we had great chemistry on stage."

"But not off stage?"

She nodded. "It wasn't Katherine sitting there in the audience, you know. It was me. I'd rather sit with my amazingly smart and kind and talented and loyal friend than with my amazingly talented co-worker. And don't forget, he let me down in the duo acting competition. *You*, on the other hand, did not."

I blinked–several times– and looked at her carefully. "I'm so glad to have you as a friend," I said simply. "I've never had a friend like you."

"I've never had a friend like you either," she said. "You remember, you had to explain to Benny what a supernova is?"

I nodded.

"Well *I* knew what it meant, albeit not in as much detail as *you*."

I always *knew* she was smart. I suppose she thought I was as well. I wonder if that had any bearing on her decision to hang around with me so much.

"You know," she said suddenly, "There's not much call for astrono-mers in Hazard, Kentucky."

"I know that." I told her the story of how I went to the local Christian bookstore (the only bookstore in Hazard) when I was in the 7th grade, seeking to purchase a star map (Asimov claimed that good star maps were as close as your local bookseller). I asked if they had any star maps, and they said they didn't carry anything from Hollywood. Once I made myself clear, they kicked me out of the store, saying they had "no truck for those devil-worshipping charts."

"You're going to have to leave Hazard if you're going to study science," she said. "Or drama, for that matter."

"I've known that for years," I said. "My *mother* doesn't know it. My father doesn't understand my goals, either."

"No one's father understands them," she said cryptically. "I'm sure he's just wanting you to be happy."

"Well, I think that's what he wants too," I said. "That's why he doesn't like drama. He thinks it won't lead anywhere."

"He might very well be right," said Lyn. "Actors don't make much money."

I raised my eyebrows at that. "It's true," she said. "Only a very few of them make any substantial money. Most of them have to work as waiters or taxi drivers or something to pay the bills. You do acting for love, not for money."

I had no idea there were poor actors. I thought they were all wealthy like the people you saw on T.V. That one required further thought, and I filed it away to churn in the back of my brain for a while. Later on in my high school career, Miss Caudill reinforced Lyn's point vigorously. It certainly was a factor in my eventual career choices.

"On the other hand," Lyn said, "You're one of the most talented and gifted actors I've ever met. *You* could do it. "

"I don't know about that," I said. I looked directly at her, and pointedly said, "I've been pretty lucky, I think."

314

"So have I," she said. "I'm lucky you're my friend." She regarded me thoughtfully. *There's something she wants to tell me but she can't,* I thought. *And it's not about mushy stuff.* "Where will you go?"

"Excuse me?"

"Where will you go to college?"

"I have no idea. Miss Carpenter says I could go anywhere, like Harvard or Yale."

"Who is that?"

"Miss Carpenter? She's the new algebra teacher. She's new this year. You never had her."

"Oh. Well, Harvard and Yale are *expensive*."

The expense of college was a problem that hadn't crossed my mind. I was only a freshman; paying for college wasn't exactly on my radar yet.

"I think Harvard and Yale are somewhat out of my league. I mean, we don't have physics, or calculus, stats or *anything* here. But I could maybe start out simpler and work my way up. How do people pay for college? I mean, if they aren't rich?" *like you,* I almost added. Lyn clearly didn't consider herself rich; her parents were well off, I guessed, since they lived in Louisville, but cities must have poor people too; it was a relative thing. I knew that already.

She was looking at me incredulously. *Physics? Calculus? When I was a freshman I barely knew what algebra was. Who is this kid?* "I wish I knew," she said, half joking. As a senior she must have already contacted colleges and arranged for whatever money she needed. "Scholarships. Grants. You get a job and work while you go to school. Loans, mostly, I guess. Maybe you'll get an acting scholarship," she said, with a twinkle in her eye.

I let that pass. "Where are you going to college?"

"University of Louisville," she said. "That way I can stay near home and save some money. I'm getting some loans too. " I didn't need to ask what her major would be; that was obvious.

I didn't want to contemplate the idea of her being in Louisville, which seemed like it was light-years away as far as I was concerned.

"I wish I could go there," I said. *Now,* I added to myself.

"I'd invite you to stay with me and do that," she said, "But I can't."

I just looked at her, waiting for an explanation.

"I just can't." she said. "It's complicated." Someday, I was going to have to ask her about that, but she clearly didn't want to talk about it now. She told me much much later that she couldn't be that good to herself, which for one thing told me that she had seriously contemplated the idea. As for why she didn't, I think the ghost of her sister's marriages haunted her.

"It's a little early for me to talk about college anyway," I said. "I've got to get through high school first."

"True," she said. "Although it's not much of a challenge, is it?" Lyn, I learned later, had missed *months* of school during the Louisville-to-Hazard transitions, and still graduated on time with no problems and a 3.6 GPA. She was much smarter than anyone knew. I don't even think *she* knew how smart she was. I was a straight-A student from *way* back. I knew smart when I met it.

"Not yet," I admitted. "I'm learning things I don't know, which is good, but it isn't hard."

"Just wait till you get Mrs. Hayword," she said. "Senior English." She mocked shivering. I laughed.

If Lyn had not been the niece of my drama coach, and I had not had the habit of being obsessive about each new hobby or project, I never would have had so many opportunities to talk to a girl like her. There was a period of time during the Spring of 1977 when she could hardly leave the house, a consequence of the incident in the Mustang and her past history. I only knew about these things peripherally; the family kept it pretty quiet. I knew something terrible had happened, I think, but I didn't know what it was. Anyway, it was during this time that I spent a lot of time with Lyn and her aunt, especially during the early part of *Charlie Brown*, and I got to know her better as a person, and as a friend. I like to think I was her friend, and she enjoyed my company. I was practically the only boy she was allowed to talk to, although I'm sure she made opportunities for herself at school of which Cheryl was not aware or could not monitor.

But *Charlie Brown* was getting ready to start rehearsals, and what part could there be for me? Maybe something technical? I'd take any job available if I could keep seeing Lyn as a side effect.

Miss Caudill asked me to audition by singing. I had done a lot of things in my life, and believed that a liberal education was the best way to cover all my bases. But *singing*? Never tried it, beyond singing Christmas carols.

My successful audition for the play consisted entirely of *imitating* the singers on the broadway musical version we had on album. Whether it was my newfound singing skills or my still youthful appearance (I was still the youngest person in the drama program), Miss Caudill cast me as the relatively naive and innocent Charlie Brown.

Maybe Later

When I was younger, I flitted from project to project. For a while it was history, mainly about WWI fighter pilots and the history of aeronautics. I built model airplanes from those plastic kits that never seem to come out quite as nice as the painting on the box. Then it was art; I painted, I drew, I did charcoals. I was in the band for a while in Ohio. For a time I maintained a garden and was active in 4-H, sort of a farm version of the Boy Scouts. Sometimes I combined things as I had with the spacescapes. I maintained an ongoing interest in only a few things: science, science fiction, drama, and art. It was drama for now. It might be drama forever. I put my heart and soul into each new obsession; stopping was an option only when I felt I couldn't learn and grow more from it. This wasn't a conscious thing on my part, and most other people would say they quit when they were *bored.* One thing about acting at Devitt H. Caudill: it was *never* boring.

Lyn and I talked; not every day, and every conversation wasn't an earth-shattering revelation or a heartfelt exchange of compliments. By this time, late spring, perhaps in early May of 1977, my initial flush of love for Lyn had begun to be replaced with an appreciation of her as a *person.* I could still feel my heart pounding when she drew near, and given a choice of being anywhere else in the world and being with her, I'd choose her; but she obviously led a life beyond her brief contacts with me, and I was becoming content with the idea that it might just be OK to have a friend who was girl, but not a *girlfriend.*

This wasn't a dramatic epiphany, or something I think I could have articulated quite as clearly as that at the time. It just became easier to *talk* to her without being distracted by my pounding heart and sweaty palms and shaking hands. I knew at some level it was a good thing, a sign of maturity and respect for her, and that if teenagers and adults older than I (whom I respected) had one thing in common, they weren't impulsive as I had been with Millie. They were patient, took their time, and didn't push. Maybe Lyn would never fall in love with me. But she was already my friend–my *best* friend, perhaps, and by God, I was never going to jeopardize *that.*

She claimed not to remember years later, but in fact I did ask her out, kind of obliquely, at least once during my freshman year. (She liked that word, *obliquely*, I think. She said it suits me.) We were driving somewhere to work on *Charlie Brown*, maybe to perform a skit for an elementary school for publicity purposes. Sometimes the entire school would turn out and sit in bleachers to see us perform. We did short selections from *Charlie Brown*, sang a couple of songs, made a pitch for our Spring play, and departed. The students seemed to enjoy the shows, and we got out of class, and we got bigger audiences for our performances.

The school didn't provide transportation for any of this; we usually just crammed into a couple of cars, shielded only by the lack of traffic in our rural community and a slip of paper (no forms in triplicate six weeks in advance with Spanish on the back in those days) with a scribbled note, more often than not written by the kid and signed by the parent: *I give permission for Pam to go to drama performance at RW Caudill Elem.*, and, occasionally, we'd get one marked with an X. Even in the 1970's, not all of the parents of our students could read. People in Eastern Kentucky today got their hackles raised whenever confronted with the reality of the prejudiced view the rest of the country held of us, but there were elements of it that were real nonetheless. We had a fundraising drive to drag off abandoned cars from backroads and people's yards. I had a newspaper route for a while, selling a bundled newspaper called *Grit* to my neighbors. One old man, grizzled, wearing a sleeveless T-shirt and old, weatherbeaten work boots, refused to subscribe.

"I don't need no paper, boy," he said, unaware of the pun he had created.

"Well, sir," I said, following the *pro forma* suggested by my paperboy's manual, "Why not? It's only pennies a week."

"I cain't read, son, " he said gruffly, and then shut the door. I was shocked I stood there for a moment with my mouth hanging open. I couldn't recall the last time I'd met an adult who couldn't read...maybe never. My parents didn't read much–but they *could* read, enough to be functional in society. My mother would even occasionally scratch out a letter with invented spelling and no punctuation to a relative. My father dropped out in 7th grade to work at home, and I don't think my mother did much more. Eventually, using the skills I learned in my algebra class, I computed that there was a point of diminishing returns on expanding my route: According to my estimates if I continued adding customers the cost driving around to deliver the papers was going to exceed the profit I made (despite the fact my father or mother drove me around when needed and didn't charge for the gas, they were starting to complain about it) so I figured it wasn't worth the effort required. "I coulda tole you that a month ago, boy, without no fancy math-a-matics," said Dad. I dropped the route.

Anyway, we were going to a *Charlie Brown* promo, I think, and we didn't fit in CC's tiny car; so some of us piled into Bobby White's El Camino. The El Camino couldn't decide if it was a car or a truck, and was sort of a blending of both. The back end was open, and in this particular vehicle someone had placed some milk cartons and crates upon which some of us were perched. Not me, though; I'd just read a summary of Newton's Laws by Isaac Asimov, and while it hadn't persuaded me to not ride in the back of the El Camino (*Lyn* was there) it did make me sit down in the bottom and not on a milk crate or wheel well. In fact, I had to have a short, heated argument with my sister that I *wanted* to ride in the El Camino, despite the fact my mother would have a heart attack if she saw me sitting in the open back end without a *seat belt*.

Such was my life at the time and my status within the group that I am reasonably certain that no one was aware of these machinations on my part, except perhaps Lyn. Maybe Miss Caudill. Maybe not. My sister didn't have a clue, she told me later.

People were talking about the upcoming senior prom, and Lyn lamented that she didn't have a date, and there was no one she thought was worth the time, except maybe Halsey Caudill, and he was being a jerk about the whole thing, for reasons I can no longer remember.

I do remember consoling her; we were riding in the back of the El Camino. A couple of other students were there as well.

"Any guy would be lucky as heck to take you to the prom," I said. I knew she didn't have a current boyfriend. I also knew that the couples at prom were not always involved romantically, striking liaisons of convenience to gain access to the big night. *Maybe that would work for me,* I thought.

"Oh, I'll go with someone," she said. "These things have a way of working out."

"I'm sure," I said. There was an Awkward Pause. My heart pounded. I felt as though I were almost developing tunnel vision. My hands felt *cold.*

Time passed.

Finally I said, "I'd be happy to go with you to the dance."

"What?" she said. The wind from the motion of the car-truck-thing along the road had swallowed my words. That meant I had to summon the will to say it *again.* I leaned closer to her so she could hear me.

"I'd be happy to go with you to the dance."

She gave me a long look, smiling. "You are sweet beyond words," she said. "They don't let freshmen go to the prom, though."

"Why not? That doesn't seem fair."

"Not every freshman is as mature as you." My birthday had come just a few days ago. Lyn had given me a little plastic cartoon figure of

Charlie Brown with Snoopy taking a nap on top of his head. On the side of the base was a little plate that read *Love one another!*

Her expression darkened, and she added, "Not every senior is, either, as far as that goes." Then she did that ruffling my hair thing which both delighted and infuriated me. I left my mouth shut, accepting the compliment quietly, the rejection as well as I could, and wondered what was bothering her.

She leaned over, so only I could hear her speak. "Tell you what. When you're a senior, ask me again, and I'll go to the prom with you then. I'll be 21, and you'll be what? 18?"

"I'll hold you to that," I said. I would likely be only 16, maybe 17 depending on the date, but decided not to mention that.

"I know you will," she said, after gazing at me for a moment. I thought she already knew how old I was, but perhaps she didn't remember I was The Boy Who Skipped 8th Grade. The visible age difference between other freshmen and me had essentially evaporated during the year– I was a wee bit taller, and with the addition of a scruffy little beard, I no longer looked younger than *all* of my peers. *I wonder if it would bother her knowing how young I was when we did* Oh Dad, Poor Dad *just a couple of months ago.*

"I'll do it, too. I'll remind you."

"I believe you."

Then the conversation changed direction and I let the moment drop. To be honest, I wasn't really sure it could happen. She'd be three years long gone by then, in another state maybe, and I thought realistically it would be too much to expect her to come all the way back to Hazard just for me. After all, we were both working hard to escape Hazard, our families, or both. Coming back would be problematic. But it was nice not being rejected out of hand. They say that it's the thought that counts, and that's what I took home from the conversation.

I had nothing further to add, and the conversation drifted elsewhere, and so I made no further comment about it. We proceeded to our destination, did our job, and enjoyed the applause. My thoughts were elsewhere, though.

We continued to prepare for *Charlie Brown*. It was a really fun show for me; the only show so far where I had significant stage time with my sister. Acting with her was fun, actually; we didn't do much playing together since we were little kids except for board games. We played a lot of Monopoly, and Life, and when we were little, Trouble and Candyland. This play was something we could share together.

I managed to bleat out the songs that Charlie had to sing; I even had an almost-solo scene, singing and flying a pantomime kite. Cheryl Ann played the non-speaking kite-eating Tree, and I think we both unconsciously viewed that scene as a metaphor for *our* relationship. For some reason, Miss Caudill didn't direct us as obsessively as she had during *Shrew* or even *Oh, Dad*. A lady named Nika came and coached us quite a bit, worked on blocking, helped us follow along with the music as we practiced. Apparently she was a friend of Miss Caudill, and she lived in Louisville, or Lexington. She and her husband were helping out with the play, and for my part I thought it was interesting working with another director. I think Miss Caudill was just tired and drained from the work load and excitement of *Shrew* and the speech competition.

Lyn could actually act, sing, *and* dance, and she really shone in the part of Snoopy, especially during the "Suppertime" scene, where Charlie stands on stage and watches Snoopy do an entire song and dance number celebrating his supper bowl. *Suppertime, suppertime, oh it's suppertime, super pepper uppertime, the very best time of day.* Lyn did a nice soft-shoe dance, and she leaped from the top of the doghouse we used for the scene to the floor with a dancer's grace. I realized that to be a good, versatile performer, acting silly or developing a silly voice were not enough; it was obvious that to be really good, I would have to develop a repertoire of skills. I'd been working like a demon all year;

and it was apparent, watching someone who'd been at it for years, I was just barely getting started.

Three years later we decided to do *Charlie Brown* again, since there was a whole new crop of schoolchildren who hadn't seen it. Some of us, like Cheryl Ann and I, were still around and remembered enough about how we did it that we could essentially recreate the earlier version. Although I received many compliments for how I interpreted Snoopy the second time around (for that was the role Miss Caudill assigned to me), I personally felt I never approached the skill and joy that Lyn put into it. She was certainly my inspiration for it – even then I regarded her as my muse.

In fact, as *Charlie Brown '77* came to a close, Lyn and I continued to have our occasional chats, once or twice a week maybe, sometimes having dinner with Miss Caudill at a local Jerry's (think IHOP). Lyn even presented me with a small gift as the show came to a close: a small metal car with all of the Peanuts characters on board. When I opened it, Charlie Brown and Lucy were in the front seat, Snoopy and Woodstock in the back. I rearranged the characters so Charlie and Snoopy were in the front seat together. She asked me who the Lucy and Woodstock characters were supposed to represent.

"Chaperones," I said, rolling my eyes in mock disgust, and aiming a thumb at my sister and Miss Caudill. That earned me a laugh out loud and one of those heart-melting smiles.

XOXOXOXO

As the years passed she would occasionally send me a birthday card, a Valentine, or a letter, and she usually signed these the same way, with a looping, swirling hand I have forever since associated with cheerleaders.

> *xoxoxoxo,*
> *Snoop*
> *(Lynnie)*

The first time she did it, I kid you not, I had to ask what the x's and the o's stood for. No one had ever given me a note with that on it before. The first one came before the end of my freshman year.

"Hugs and kisses, silly," she said, pantomiming an "x" by hugging her arms across her chest and an "o" by puckering up for a kiss. Naturally, I blushed, which earned me another laugh and another wonderfully tortured head rubbing. It was apparent to me, as the year drew to aclose, that she regarded me as something like a little brother, to be looked after and cherished, but not thought of as a source of romance. More than a little brother, perhaps. But not a boyfriend *per se*.

I once asked her if she had a boyfriend. I was worried it would seem sort of impertinent, but she replied matter-of-factly to the question, which further cemented our strengthening relationship as close friends in my opinion.

"Not at the moment," she replied.

"I don't understand that," I said. "You ought to have people standing in line."

She smiled. "You are insufferably sweet," she said. "I've had boy-friends, but ... well, it didn't work out."

"What do you mean, 'didn't work out'? Did you break up with them?"

"No," she said. "Well, sort of. A couple of years ago I went out with Henry Castilla. I *called* him my boyfriend," she said.

"What happened? If it's none of my business, just say so."

"No, that's OK. I went with Henry to a movie during a drama trip, and we were sitting there, holding hands, and I looked down at our hands–" She stopped, took a breath; I could tell that whatever had happened still bothered her.

"And?" I said, finally.

"And he was holding hands with Pat *at the same time.*"

"What?!" I was aghast. The only Pat I knew was Pat Hatfield, who had given up the role of Grumio because of the whole gender issue thing. How could a guy have the *nerve* to do such a thing? Then I looked at the glistening tears accumulating in her eyes. Confessing such a thing must have been difficult and painful. "What a jerk... what did you say? What did you *do?*"

"What could I say? I couldn't think of a thing that would hurt him as badly as he hurt me. I jerked my hand away, and when he looked at me, I said, 'Have a great time,' and I just stood up and walked out."

"So." I said carefully. "No boyfriend now, eh?" I arched one eyebrow and stroked my chin melodramatically. "Hmmm."

"Yup," she managed to say. "No boyfriend now. Actually, I've been feeling pretty isolated and lonely for a long time now. Until lately."

I stuck out one hand, palm down, suspended in midair between us. I held the other in the air, and wiggled my fingers. *See? No extra girl-friend attached.* I wiggled my eyebrows up and down and twitched an imaginary mustache like Snidely Whiplash. *So now my nefarious plan comes to fruition,* I tried to communicate nonverbally.

Of course, I was too afraid of what she might say if I made a serious pitch to be Henry's replacement, so I *had* to yuk it up.

Lyn sniffed, looked at my antics, and giggled. *Giggled.* What a joyous word. All my life, I have *loved* making girls giggle. It's like music to me. This time, it was bittersweet.

She took my offered hand in hers, and we held hands for a few moments in silence. Then she and I had to return to our various theatrical duties, and she stood, and gave me a quick hug.

"Thanks for listening," she said. "You really are my friend, aren't you?"

"I yam what I yam," I said, in my best Popeye. "And I yam your friend." I think I knew then, regardless of how our relationship might evolve in the future, that I was an important, *trusted* friend in Lyn's life. That was a kind of relationship I'd never had with anyone until our orbits intersected that spring in the hills of Eastern Kentucky.

I was becoming used to the idea. The thing was, I didn't feel resentful about the situation or sad. She was so much *fun* to be around, one of the few people I knew who was interesting just for her own sake, and as wise as anyone who was still regarded as a teenager could appear to be, from my perspective. When excited or nervous, she jabbered nonstop. It was charming, and a joy to behold. When overwhelmed, she cried, but not at the drop of a hat. She was attentive, and made an effort to ask about *me*, and my interests, my goals and dreams. I was quite aware that she was not regarded as particularly mature or wise by her aunt, or her other teachers (as evidenced by Mr. Carpenter's moniker for Lyn in typing class, "Little Miss Popcorn Brain," which ejected him from the "somewhat cool teacher" category and deposited him in the "total dork" bin as far as I was concerned.)

Nevertheless, it seemed to me, she always gave me thoughtful answers; she was considerate of others' feelings (especially mine) and she was hardworking, so she knew the value of that; what else did an adult need to know? As it turned out, she'd had a much harder time getting to this point in her life than I or most of her classmates knew. I wish I had known more at the time; I could have been more of a friend to her than I was. She always seemed to be content with our status as friends. Maybe it was nice for her to have a friend who didn't know all the complex details of her life, judged her by her own merits and not her history, and *still* found her worth knowing and loving.

In retrospect, I think she really appreciated that there was someone who didn't require her to do something for her affection. There were no expectations that if we went on a date, she'd be pressured to offer something in return; no social obligations, because only a few people knew we were friends at all. I never really wanted her just for her looks or her body (though *Oh Dad* had really just about driven me mad); I wanted her *heart*.

I eventually figured out I already *had* her heart. She told me as much, although I didn't understand completely at the time.

I never asked for anything she wasn't willing to give. I don't think there's any man on Earth that can claim to understand women, deep inside. We can't grow a new life in our bodies. We can't command attention with just a glance like they can. But if I knew anything, I knew the heart of any real relationship with a woman was *respect.*

"Men have objectified me all my life," she told me. "You don't have any idea what it means to me to be looked at like a *person*. To be treated with *respect.*"

Lyn *taught* me that, as much as Miss Caudill ever taught me how to speak or project. It wasn't really an explicit lesson. I just sort of got it from the aura surrounding her.

Some years later my sister confessed that she had witnessed some of the upperclassmen teasing Lyn about my attentions.

"So," said Henry to Lyn one day, not noticing that Jane was nearby, "How's things between you and the Perfesser?"

"What are you talking about?" asked Lyn.

"Everyone knows Jeff Mason has the biggest crush *ever* on you," said Castilla. "We were just wondering if the feeling was mutual, or were you just stringing him along for fun."

"That's not funny, Henry." She glared at him. "He's a nice boy. You leave him alone." She glared at him. "Leave *me* alone too, as far as that goes."

"I notice you didn't answer the question," said Henry, folding his arms and smiling. He knew who had the upper hand in this verbal jousting match.

"My feelings about Jeff are complicated...and..none of your business." Lyn said through clenched teeth.

"Complicated?" sneered Henry. "What's it like going out with a *younger* man, Lyn?" He sneered at her with a lecherous grin. "I think you'd be better off with someone more, how can I say this, *sophisticated* and *experienced,* considering your own background–"

The sharp *crack* of a slap across the face ended the conversation.

"Jeff Mason is my friend," she said, between gritted teeth. "He's the only friend I ever had that's never let me down," she continued, telling Henry with her eyes. "*And that includes you.*"

"Jesus Christ, Lyn, you don't have to get all *violent* about it!" cried Henry, touching the red welt on his face. "I was just teasing!"

"You leave that boy alone, Henry, or I'll start circulating some rumors of my own regarding *your* behavior with girls," Lyn growled. "And just for the record, Jeff Mason is a heck of a lot more sophisticated than *you.*"

Henry held up his hands in surrender and looked around at the audience which had developed during this exchange. *What is going on with her?* played across his face.

Jane watched this exchange in astonishment, and left the room. *Jeff has a powerful ally in that girl,* she thought. *I wonder if he even knows she defends him.*

As it turned out, I didn't. Not for a long time afterward. I suppose if I had known, I wouldn't have confronted the upperclassmen as a matter of sheer physical practicality; the actual result would have been I would have left Lyn alone to spare her the embarrassment. Henry wasn't in *Charlie Brown*, anyway, so I didn't see much of him through the rest of the academic year.

Since *Charlie Brown* was the first major production we'd put on since *Shrew*, we enjoyed a considerably larger audience for it than we had had all year. Even though the audience was farther away, they were more involved in the story, and clapped more frequently. For the first time I didn't feel paralyzed with nerves as I prepared to make an entrance. This was my third play, and I actually began to feel like an actor rather than as a curiosity.

My costume for Charlie Brown was a pair of short pants, which revealed my short, hairy legs. At the age of 14, I already had a light mustache and a small goatee for a beard; Miss Caudill instructed me to shave these off, and I dutifully complied. My leg hairs were another matter. I had heard shaving stimulated hair growth, and I was plenty hairy already (and it was becoming apparent more was on the way. *Everywhere.*) So I put my foot down and refused to shave my legs.

"Listen," she said. "Charlie Brown is a kid. He's maybe 6 years old. He can't have hairy legs."

"No one will care," I said. "If we're doing our job, they won't stare at my legs."

"Some people will," she insisted. "It'll grow back, I promise. And it's only for a few days."

"No," I said. "It'll grow back thicker and more *luxurious*, and I'll have to live with it *forever.*" I reminded her that the male cast members of *Shrew* had nearly carried out their threat to write dirty words in my back hair with hair removal gel. Everyone in drama knew I had hairy legs (and a hairy back, for that matter). If I removed my leg hair, I'd never hear the end of it.

She finally relented–surprised, perhaps, that I had finally said *no* to anything she suggested, and as Charlie Brown I wore short pants, a horizontally striped shirt, and my old Grumio hat (turned inside out). I don't know why she let me wear that; Charlie Brown always wore a ball cap or a winter cap with ear flaps in the cartoons and comic strips. Years later she told someone, "It was kind of his signature during his freshman year. He wouldn't take the godforsaken thing off."

I was teased by nearly everyone in the cast (*especially* Cheryl Ann, who played the kite-eating Tree: "*Was it an accident in a science lab or did you just un-evolve like that all on your own?*") about my hairy legs anyway, but no one in the audience ever said anything to me about it afterward. Miss Caudill, on the other hand, treated it as the little brother of the ass-scratching story: she told everyone who ever met me about it. Sometimes twice.

Ironically, when I played Snoopy years later, I wore a full body cos-tume of white cotton, which hid my legs. Only my beard protruded from a dog-shaped hat.

Lyn herself created the program we used for Charlie Brown. Seeking to capitalize on our newfound fame, we went to various local busi-nesses and told them of our success and sold ads. The money financed our awards banquet.

In those days most schools had exactly one copy machine, and it was jealously guarded by the school secretary. Ordinary souls like teachers had to use a ditto machine, which used a sort of carbon paper with some sort of alcohol-based fluid to produce blue print on the papers that cycled through it, *ka-thump, ka-thump, ka-thump.* I made so many scripts for Miss Caudill over the years I can still remember the smell of ditto fluid and the sound of the aging machine. So our program was produced on a ditto machine, with the pagination figured out and drawn by Lyn so that when copies were made back to back, the half-pages laid out so that the pagination would work out when they were eventually stapled. It was actually pretty complicated to figure out in advance, and she did mock ups with regular paper to plan it correctly. *Popcorn brain, indeed.*

Lyn did the layout and design, and typed the cast bios and drew the cover. I did some of the ads which mostly consisted of the company's name (*Home Office Supply, Food Fair, Hatfield's House of Guns, Bill's Market;* and drew a couple of logos for her: *FDIC Insured, Burger Queen)* and she did the rest. There were cute little accents on her y's and H's. She had lovely handwriting, I noted. In comparison my writing wasn't entirely straight, but ditto masters were expensive, and we tried not to waste them once we started.

Lyn and Miss Caudill collaborated on the cast bios.

For my sister Jane, they wrote:

> Jane Mason (Lucy) performs tonight in her first leading role at Devitt. Although Jane is a second year speech and drama student, her previous work has been done primarily in speech and in technical work (including the highly demanding position of stage manager for TAMING OF THE SHREW in which she also performed the supporting role of Curtis). It has taken much time and work, but Jane Mason finally has "arrived."

When you are preparing content with a typewriter with only one font, capital letters are the closest thing to italics you can generate.

For Lyn, they wrote:

> "Lyn Anderson (Snoopy) is a Senior at Devitt, and this perform-ance marks the end of a long and successful career in Theatre at Devitt H. Caudill. Lyn has multiple local, regional and state awards in speech and theatre, but this year surprised many people by winning 2nd place in State Competition for best actress with her superior performance as Katherine in TAMING OF THE SHREW. Lyn has also been seen as Rosalie in OH DAD, POOR DAD, as Lizzie in THE RAINMAKER, as Marilyn and as Gretel in SEE ME, I AM A PERSON, as Ismene in ANTIGONE, and as Snow White in SNOW WHITE, in addition to speech events and much technical work. Lyn plans to attend U.of L. next year. Con-gratulations and good luck, Lyn. We hate to see you go!"

We hate see you go. I looked at that sentence a long time, facing for the first time that perhaps my dearest friend in the world would be leaving for U.K. soon. U.K. was the University of Kentucky, one of the two major universities in the state. Or maybe she might go to U of L, to be closer to her parents. Just as far away, as far as I was concerned.

I figured there wasn't much to say about me; I'd won a couple of awards for Grumio, and I'd been in one play and one skit. JEFF MA-SON, I thought I'd see. IS A BEGINNER IN THEATRE AND HAS BEEN FAKING IT ALL THIS TIME. BE NICE TO HIM. Instead, I discovered the following.

> Jeff Mason (Charlie Brown) is a list of firsts at Devitt: First Freshman to carry a leading role; first Freshman to win regional Best Actor; first freshman to place at state competition (4th); first freshman to pull off a superior rating in Speech Competition (he got TWO). Heard enough? Just wait! This guy has three years to go.

Apparently, I thought, there had never been a freshman in drama before. Given Mr. (Byron) Caudill's attitude, I could see why.

The best part of the thing is that I was billed *under* my sister Jane and my bio was shorter; that helped mollify her that I had obtained a leading role before she had, relatively speaking. In truth the listing was probably in order of appearance, but while *we* knew that, the *audience* likely didn't.

We performed *Charlie Brown* on the community college stage, and had several packed houses. Music was provided by an offstage record player cued up by Pam Tilden and an onstage piano we'd hauled out of the music room. We even used the lights to trigger scene changes, such as they were. Most of the time, like with *Shrew*, the stage was empty. We had a doghouse for Snoopy, which if I recall correctly was merely a table. Three years later, we had a real doghouse, built by my father, if you can believe that. He eventually came around.

We continued to rehearse just as hard as we had for *Shrew* even though we were never going to enter *Charlie Brown* in a competition.

"Miss Caudill," I said one afternoon at Jerry's, "Why are we working so hard when we won't be winning awards for this show?"

"Because, Hoss, winning awards isn't the *point,*" she said. "What's the point, Lynnie?" I gaped at her. Not the *point?* What was all that drama after *Shrew*, then?

Lyn regarded me carefully. I noticed my sister frowning because *she* hadn't been asked.

"Performing is its own reward. It's *fun,* for one thing. Don't you just like living like you're someone else, really getting into a role? And isn't the applause great? You've affected people's lives when you act. Escaped the drudgery of everyday life. Made them happy. Made them cry. Changed the daily routine of their lives a little bit."

This earned her a hug from her aunt. Smiles from Lyn. Despite their differences, I knew that they loved each other as aunt and niece. It wasn't an easy relationship, but it seemed to work as far as I could tell.

I noted, as fun as Lyn was to talk with when Cheryl was not around, she was usually silent unless asked something specific when she and Miss Caudill were together. It wasn't that Lyn had nothing to say; Miss Caudill just sort of dominated the conversation. Heck, she even dominated the conversation when *I* was a senior, and in high school I had an ego some people mistook for a small moon. (Just had a vision of Cheryl Ann flying an X-wing. *You're all clear, kid. Let's blow this thing and go home.*) Miss Caudill had a powerful personality. She had to, to make us do the things we did.

"Winning awards is just a side effect," Miss Caudill continued. "It's a *nice* side effect, because winning awards is leverage you can use to justify what you're doing. The real reward is...just creating a new world. Getting the audience to suspend their disbelief, for a while, and accept that the play's events are important. That's the point."

I scratched my chin where my recently shaved beard itched. *Suspension of disbelief*, I thought. *It's like a skeptic who goes to a magic show. He knows it isn't real, but he doesn't care.*

"You know, I might just be beginning to figure this acting thing out," I said.

That earned laughs all around.

Charlie Brown closed, people clapped, and I had a great time doing the show.

The Awards Banquet

At the annual awards program for the drama program, we did several different things. Sort of like the Oscars, Miss Caudill arranged awards in a variety of categories; Best actor, best actress, best voice, best technical, best supporting actor, best supporting actress, comedy and drama subcategories, speech awards, and everything else she could think of. She was not above inventing a category just so some student she felt was worthy would walk home with an award. She also went to great lengths to obtain trophies for us. It was not an insignificant expense.

Part of the work we had to do for her was raise money to pay for buses, makeup, even the rights to perform shows from publishers, and trophies. I sold (and bought) far too much candy. We charged admission to public performances, and wonder of wonder, people paid. We sold advertising in programs. Word on the street was that graduating seniors who won the Hall of Fame award and Esprit d'Corps award (the highest two honors) were allowed to *design* their own trophies and got whatever they wanted.

I also learned that the award event was a dinner, with a catered meal, and formal dress expected. I didn't even own a suit–for what purpose would I ever need it? We didn't go to church since my mother had induced a schism with the local church elders over my "ambush baptism" – I was *drafted* into the church at age 12 and nearly baptised (full-immersion *in a creek*) without consulting my parents. *Do you believe that Jesus Christ is the son of God?* our preacher shouted at me, standing next to me with the entire congregation watching. *DoyouacceptJesusChristasyourlordandsavior ? Do you bleeve thathediedforyoursinsonthecross?* Like all good Sunday school students, I knew all the answers the preacher wanted to hear. I didn't know if I actually believed any of them. From a practical standpoint my fear of my mother's wrath was stronger than my fear of God's, and I deferred to her suggestion to skip the baptism until I was older.

I dressed in dark shoes and pants, and a white button-down shirt. During the school week it was jeans and beat-up sneakers, and more often than not, a plain white t-shirt. I got basically one pair of shoes a year, at the beginning of the year when we bought school clothes, and that was it. I still only own three or four pairs of shoes, but maybe that's just a guy thing. Sneakers, dress shoes, sandals, slippers. One pair of each. For all the jokes about shoeless Appalachians, I never knew anyone so poor they could not literally afford shoes, but in college (I went to college in Eastern Kentucky, eventually) we used to tell visiting tourists they could leave extra shoes from their luggage in the library for poor students to check out for the semester. We did buy used clothes from Goodwill, but that seldom included shoes.

My mother thought I should be equipped with a suit for her own reasons, and I got (funded from her stash) a simple blue shirt and dark slacks, my first tie (a clip-on) and a blue polyester jacket. It wasn't fancy, but given who I was and where I was, it fit in, which was the point, I guess. And certainly no one had ever seen me in a tie before.

Another function completed at the award ceremony was the induction of new members of the local chapter of the International Thespian Society. *With all the rights and privileges thereof,* the certificate read. I never knew exactly what those were. It was a lifetime membership, so I suppose I'm still a member. A nominal fee brought a magazine subscription, and a small lapel pin with the faces of Comedy and Tragedy on either side of a capital T.

Lyn was a graduating senior at the ceremony, and she handed out the certificates for new inductees. When she came to me, she placed the certificate in my hands with a smile. I looked at her, puzzled. She responded by turning her hand over, indicating I should flip over the certificate. I waited until she moved on, handing out certificates, before sneaking a a look. On the back, she had written me a note.

> *I don't have time now to say everything–* she
> wrote. *But if you ever wonder–or ever feel
> lonely!- You better know that I love you honey!!!
> AND I ALWAYS WILL!! You are a light in my*

*school career and in my life! And you better be-
lieve that you won't get rid of me too easily. I'll
<u>always</u> keep in touch–if not by letter–by heart
and by mind!*

All my love always,

Lyn '77

I was speechless. I looked up at her, but she had moved on, still passing out certificates. My hands were shaking. Tears welled up in my
eyes. That seemed to happen to me a *lot* when she was around. Normally, I wasn't quite so weepy.

"What's wrong?" asked my sister, glancing at the handwriting on the
note.

"Nothing," I choked out, flipping the certificate over. "I'll – I'll be
back in a minute." I got up, and managed to walk to the foyer leading
to the bathroom. I went into the bathroom, and found an empty stall.
Silent tears streamed down my face, and I shook with sobs. *She loved
me. She loved me. All this time, I thought– I thought– she was just being nice, tolerating me, just because she's nice to* everyone. Then I
thought, *maybe it's just love like a little brother.* Yeah, that was it. She
loved me like a little brother. That's what she meant. Had to be. *Keep
your mouth shut, there's still some time left in the year. You don't even
know what love is. You're too young. It's not like that.*

After a few moments, I calmed down a bit, dried my face. I hoped I
wasn't all red-faced and blushing again, because the awards were going to start soon.

I returned to my seat. Miss Caudill made a speech about how proud
she was of us, and how much the awards for Shrew meant for her, and
her program. She said she was glad to have been our teacher, and
hoped we all carried something away from the experience.

Everyone was there. Charmaine, Pat Hatford, Benny, myself, my sister. Lyn was there of course, and Bobby White, Jensen Tilden; Randall Smith even made an appearance. Mrs. Williams, Cheryl's staunchest supporter among the faculty, was there, as well as Mrs. Rice and Mr. Simmons. Some parents were present, but not ours; Mom was at home, and Dad had dropped us off earlier so we could help set up. He was due back to pick us up after he went to the lumber store for some supplies.

The awards began. I had no idea if I was even eligible for anything. I figured, all the upperclassmen would get the awards...my turn, if I had one, would come later, if I stuck with it.

"Best supporting actor in a comedy," said Lyn. "Jeff Mason," said Benny.

I walked up to the front, hearing the applause, receiving the award from Lyn, hardly noticing the peck on the cheek she delivered with the trophy; I looked into her eyes and she could tell, I think, I had been crying.

"Thank you," I said to her, speaking only to her. We didn't make acceptance speeches for the minor awards. Everyone else thought I was talking about the award. I wasn't.

Other awards continued. Benny got best actor in a drama; Lyn got best actress. The awards were selected by a committee of teachers including Miss Caudill, some teachers who attended most of the performances, and senior students. You couldn't vote for yourself, though. That meant that more than one person thought I was good at this drama stuff...maybe I ought to stick with it after my *muse* departed.

"Best voice," I heard. "Jeff Mason for Jonathan Rosepettle."

"Best...best...best..." the awards continued. Miss Caudill had a healthy supply of trophies– probably more trophies than people, and I expected that meant that everyone would get *something,* but they kept piling trophies on my table. My sister Jane received several awards as well, including best technical for stage managing *Shrew*. At the end, she and I accumulated something like over a dozen awards, when some upperclassmen hadn't gotten anything. The only thing I could think of was *How will I carry all these home?* That problem eventually got solved when Miss Caudill loftily deposited the delivery box from the trophy shop on my table.

"I thought you might need this, Hoss," she said.

"Miss Caudill. I– I don't– don't know what to say–"

"Well, that's a first," she said, grinning. My sister seemed genuinely happy for me, not jealous at all. "Good work, kiddo." She pounded me on the back.

The awards were not quite finished. The two biggest awards, Esprit d'Corps (Spirit of the Company) and Hall of Fame were last.

"This next awardee," began Miss Caudill, for she always reserved the big award announcements for herself, "Has worked harder than I thought a high school student could work. She started in drama before she met me, and sacrificed more than you will ever know to join us here and enrich our program. She has stage managed, made costumes, acted, directed, and choreographed. She has had more leading roles in two years than most students get in four. She probably felt put upon, from time to time, but we all know that the person who has given more to us than anyone else, who best exemplifies the spirit of the company, and the recipient of this year's Esprit d'Corps award is– my niece, and my best student, Debra Lyn Anderson."

Applause erupted from around the room. I clapped as hard as I could without trying to draw attention to myself. The corner of the room behind me was silent, however. I turned to look and saw the backs of Charmaine Marshall, Pam Hatfield, and Jensen Tilden leaving the room. Why would they leave *now*? I thought. The awards aren't over–

Oh. I thought. *It's because it's Lyn.* I looked at Lyn, who was crying, dabbing at her eyes with a napkin trying to keep her makeup under control, struggling with a beautiful trophy she probably had designed herself. I saw her glance at the exit, as people she once called friends left in protest. *They probably think she got it just because she's Cheryl's niece,* I thought. I remembered with some shame that I had once suggested the same thing.

The Hall of Fame award was announced. Benny got it. Miss Caudill made a nice speech about him, but such was my emotional state that evening I don't remember much of what was said.

Benny and I had some adventures in the year that followed. In particular, he and I did the show *The Sunshine Boys* in his senior year and my sophomore year. We did a good job that year, and won some more awards. Benny was always convinced that he was going to seek out fame and fortune through a career in acting; but somehow that never worked out. I suspect it was because he had more responsibilities at home than any of us ever knew. If anything, his home life was just as difficult as mine, if not more so, but he never complained about it.

He maintained his tough exterior facade and wore it like a shield, and was the life of the party wherever he appeared. Part of his persona was a studied indifference to the more academic requirements of high school. That was not to say he was irresponsible. At home, he worked at jobs that paid the bills but allowed little free time for pursuing extraneous pursuits such as acting. Even at the height of his high school acting career he would often miss rehearsals for one reason or another, and I often accompanied Miss Caudill as she dropped him off at his home numerous times.

Benny's sister Penelope, who had played Bianca in *Shrew*, did some shows as well, and picked up the mantle of the young ingenue after Lyn left. I did a couple of shows with her, most notably *Antigone,* and we enjoyed some success in various venues.

I occasionally ran into Benny from time to time after that, and we always shook hands and reminisced about the good old days, even while I was still in high school. After *The Sunshine Boys* we didn't work together again.

Whatever talents I may have had, I never could stand up to the raw stage presence that Benny commanded. I always admired and envied him for that.

Finally the awards ceremony ended, with Miss Caudill thanking everyone for their hard work, and the tables were cleared as the remaining people began gathering their things. My sister appeared suddenly and said my father was there to pick us up. I gave her my box of trophies and told her to add hers into it, and I would catch up in a few minutes. Jane looked at me, looked at Lyn, and for once didn't tell me Dad would be pissed or I should hurry up. Occasionally, she could actually be pretty cool and with it. She smiled, nodded, and departed.

I found Lyn talking quietly, still trying to control her disappointment but hiding it well–mixed with pride over the Esprit d'Corps award– with Cheryl and a couple of other upperclassmen. I waited patiently nearby, as I nearly always did when confronted with my elders, until I could speak to her. She saw me between two people, and said, "Excuse me," and pushed through to me and took my hand. She led me to a quiet corner of the room.

"Congratulations, Jeff," she said. *For what? Oh, the trophies.*

"School's almost out," I said. "I may not get to see you again." *Ever.*

"Did you read my note?" she said. "You'll see me again. I promise."

"Lyn–" I began, and changed course before even beginning. "I'm sorry about your friends walking out."

"They aren't my friends," she said. "Not anymore." She looked pained, though. "Consequently it doesn't bother me as much as they think it does."

"Well, it would bother *me,* " I said. "It was rude."

"It was that," she said. I think I could tell she was hurting but didn't want to burden me with it. *Always thinking of others before herself,* I thought. *Almost to a fault.*
342

"You'll have to tell me what happened between you and them some-day. I can't imagine anyone having a reason for not liking you."

She laughed out loud at this. "Somehow, I don't see them agreeing with you."

"Well, anyway, I just wanted to say–" I started again, and stalled out, unable to select the right word. *I used to read whole dictionaries for fun,* I thought. *Why can't I pick the right word?* "–uh– say, th-th-that, well, you know..." *Damn and double damn this stutter!*

She grabbed me and held me in a close hug. I wrapped my arms around her too. She was wearing *that* perfume, the kind I always asso-ciated with her, that smelled like I was swimming in roses. She always *smelled* like a girl. I breathed it in deeply, almost gasping from it.

"I already know, sweetie," she said in my ear. "I already know, believe me."

"I'm going –to miss– you. You don't have any idea."

"Oh, I do," she said. "You're going to miss me just about as much I'm going to miss you. But not quite as much."

I leaned back from the hug, looked her in the eye. Her *electric blue* eyes.

Really? I tried to say. The signal was being generated in my brain, but never made it to my mouth.

"You're the one person who has stood by me, loyally, all this year," she said. "No one else in my life can say that. *No one.* And I won't ever forget it. You made me feel...*special* again. Loved. *Cherished.* Just when I needed it most."

"Loved? Special– I – you have no idea how much you've meant to me, made me feel *important*, and *worthy*– I– I–" I choked. I was babbling, why couldn't I have forseen this moment, and tried to prepare to say something that more clearly communicated how I felt? It was as if my brain refused to engage, like a recalcitrant tiller chewing on a boulder too big for its tiny blades.

She could tell I was about to cry. She placed a finger on my lips to say, *It's ok.* She produced a pencil, one of the giveaways we'd scattered on the crepe-paper covered tables at the country club. My eyes filled with tears, but miraculously, none fell upon my face. Then she took my certificate, the one she had signed and was still, somehow, in my hand, and wrote her home address on it. Her home in Louisville.

"Write to me," she said.

"I will," I managed to gasp. "I promise."

"I believe you," she said, smiling. No star ever emitted light like her eyes when she was smiling.

Somehow I walked away, got in the truck. Dad didn't say anything about having to wait, for a change. I sat and stared out the window. Jane, bless her heart, jabbered all the way home, bragging about me, listing our awards for Dad, saying how I had more awards than *anyone*, and saying how I was just overwhelmed by all the attention and that's why I wasn't talking and wasn't it *great*, and I sat and looked out of the window, at the inky blackness of the unlit hills, and at the sky, spangled with distant suns peeking between the trees above the ridgelines, and counted the stars.

Three Orbits Later

The school year ended. Lyn graduated, but I wasn't allowed to attend the ceremony for some reason. I think if I had insisted, I would have been allowed to go. I honestly don't remember thinking about it; perhaps I was afraid of crying in public.

The summer of my freshman year was one of the last ones I ever spent not working on *something*. Starting with my junior year, I worked every summer and never again enjoyed the timeless freedom children enjoy when it seems like summer would last *forever.* Part of growing up, I guess.

Star Wars came out. It was the first movie I ever saw in an indoor movie theatre. (The first movie I ever saw anywhere aside from television was *2001.* I suppose that explains a lot about my early fascination with science fiction.) When I arrived at the theatre, word about the movie had already spread. *Everyone* wanted to see *Star Wars.* Back then, it was just that, no numbers or volumes or episodes. It was the only one. I arrived to a nearly packed theatre. I went alone; no significant friends with whom to share the experience, and no one in my family saw the potential of the movie from the ads we'd seen on TV.

The only free seat was in the *front row.* Imagine what it was like, seeing *that* movie with a screen taking up your entire field of view, right next to the speakers, as the *first movie you ever saw on the big screen.* When the first Star Destroyer spent that interminable interval scrolling by overhead, I thought *science fiction movies are never, ever, going to be like they used to be. This one will change everything.* I *loved* that movie; the rough edges, the worn look to the universe, in contrast to the antiseptic future seen in *Star Trek,* was enthralling. I loved it despite the violations of physical law (in space you can't *hear* the ships scream as they zoom by). I didn't go to movies much that summer even after that; it was the only movie I saw that year.

In art class the following year, I annoyed my art teacher Mr. Williams by picking subjects and themes which invariably led to astronomy and space. I painted several spacescapes, from various places around the

345

solar system. I even painted a landscape, as directed, on the surface of the planet Tatooine, which was most certainly not directed. It showed blue sky, two suns, and everyone's favorite droids. I sketched endless views of the Starship *Enterprise*. I used to think that there really was a real *Enterprise*, and some weather satellite had taken the pictures that were beamed to the earth for use in the TV show. Like every other *Trek* fan I was thrilled that NASA named a space shuttle *Enterprise* but infuriated that it was one destined to never fly in space.

To pass the rest of the time and take my mind off of weightier matters during the summer of my freshman year, I read books. I read a *lot* of books. *Hundreds.* Every two weeks in the summer, the pale blue bookmobile from the Hazard public library would trundle down Maces' Creek and park at the end of the hollow. Sometimes my sisters Brenda and Jane would join me; sometimes I was alone. Occasionally neighbors would climb on board as well.

After a couple of visits, the bookmobile operator got the idea that I liked science fiction. I read everything resembling science fiction on the bus, including the children's section. I knew the Big Three, Asimov and Heinlein and Clarke, and had read about robots, and immortality, and exploration. They say that science fiction is escapist literature. I certainly lost myself in it. One week the operator just gestured to the bottom shelf in the back. The entire shelf's contents had been replaced with science fiction, none of which I'd read yet. The librarian had screened each book to see if my name was on the little check-out card in the back.

"Can I check out more than usual?" I asked, wide-eyed, and appreciative of the consideration.

"You can get a bunch if you want," came the reply. "Might take you a while to read them all."

"I'll be right back," I said, and flew back up the hill to fetch my little red wagon, still stored in the shed, unused since the move from Ohio.

I filled the wagon up with books. "You know, you only get two weeks to read those," said the operator, realizing that I intended to take *all* the books instead of picking and choosing.

"It's OK," I said. "I read fast."

"Ok," the librarian said, doubtfully.

Two weeks later I had read the entire wagonload. I didn't think it was any big deal to read a whole book in a day; someone once said good books are meant to be devoured, not sampled; I gorged myself. My parents weren't well off, as you know if you've read this far. But anything academic–even putting up with drama practice or reading "useless" science fiction– was tolerated, to the point where my mother insisted we didn't have to do much in the way of chores. Just keep our rooms clean, help in the garden a bit, token stuff really. Considering the condition of my office today, it would probably have been better for me to develop a little bit more of the obsession with organization exhibited by neat-freaks, but hey, no one's perfect.

It's remarkable and amazing to have parents who just gave you free reign to study whatever you wanted. I knew any number of students trapped into the plans laid by others for their academic choices and eventual careers. I knew how lucky I was and how unusual my parents were in trusting my judgment–eventually– in such matters. Even my father backed off after I started making money acting. My mother always defended all of our academic efforts.

"When I was in school we had a pencil tied around our neck, and we got one piece of paper a day for school work," she said. "If we lost or broke the pencil there was hell to pay. No child of mine is ever going to have to scrimp and save and use the backs of grocery bags to find something to draw on," she said. Every school year started with a box of pencils and several packs of paper.

So I had plenty of time to read.

I think I learned more physics in those books than I did in my first month of a real physics class. I understood Newton's Laws for the most part, spacetime, some idea of what relativity was about; I knew what angular momentum was, and the consequences of conserving it; I learned that physicists, bucking the trend of other scientists, did not invent new technical vocabulary (deoxyribonucleic acid = D.N.A.), but rather *changed the meaning of ordinary words* such as force, and weight, and acceleration to match what the equations *said* they were. I learned of the theory of evolution, and ideas about gravity and black holes and time travel washed over me like a tide.

I began to realize that there was perhaps a larger world to learn about besides just Hazard, or Devitt H. Caudill for that matter; larger perhaps than Kentucky, or even the whole United States.

To me, Mars became a *place.* People could *go* there, and live a normal life. People had been to the moon; Mars was practically inevitable. I read Bradbury, puzzled about his curious lack of respect for physical reality. Asimov taught me to respect the sweep of history with the Foundation series. Logic came with the stories about the Laws of Robotics–modeled after the Laws of Motion–and the logical consequences of implementing them. Clarke stoked my sense of wonder. I may have been one of the few people who understood *2001* when I saw it, because I read the book *first.*

In these stories, scientists were not evildoers bent on ruling the world; they were the *heroes*, the ones who figured things out, the ones respected because they were *smart.*

All this I had to absorb in silence, because my father was no fan of science fiction, and my sister wasn't interested. At home, we watched 1. *Gunsmoke*, 2. *The Beverly Hillbillies* and 3. *Hee Haw*. In that order.

"I don't see what you see in that damn 'Star Track,'" he said to me once. "None of it's *real*. It's all made up stuff. Don't do no one no good to watch that."

"It's based on real science," I said.

"I'll tell you about *science*," he would say. "Half the problems this world has is because of *science*. Them scientists don't know nothing about how the workin' man has to live. They just take a man's tax money and shoot it off into space for no good reason. It's a damn *waste*." The closest he wanted me to get to science was architecture, which he thought was my ticket out of the grind of poverty. I dutifully drew floor plans to scale for math projects, and it seemed to keep him happy. On the backs of the diagrams I designed moon bases and star-ships. That kept *me* happy.

My uncle Howard had actually recorded a musical song about wasting money exploring space. "All our tax money done shot up to Mars," he wailed on a scratchy 45 RPM record. "Shot up to Mars."

I kept most of my viewpoints about space travel to myself.

Every week, more often than the bookmobile, another truck stopped by to deliver ice cream. I *love* ice cream, and never met a flavor I didn't like except mocha. Can't eat as much of it now, but in those days I begged a quarter, sometimes a dollar, and that was a highlight of my week. The ice cream truck – and it was a *real* ice cream truck, not these white and rust colored, poorly labeled, overly loud, run down excuses filled with half-melted, half-refrozen product you see wobbling through suburban neighborhoods these days–a *real* ice cream truck with nothing but name brand stuff and Mickey Mouse ice cream bars and push ups and fudgsicles and bomb pops and little cups of strawberry ice cream you eat with a wooden spoon. That's *real* ice cream, not overpriced lumps of sugar with chunks of jelly beans hand-dipped by some acne-ridden teen in a strip mall. If you wanted ice cream, you had to go out in the hot, humid summer day and *be there* waiting whenever the truck showed up; if you missed it, there went a week without a cool break from the stifling summer heat in Kentucky.

We never had air conditioning, even with 100 degree days and near 100 percent humidity. I still sleep better with a fan blowing air over me. My father still doesn't use AC; but my little sister, who lives up-stairs, has a window unit.

The summer passed, and school started again. I had Miss Caudill, officially or unofficially, every year till I graduated.

My classes grew more challenging, and enjoyable. I had Mrs. Mason (no relation) for biology and did some dissections. Mrs. Williams taught chemistry (I managed to cause a thermometer to explode, and caused a minor evacuation by making too much hydrogen in the lab one day.) We reorganized the chemistry shelves and removed old chemicals, grouping by type instead of alphabetically. There was no physics or physiology or God help me, astronomy, so I was finished with science as a junior. In math, I took Algebra II and Geometry and stalled out again due to a lack of offerings. Someone gave me a self-teaching course in the early computer language FORTRAN, consisting of 5 self-paced books produced by the University of Kentucky press, which I walked through in a week. Having no computer or card-punching machine with which to practice my newfound knowledge, I put that on hold. I had missed the beginning of the computer revolution by only a few years, and a couple thousand miles.

I took my first college class at Hazard Community College. It was a survey of science fiction. There were only five people in the class, but I did enjoy having someone to talk to about the books I had been reading. They taught me about the Big Three science fiction authors of so-called "hard" science fiction (Clarke, Asimov, and Heinlein). I remember distinctly being told that any so-called fan of science fiction *had to* read the Dune series, the Foundation trilogy, Rendezvous with Rama, and *The Man Who Sold The Moon*. I'd read some of these. They introduced me to other works, by other authors, and I enjoyed listening to the discussions about science fiction as a form of literature rather than just a source of ideas. (Although some of those ideas can be really cool; modern fans of *Halo* should consider *Ringworld* by Larry Niven required reading.) Writing good science fiction is *hard*, because you have to spend so much time cleverly working in the exposition and explanation of an entire *world*, you don't have as much room left for character development and plot.

Because I was a high school student, I could attend the course for free– and no credit– called *auditing*– and I got rides to the class from Miss Caudill. She was teaching a theatre class at the college and after the science fiction class, I would go to her room and listen to her lecture, and run all the AV equipment she needed. I did film strips, 16 mm movies with sound, and record albums with ultrasonic triggers that automatically advanced film strips. A film strip was a series of photos or slides in a single strip of film that you cranked through the projector one frame at a time. It was the equivalent of a modern Powerpoint, except you couldn't make them yourself. We didn't have any equipment like that at Devitt, although we did watch the occasional film strip.

That experience as the "AV kid" was probably what led me to have an appreciation for computers when I finally got access to them in college, but it wasn't why I was interested in electronics in the first place.

Problem Solving

During my sophomore year, Mr. Byron "Bear" Caudill was visited by Mr. Caldwell, who had been promoted or voted into office as superintendent.

"I have some good news for you, Byron."

"What's that? Is Cheryl Caudill retiring?" He laughed, emitting a little squeaky *henh-henh-henh* that annoyed everyone who met it.

"Got a job for you down to the district office, Byron," said Mr. Caldwell.

"Well, I appreciate the offer. What's the job?"

"Assistant superintendent of transportation." Mr. Caldwell smiled. "Plenty of room for advancement."

I think I saw the end of this conversation, as I have a vague memory of seeing Mr. Caldwell in the hall shaking Byron's hand. The rest of what was said I inferred from later conversations with Caudill's replacement.

Caldwell drew me aside as Mr. Caudill retreated to the office, hunched over and marching with intermittent mincing little steps, to tell the staff of his impending departure. I think that is quite possibly the only time in my entire life I have used the adjective "mincing" about anyone and meant it.

"I hear you're making quite a name for yourself down here at Caudill High School," said the superintendent.

"They have some good teachers here," I replied. "I like Cheryl Caudill, for example."

"Why is that?" I liked how he asked my opinion instead of feeding me his, as certain other administrators would have been likely to do.

I considered his question carefully, aware of both to whom I was speaking, and about whom I was answering. I answered, "She knows what's important. "

"That she does, son," said Caldwell. "That she does. You take care and keep up the good work."

"Thanks." I waved and went on my way.

It is one of the great ironies of bureaucratic politics that the only way to remove someone from a civil service position is to promote them to a higher-paying, if less important job. Mr. Caudill, in the parlance of the 90's, had been *dilberted* into a position exceeding his level of competency. Removing his talent for obstructionism was as simple and anticlimactic an act as that. I never saw the man again.

Mr. Caudill was replaced by Mr. Carpenter, my freshman typing teacher, and our bus driver to the state competition. He liked me; he liked Miss Caudill, and for a time, the Devitt H. Caudill Drama Club and "CC & Company" (for that is how Miss Caudill referred to her collective enterprise) enjoyed a Golden Age.

I nearly forgave him for the "popcorn brain" comment.

The only place I could keep pushing and growing was in Miss Caudill's drama class, and so I did.

Girlfriends came and went (always went, never sent; I have never ended a relationship with a girl in my whole life). Some parted in friendly terms and remained friends, others just ended; none of them were bitter, angry duels for Most Offended like you see with some couples. Each one hurt a little, though. I had no car, no money, and participated in no sports teams, not even in band; all I had to sell myself was my winning personality and hair.

Lots of hair. It was the 70's, after all. The BeeGees wore shoulder-length hair. Looking back, it looked like an unholy explosion of hair. My beard filled out and I kept it throughout most of high school, because I thought it made me look older. I'm sure that "he needs a *hair-cut*" became sort of my unknown catch phrase. I didn't get haircuts often, and when I did, it was because my mother insisted and she did the cutting. She stopped insisting when I was a teenager, so for the most part, I quit getting haircuts. It itched; it took time I didn't have; so I ignored it until people wouldn't quit bugging me about it. I'm pretty sure I got half of the haircuts I did because Cheryl Ann wouldn't quit picking on me about it. The other half were ordered by Miss Caudill for one reason or another.

The odd part was I wasn't making a decision not to cut my hair on purpose; it just never occurred to me most of the time. When I did get haircuts, it was for a part in a play; the first time I ever visited a bar-bershop (like so many other experiences I had) it was because Miss Caudill took me to one, and directed the barber.

We did one play, called *Antigone*, by Joanne Anouih, where I played Creon, the King of Thebes. While getting ready for a performance at the school I wore a black turtleneck sweater, a gold bling-y like chain around my neck with a lion's head belt-buckle as an amulet, and dark pants and platform shoes. Some kid walked in the boys bathroom where I was changing and asked who I was. I replied, in a deep voice, "I'm Creon, King of Thebes." My voice echoed in the bathroom stalls. The kid scurried out of the bathroom and ran to Miss Caudill's room and declared to the class, "Miss Caudill, Miss Caudill, there's a king down the hall in the bathroom!"

Eventually, we won 2nd place in the state with that play, and Kentucky Educational Television had us recreate it and filmed it like a real, live movie. The set was the porch of some antebellum mansion, the build-ing long since destroyed, marble columns standing like a monument in the rolling hills of a horse farm.

We had many adventures (More than enough for a sequel, Miss Caud-ill!), and new members of the troupe came, and others went.

We did *lots* of plays. I was in *The Sunshine Boys*, and *Antigone*, and our revisited version of *Charlie Brown*. I played Roy in *Plaza Suite* by

Neil Simon. We did scenes from Chekhov, other works of Shakespeare, Poe, and many more. We did skits, we performed at elementary schools, in Room 111 and at the local community college stage several times. We did announcements for the school on the P.A. system. We visited the local television station, located at the top of a mountain and accessible only after a long and twisting journey up a road that was ridiculously narrow even by Perry County standards, and taped a little segment using a teleprompter. We dressed up in costume and participated in parades and performed, an old news clipping tells me, on the county courthouse steps for some sort of tribute to the hostages being held in Iran, a community event that I have absolutely no memory of participating in despite the photographic evidence to the contrary.

We won more awards at various state competitions. I improved my storytelling skills and eventually won a first place at the state competition. (I wasn't the first one from Devitt to do it, though; Benny had led the way with his version of *The Tell-Tale Heart*. I told *Choo Choo The Runaway Train* one year and won first place with *Where the Wild Things Are* by Maurice Sendak the next. I did scenes with Penelope Dougherty, Benny's sister, and later with Cheryl Ann, and we were *good*. Cheryl Ann and I won first place in duo acting at state, the same competition I had entered with Lyn when we did *Oh Dad, Poor Dad*.

"You were the only student I ever had that placed in the top 10 actors in the state one-act competition, every year you were in high school," Miss Caudill told me recently.

"Really?" I asked, surprised.

"It's true," she said. "I had some good students, and we won more awards, but I never had another one quite like you," she said.

In the summer of my junior year Miss Caudill persuaded my parents to let me audition for a role in *Wilderness Road*, an outdoor drama performed each summer at Berea College's Indian Fort Theatre, a two-hour drive away. I made the lowly sum of $70 per week for a small role, Doc Merritt (*He's dead, Jim*, pretty much described my function), and understudied one of the leads– Squire Sims, a 50-year old patriarch of the family. Halfway through the summer, the actor portraying Sims had to depart to deal with a family emergency, and I became Sims–at the age of 16. I had to use silver spray in my hair, and adopted mannerisms like turning my head more slowly; everyone was always surprised when they met the cast because they didn't recognize me without makeup. I also got a raise, taking home $100 per week. I could support myself on that, living in a dorm at a reduced rate, buying my own food, even purchasing my own school supplies for the fall of my senior year.

That first paycheck *finally* silenced my parents' objections to my current career path; there was money in it, and $400 per month wasn't bad for a teenager in the 1970's, in that place, at that time. It was certainly the most money I had ever been responsible for. And I started my senior year as the only professional actor in the school.

The small pittance I brought home finally directed my attention to the fact that wherever I went to college, I was going to have a tough time finding a way to pay for it. I had only a theoretical knowledge of scholarships and grants at the time. Nearly all my teachers regaled all the junior and senior class with stories of how they had worked in pizza shops, cut lawns, endured endless hours behind the counter of convenience stores, and pumped gas to pay the bills, and some of them were still paying for the college loans that got them through school.

I'd spent an entire summer working and only had some token funds left over to show for it. Not that I wasted money, but summer outdoor theatre hardly was the path to fame and fortune. I began worrying about how I would eventually pay for college.

I even missed the first two weeks of school doing the final performances for *Wilderness Road*. Such was my reputation that some teachers insisted I not bother with making up the work; others let me, and the other students were only mildly annoyed when I returned two weeks of makeup work the next day. They just rolled their eyes and said, "That's the Perfesser for ya."

Roger William (Wilbo) Fine, as I recall, coined that name for me. My classmates in the school were convinced I was going to go off and become a Professor of Science, or an actor, or a TV star. Or all of the above; Wilbo suggested I play the next Perfesser on a sequel to *Gilligan's Island.* I was voted Most Likely to Succeed, against all traditions of popularity. By the time I had graduated, I had grown out of the habit of raising my hand for *every* question. The teachers knew I was smart; the students knew; and all I was accomplishing by volunteering continuously was annoying the teacher and shielding the other students from having to think for themselves. Occasionally, when no one would answer a question or volunteer a response, someone in the back of the room would mutter "Just ask the Perfesser."

I was ambitious, all right, but my ambition was tempered with a dose of reality; I had lived alone for months, but I knew I had had it easy even then. There was rent, utilities, taxes, car, gas, food: how was I going to manage all of that and go to school?

Sometimes a little knowledge is dangerous. It might have been better for me if I didn't try to think through the consequences of my choices so much. Trying to solve every possible problem in advance of making a decision sometimes almost paralyzes me.

I confessed my uncertainty about how to pay for college to Miss Caudill one day after rehearsal.

I found Miss Caudill sitting on the floor in the back of the room. I didn't ask why; she just seemed to appear in different locations every time I entered the room. Something about finding a good place to concentrate.

"Miss Caudill, I can't even afford to pay you for all the times you fed me," I said. "How in the world am I going to pay for college?"

"There are scholarships, and loans for when the scholarships dry up," she said. "You could work and go to school at the same time, you know."

"I could," I said, "But I'd rather concentrate on going to college to learn, rather than work."

"Welcome to the real world, Jeffery. College isn't like high school." She shook her head. "Where are you thinking of applying?"

"Well," I confessed, "I only applied to a couple of different places so far. University of Kentucky in Louisville was one. I was looking at this place in Maryland–"

"Why Maryland?"

"I always wanted to visit the east coast," I said. People in California consider Kentucky to be one of those "Eastern" states. People in Kentucky think of themselves as living in the center of the country and consider Maryland to be an "Eastern" state.

"Anywhere else?"

"Harvard has a great reputation in astronomy, but it's somewhat out of my league."

"Financially or educationally?" she said, unfolding her legs and starting to rise. I offered her a hand up, and lifted her to her feet.

"Both," I said. "I've got a lot of catching up to do."

"You're going to need maybe 6 to 10 thousand dollars a year just for tuition," she said. *Damn. That's even worse than I expected.* "Big loans. Big debts."

"Don't I know it," I said. "Maybe I should work for a few years, save up some money."

"Maybe," she said. "What do you know about Berea College?"

"All I know about Berea is what I learned from being in the dorm at *Wilderness Road.*" Berea, Kentucky is a small college town about an hour's drive south of Lexington. While I had stayed on campus, the only people I hung around with were actors in the play. All the students had gone home for the summer. And all I knew about private colleges was they they were *expensive*.

"Not much," I confessed.

"I graduated from Berea College," she said. "Class of '68."

"How did you pay for it?"

"That's the odd thing," she said. "I never really did." She smiled at me, as if she knew a secret that I didn't.

"Uhm, you didn't pay for it?" Visions of loan officers cruising the hollows of Perry County looking for That Woman Who Absconded With Our Money flashed in front of my eyes. Was *that* what she meant?

"No," she said. "Berea doesn't charge tuition. It's free."

Free? Sounds like a good deal to me. "*Free* free?"

"*Free* free," she replied, smiling. "They don't charge tuition. But you have to work to help defray those expenses, and keep your grades up."

Miss Caudill went on to explain how the college raised its operating expenses from fundraising, grants, and money accrued through investments. Freshmen who were admitted weren't even allowed to have a car on campus–on the theory that if you could own a car, you could afford drive to work and go to some other school.

"Every student has to work for the college," she continued. "There are lots of jobs in all the different parts of the campus...things like waiting tables at Boone Tavern, working in the theatre shop, and being a tutor to younger students."

I got an application from the counselor, and filled it out. I mailed it in, and crossed my fingers.

The senior year passed on. I worked on the yearbook, and found in an old box in Mrs. Williams' room a picture of myself and my sister sitting at a table during the awards ceremony my freshman year. On the edge of the picture was a girl's shoulder, with curly blonde hair flowing down her back–it was *Lyn's* shoulder in the picture, and seeing it brought back a flood of memories. I slipped the picture into a book and took it home. *You're pathetic,* I thought. *You just stole a picture of a girl's shoulder.*

In the picture, my head is down, as if I am afraid the photographer would catch me staring at Lyn.

The other thing I did in journalism class was found the school paper. I was given a flyer outlining the basics of journalistic style (inverted pyramid, lead with the most important idea, don't forget the five W's and one H (who, what, where, when, why, and how), writing in third person, etc. Once the school newspaper was approved to go, it had to have a name; I decided to call it *De Witness,* but was always disappointed that no one seemed to appreciate the pun. Our journalism teacher, Mrs. Williams, even assigned a couple of students to help me. I assigned them sports, which I knew nothing about, and music and fashion, about which I knew even less. The paper was printed on an old mimeo machine and featured a hand-drawn masthead and a cartoon strip (which I drew). Mrs. Williams even arranged for me to teach a two-week unit on journalism in a freshman English class, an experiment that came to an abrupt end when the principal fielded a complaint from a parent that a teacher was letting some *boy* teach her class. The quizzes I had created, administered, and corrected were never counted towards anyone's grade.

Still, that was my first teaching experience, and it did teach me one thing at least. If I needed to, I *could* teach.

As the years passed, Lyn and I wrote to each other occasionally. I sent her a Valentine; she sent one to me (*My calculator can't add up all the ways I like you,* it read.) We wrote letters, too; not long ones, and not filled with long expositions of our emotional states; just I'm-fine-how-are-you, how's-college-going, I-just-started-a-new-show,

Mrs.-Hayword-says-hi. Eventually these tapered off as well. I gradually resigned myself to the obvious fact that she had her own life, probably had dozens of boyfriends, was on her way to greatness in stage and screen. Maybe I had made too much out of our friendship during that year; perhaps she had *other* friends, just as important as I was, maybe *more important.* Probably, she had better friends than me *now*, which is what mattered to me at the time.

While I didn't suffer for lack of girlfriends, none of the relationships turned out to be lasting. I had incredibly good luck picking up girls; one I met because I had an umbrella during a downpour and offered to walk her to her bus; another sat with me on the only empty seat on a ride home from a competition. Some were friends already and remained friends afterward. All ended when the girl uttered one of the fateful phrases boys dread to hear (*let's just be friends, it's not working out, I'm busy this weekend, there's someone else* and, I swear to God, *I forgot to tell you I was getting married.*)

Perhaps my best relationship during those three years was with Meredith Campbell. Meredith was slightly taller than I and had, from my perspective, all the ingredients of a great girlfriend: great figure, good self-assured personality, intelligent, and a charming, if subtle lisp when she talked. Her feet were pointed ever so slightly outward when she walked, and it gave her gait the most *interesting* sway; being the gentleman that I was, I *allowed* her to go first everywhere we went. It was kind of a low-key affair. We didn't go out much because both of us basically lacked the means; but we talked about serious things, and got to know each other, and didn't settle for a just physical relationship. We never did more than hug and participate in some serious tonsil-hockey kisses, but we did a *lot* of that; nevertheless we found that the emotional relationship was more important in the long run. Although, Meredith, if you're reading this, you should know: You're a *great* kisser. Really.

Eventually the romantic part of that relationship faded, but we remained good friends afterward, even calling each other occasionally through my college years. Apparently, I could maintain friendships beyond romance; after all, I'd had practice. Meredith was certainly my best friend for the remainder of my high school career after Lyn departed.

She was, as many of us in "the theatre" often are, a misfit within the larger school population. I think it is not too much of a stretch for me to state that we viewed each other as one of the main reasons that the latter parts of our high school careers were happy and enjoyable, for the most part.

I have to say, my relationship with Meredith was the only one that ended with me walking away happy, because even after we stopped dating we always were friendly together. That is a special thing to be cherished.

My relationship with Cheryl Ann (the student not the teacher) remained basically friendship-at-arms-length or sometimes just professional. It had been suggested to me (by more than one person) that her unending criticism was not merely jealousy, but a secret ploy to gain my attention because she liked me. I had my doubts about this theory but conceded I was not the most perceptive person, and that it might be true.

Once, when we were juniors or seniors, I tried to initiate something more significant with Cheryl Ann by holding her hand while we were listening to some music (I forget where, but we weren't alone.) She tolerated it for a minute or two, and then removed her hand, saying, "Whatever you're getting out of this isn't working for me," and I never hinted at trying to get closer to her again. At least it was short and quick, if painful. *No means no.* Still, I counted her as one of my best friends in school, because she was always honest with me, if blunt. Not every relationship with a girl has to end with romance, a fact with which I was intimately, and painfully, familiar.

I (due to my ongoing theatrical and academic success) also suffered from a, shall we say, well-endowed ego. My head was so big in those days, I'm sure she's about the only thing that kept me in check and let me fit inside the doorways. I did things like order my senior yearbook embossed with the name "Superstar!" on the cover, and I was the only senior who insisted on having his senior portrait done lying in the grass wearing a Seinfeldian "puffy shirt" and a rakish cap set at a jaunty angle. All of the seniors had individual poses outside, but I was the only one reclining in the grass. If any of my current friends are reading this, they're snickering because I could name a couple who perform the same role for me now in Cheryl Ann's stead. Eventually she married, and I know she has a happy life, for which I am glad.

If you *don't* know me and you're reading this, you probably think it's odd that none of my friends was male. That's not true; I had several (not *lots)* of friends I hung out with, and occasionally visited. Todd Williams was probably my best male friend; there was Dan, and Tim, Chris Petersen and Wilbo and a couple of others I called my friends. Some were good friends, some acquaintances, but they were not–strike that– *I* was not the kind of person who could reveal close personal intimate details easily to a guy.

For some reason, I've always had closer *friendships* with girls than guys. Cheryl Ann, abrasiveness aside, was always my good friend. We talked a lot, probably more than Lyn and I ever did. So was Meredith, with whom I maintained contact for several years after high school. They were all good friends; I enjoyed their company and had wonderful adventures with them as well; but this isn't a story about that, and for that I must apologize to them.

I thought of Lyn from time to time, and Miss Caudill obliged by keeping me informed about the shows she was doing, her progress in college, the fact that an entirely new fleet of young men (more her age) followed her around wherever she went on the campus. I accepted these stories as my due as one of her friends from high school, but carefully avoided thinking about scenarios of What Might Have Been, or even more unthinkable, What Might Yet Be.

Miss Caudill told me that Lyn asked how I was doing, and was regaled with tales of shows and academics and the promise of my future in the theatre.

I thought about Lyn asking after me, for weeks on end.

My senior year began to draw to a close. I auditioned for *Wilderness Road* again, and was accepted in essentially the same role with the same understudy opportunity. This year I would get a small bonus for participating in *preshow*, the warmup acts used to keep the audience occupied before the actual production began. School wasn't quite out yet; I would be leaving for Berea literally the day after graduation, and arriving one day later than everyone else to start rehearsal for the summer opening. Once *Wilderness Road* ended, I would be entering my freshman year at Berea College. The day after graduation would be the day I left home, but my parents had not yet given up on the idea that I would return home after college supposing that I could find some job locally that would grant me a living wage.

People began slipping me cards, congratulating me on graduating. Several teachers gave me money. Even my grandmother, virtually estranged from us and notoriously stingy, slipped a twenty into an empty envelope and had it delivered by one of my cousins. I appreciated all of it. I spent money *carefully*. After my first summer at *Wilderness Road*, I came home with over a hundred dollars in savings. I used this to buy school supplies: a briefcase, a two-drawer filing cabinet, some paper, my first scientific calculator. I used my graduation money the same way.

I still had little to no idea of how much money I would need for just everyday living expenses at college. I did remember a rather tense week-long period at *Wilderness Road* where I had overspent my budget and had to survive a week on nothing but peanut butter and jelly sandwiches. I used to laugh at the stories of starving actors in New York making soup out of sugar packets, water, and ketchup packets, but that week convinced me that if you were hungry enough, desperation can turn into inspiration.

I'd done so much with so little for so long... a week of peanut butter and jelly was *trivial*.

It's possible that I learned that lesson long before I worked in summer outdoor theatre.

Negotiations

Near the end of my senior year, I did some token support work for the prom committee; prom was managed by the popular and wealthy, and I was peripheral at best. My meager involvement reminded me it was time to start making decisions and begin the dance before the dance: negotiating a date for senior prom.

I had somehow carefully avoided thinking about it; with no current girlfriend at the time, I might be forced to go alone, or ask someone who didn't have a date and viewed me only as a source of a ticket; or even worse, take my sister along, which happened from time to time.

One day after one of the final *Charlie Brown '80* performances, I sat at Jerry's with Miss Caudill. It might have been the last time I did that; I don't specifically remember. It was just us; Cheryl Ann had been there, but left, I think. Jane was not there, having departed for Alice Loyd College in the tiny village of Pippa Passes, Kentucky two years earlier. We talked about graduation, and Berea, and Miss Caudill abruptly asked me about the prom.

"Who are you taking, Hoss?"

"Hah?" I said, not tracking the question.

"To the prom."

"Oh. I dunno. Meredith maybe."

"She has a date. What about Cheryl Ann?" I looked at her over my glasses. *No.*

"Ok, then, who?"

"Oh. Well. I dunno. Maybe I won't go. Could be proms are overrated."

Miss Caudill was shocked, and not at my diction. "You're such a la-dies' man, I'd be surprised if you didn't come up with someone." she said. "What about that girl from Hazard High you went with last year?"

That relationship hadn't survived the beginning of the football season. No car, no games, no interest in football...my school didn't even *have* a football team.

"Me? A ladies' man?"

"Sure, you're a– what did Edie say about you the other day– oh yes, she called you a *ladykiller.*" She grinned at me. Did she mention Lyn's mother on purpose, or just because Edie was her sister? "Did you know when she first saw you on stage, back when you played Grumio, she told me to keep an eye on you? She thought you were talented and special even then. She always did like you, you know."

"Huh. Ladykiller." I grunted. "It's more like *they* kill *me.*" *Lyn's mother liked me? Why hadn't I known about this?*

I wasn't exactly depressed, but I didn't think this conversation was cheering me up all that much. Discussing my love life like this, with a female teacher, would be considered sixteen ways from *wrong* today; but I thought nothing of it. Miss Caudill was fifteen or twenty years older than I and had never shown the least bit of interest in me or any other male student as far as I had ever been able to detect. She liked men, though; talked about her relationships (not in any sort of inappropriate detail) past and present; she just never found anyone who was a big enough draw to distract her from her Mission. Years later, she said, "It's a good thing I *wasn't* a pervert," she said. "You all would have been so *doomed,* considering how much time we spent together." Frankly, the thought of untoward behavior with her never crossed my mind. She fed me, and taught me, advised me and listened; she was as much my friend as a teacher, and a better friend would have been hard to find.

I also came to suspect that secretly, in her heart, she hoped that Lyn and I would get together. I think she believed it might save us both. Me, from loneliness and isolation and limited opportunities; Lyn, from the fate of her sister. Even then, I think I understood that in fact, in some sense, we *did* save each other. That was the truly magical thing about our relationship.

"I talked to Lynnie the other day," she said, piercing my reverie with her spoon by absentmindedly flipping it over and over in one hand like a cheerleader twirling a baton. I stared at it for a moment, struggling to make my brain shift gears. She accomplished this by plunging it into her Double Fudge Brownie swimming in melted ice cream. It was as if she was reading my mind.

"Really?" I finally asked, trying, and failing to be nonchalant. Knowing that Miss Caudill, if anyone, could tell. "What-what- d- did she–h- how is she?" *Damn.* I hadn't had that Jonathan Rosepettle-induced stutter in *years*.

She let it pass. "College is great, she says," she said. "She just started rehearsals for a new show, I think. School's out for summer for her, though."

Already? I thought. *College must end earlier than public school. We've still got two weeks to go, graduation, baccalaureate, and prom–*

Prom.

Miss Caudill sat there, smiling sweetly and tranquilly, not even a twinkle in her eye. I looked at her, and narrowed my eyes. I don't think I ever really appreciated how smart–no, not smart, she was plenty smart but that's not the right word– how *clever* Miss Caudill was.

"You know, when I was a freshman–" I started. "When I was a freshman I asked her to go to my senior prom. Well. Sort of. She kind of told me she would go. If I were to ask her."

"Did she?" she asked. Did I mention all directors are frustrated actors? My mind raced. Ever since my freshman year, I had carefully compartmentalized my feelings for Lyn on the assumption that I would, very likely, never *ever* see her again. My heart began pounding. What would it mean, what *could* it mean, if I had one more chance to see her... and tell her what I *really* felt about her?

"Yeah." I was astonished that all I could manage was a simple *yeah. Come on, brain, engage. Start transmitting data to the vocal cords. Go. Go.* "She said she would. She probably doesn't remember, though."

"Well then," said Miss Caudill, sliding a piece of paper to me. "Isn't it time you reminded her?"

The paper had Lyn's phone number on it, written out in Miss Caudill's slanted, loopy script.

I gaped at Miss Caudill, who was smiling more broadly now. I was, for a few moments, completely dumbfounded. *How much did you know and when did you know it* was a phrase completely familiar to me long before the associates of Ronald Reagan heard the query.

"I think perhaps you know too much about me," I finally said.

"Miss Caudill sees all, and knows all, child." she said, waving her hands like a magician above her plate.

"I believe you," I said.

Cheryl Caudill, director, teacher, friend, magician, had pulled another miracle out of her tiny, overstuffed maroon leather purse. I always did feel somewhat out of my league when I talked to her.

I laughed as I pocketed the number and changed the subject. Miss Caudill, amazingly, returned to her dessert and allowed me to redirect the conversation to other topics, such as the new TV show called *The Dukes of Hazzard*, which undoubtedly would lead the good citizens of Our Fair City to seek, and find, a way to exploit the extra attention directed at them.

To this day I still have to explain to anyone who finds out that I'm from the Hazard area that Hazard, Kentucky is not the town portrayed in the TV show, which is ostensibly set in a part of Georgia that looks remarkably like southern California. Although, in a perverse example of life imitating art, our mayor took to wearing an all-white suit on special occasions and driving a white convertible Lincoln. And every year during the annual Black Gold (coal) festival, the aging stars of the show appear to be grand masters of the parade downtown, a spectacle that I am both proud and ashamed to admit I have never seen.

It's amazing how sometimes your mouth can carry on a complete and coherent conversation with someone while you have a discussion raging with yourself inside your head about entirely unrelated matters.

Starry Night

So.

I called Lyn and asked her to the prom.

Just like that.

It's odd; as I write this, I remember lots of seemingly insignificant conversations, and can construct other ones from context and fill in the blanks by talking to people. But I don't remember this actual conversation, or what she said. It must have happened somehow, because she showed up.

She was 21 at the time, and I was 17 (just turned). She was a junior in college. She arrived driving her sister Teri's world-worn Volkswagen Beetle, which suited her just fine. I opened the door for her and helped her out. Apparently I had grown a bit. I was nearly half a head taller than she. When we met we were pretty nearly the same height.

"You've grown," She said. *You've shrunk,* I started to say, stupidly, but decided a dumb joke wasn't the best opening line. She gave me a quick hug and clutched my arm as we went in the house.

She said hello to the folks, and I put on the jacket to my dark brown suit–sort of a burnt umber thing, much more sedate than the purple-and-pink disco-inspired thing I'd worn the year before, with a girl I had met in a play competition. Lyn *beamed* at me. I gave her a corsage.

I must have gotten one somewhere, or someone obtained it for me. It was in a little clear plastic box. Other than pinning it to her dress, I have absolutely no memory of how it found its way to my hands. It might have been magic for all I know, and it probably was. I found the receipt later, but still didn't remember obtaining it. Maybe someone picked it up for me because I wouldn't have had the faintest *clue* about how to make a selection. It might have been Jane. I should ask her about that sometime.

My father, who later became an insufferable flirt after my mother died some years after these events, stood wide-eyed and silent, but smiling. I was glad he'd put on a t-shirt instead of being in his usual shirtless state. My mother told me to "be keerful," and tried to send multiple messages with that short phrase and succeeded.

Lyn was wearing a pale blue dress, modest by today's standards, but it revealed and flattered her figure. She was slimmer than when she was in high school, but not skinny. College agreed with her. Her hair was up, very curly, and tied together with a bow. Shoes with straps. A little purse. Red lipstick, not too bright. I remember noticing for the first time that she had a beautiful neck; I recall distinctly forcing myself to stop staring at her neck because it would seem as if I were not paying attention to her face. She slipped her arm into mine smoothly as we started to leave, doing so in such a way that my parents and sisters could see she wanted to be my date. As if we'd rehearsed it, some dozens of times.

I couldn't yet drive although I'd passed Driver's Ed with an A–I had had no opportunity to take the driver's test yet– so she drove. I didn't care. I barely spoke to her until we were in the car, trundling down the uneven ditches in the driveway scraped from the hillside of my parent's home.

"Thanks for this," I said.

"Thank *you*," she said. "It's an honor to accept your invitation."

I didn't know what to say to that, so we filled the time driving to the school with chitchat. I asked about college. She was majoring in theatre arts, of course. She asked about *my* college. I explained I had been accepted at Berea, and I was working at *Wilderness Road* again.

"I know," she said. "Aunt Cheryl told me."

I finally remembered to tell her she looked lovely, and crunched up in the front seat of a creaky Volkswagen, on a hot spring night in Eastern Kentucky, sputtering down the road on a little planet orbiting a nondescript star near the edge of the Orion Spur of the Milky Way Galaxy, I decided that I was pretty lucky that one of the jewels of the sky had allowed one of their number to take a short trip down to the earth to visit with me.

We talked mostly about the three shows (just *three?)* we'd worked on together when she was a senior and I was a freshman; *Shrew, Oh Dad,* and *Charlie Brown.* They were good memories, and we plucked them from the memory tree and found they still tasted good.

We arrived at the dance. It was held in the study hall, which had been draped with colored paper and mirrored balls and crepe paper. The room number, 111, was covered with decorations, but we both knew it was there. A DJ surrounded by sound equipment inhabited the stage area where we had done *Shrew.* Giant speakers sat on the floor on either side of the DJ.

We showed our tickets, and stepped inside. I looked at the ceiling. The water stains were still there. I pointed these out to Lyn, who laughed, remembering the plumber story. I thought it ironic that the room where I had first really worked with Lyn, more than likely during a *Shrew* rehearsal, was the same room where she had finally conceded to go with me on a date.

That's karmic, too.

As we entered the dance I felt the burning gaze of my classmates looking at me from various directions. Some of them knew who Lyn was– some of them had had crushes on her too; there was, after all, an entire *fleet* of boys who doted on her when she was a senior– but most didn't. She was obviously older, more mature, and she was *radiant.* And, best of all, she was with *me.* She clung to me, as if warning the other boys that there would be no accepting of invitations to dance, no tapping on the shoulder.

Lyn said hello to some of her former teachers, some of whom beamed, some of whom appeared startled to see her here. Miss Caudill was there, smiling.

"You make a wonderful couple," she said. "Edie always said so."

"I've always thought so too," said Lyn. *Me too,* I thought, unable to convince my vocal cords to participate in the conversation.

I smiled, she began to walk, and I, concentrating, willed my legs to move. It took a couple of attempts but eventually, they responded, if only for the need to keep up with Lyn. We stood in front of a backdrop and had our picture taken. I looked like I was about to explode with pride. She ... she was *amazing.*

All my teachers and friends looked at me incredulously. A few, like Cheryl Ann, had known this was in the works. Cheryl Ann smiled at me, and *winked.* I hadn't known she *could* wink. I strolled along, ignoring most of the stares, looking at Lyn. *Are they dating? Who's that girl?* I heard someone whisper, a little too loudly. *How the heck did he arrange that?*

If I had known, I would have told them.

A photographer from the yearbook came by, snapping pictures. Through the internal politics that governs school yearbooks, somehow no pictures of Lyn or me made it into the prom pages (*pages and pages)* of the yearbook.

On the other hand, I wrote the picture captions for what pictures *did* get published, and there are some pretty subtle things going on *there*, I can tell you. *This is Barry. He is holding a cup,* one read. *Anna looks as if she's somewhere else,* said another. *Terry is having some fun now. Tonya is on the verge of dancing. Justin is looking around for his date.*

We got a little autograph book, and a pencil. We got a little commemorative ticket. Somewhere crushed in my pocket was the receipt for the corsage.

We danced. Slow dance, fast dance, slow dance alternated slowly through the evening. We drank punch, ate a few snacks. Right now, as I write this, I realized for the first time after all these years we never ate dinner. It never occurred to me, and she never mentioned it.

Alan Moore punched me in the shoulder as he drifted by with his date, Tammy. *Wow*, he mouthed silently. *I know, I know*, I replied in kind. Chris Peterson asked to be introduced. I did, and he blushed, his scalp showing through his thin blond hair.

"Who do we have here, Jeff?" he said.

"Chris, let me introduce you to Lyn, the most talented person I've ever met," I said. She smiled sweetly and shook his hand, which only intensified his blushing.

"Chris's the only guy I ever met that blushes more than I do," I said, grinning. "That's saying a *lot*." He rolled his eyes and said a few more words, and departed.

"He's nice," she said.

"One of the good ones," I replied. "I used to tease him that we could solve the energy crisis by hooking up his head to a steam generator."

"If there was money to be made doing that," said Lyn, "you could pick up some pocket change yourself." Grinning as she said it. Of course, I blushed. Again.

I introduced her to Tammy and Alan. Alan bowed low and kissed her hand. Lyn actually *giggled* at this, and I said, "All right, all right," and waved him off, silly grin on his face as Tammy towed him away. Alan had been one of the fleet of young admirers of Lyn in my freshman class. *Gotta remember that hand-kissing deal,* I thought.

Eventually we found ourselves sitting at a table, alone, far enough from the band we could hear each other speak.

"Lyn," I began. I felt like a giant was crushing my chest. "I've missed you."

"I've missed you too. You've grown up so much."

So much implied *not enough* to me although she didn't mean it that way. I smiled. I felt the same as I had three years ago, like a little kid basking in the glow of the sun. "You're beautiful tonight," I said, for the third or fourth time.

"Thanks," she said.

"You didn't– have to do this," I said.

"No, I didn't," she replied matter-of-factly. "I *wanted* to. I owe you so much."

She owed *me?* What could she possibly owe *me?*

"It means a lot to me, that you'd come all this way," I said.

"It was nothing. I would have driven farther. " She smiled again. I didn't think it was possible, but she was even prettier than she had been in high school. I hoped college life had the same effect on me as it did on her.

She told me later she never went back to Hazard after the prom. I was the only thing that could have lured her there, and it had worked–once.

A couple more people wandered by. One or two teachers passed by. Mr. "Popcorn Brain" Carpenter regarded us from a distance. Lyn tossed some daggers his way, as if to say, *I dare you to come over here.*

He didn't. He did manage to toss a wink at me when Lyn wasn't looking. I smiled back at him.

We sat in silence for a time. I thought I should say *something* more, but didn't know where to begin, or more importantly, how to end. Finally Lyn spoke.

"Jeff." she said, taking my hands. "Jeffery. For a while there, when I was a senior–" she stopped, gathering her thoughts. A deep breath. A decision flitted across her face. "For a while, you were my only friend. My *best* friend. You made me feel like I was–I was *special* and *interesting* and *talented...*"

"You're all that, and more," I said. "You know how I felt about you." *How I feel about you.*

"Yes," she said. "It's too bad we're not the same age."

We're closer to the same age now than we were then, I thought, but didn't speak. Her comment didn't seem like an invitation to me. Or maybe it was. "Yes. It is. Or at least closer to the same age."

It was the longest conversation I'd had with her in three years. Already my heart was pounding, my head felt light. Was something in the punch? Was it the pounding of the music? I hadn't felt this way in *years*.

Maybe *ever*.

"Let's dance some more," she said.

"Ok," I said. If she had suggested we dunk our heads in the punch bowl, I would have reacted in exactly the same way. We moved to a fast beat. I wasn't much of a dancer, but it didn't seem to matter to her. I did the "robot," which was popular briefly, for about seventeen days in 1980 due to some dumb TV show. She smiled and laughed and clapped. Another slow dance came, and I held her tightly, closer than before. Somehow I managed not to step on her toes, although that is probably more a testament to her skills than mine. She *was* trained in dance, after all. I smelled her hair; she was, of course, wearing *that* perfume. I never told her it was my favorite. I never knew what it was called. If I had, I would have bought some for her.

We finally collapsed into our seats, exhausted.

"Waiter!" I called to a passing teacher. "More wine here! And none of that cheap swill you serve the tourists!"

Lyn chuckled at this. Each time she laughed it was like pixie dust had been sprinkled on me; I could easily become addicted to it. Or start flying around the room.

Eventually, the silly jokes subsided, and we talked about old times, and how much we enjoyed them. We carefully avoided the present. I didn't even let my self *think* about the future, let alone discuss it.

"Jeff," she asked during a break between sets, "are you *happy*? I mean, here in Hazard?"

I was confused because I wasn't sure where this was leading.

"I'm pretty happy, I guess." I smiled at her. *I'm happier now that you're here again.*

"Are you planning on staying here?"

"In Hazard?" I asked. "No."

"What does your family think about that?"

I looked at her carefully. What was she driving at? "They've known I'm leaving Hazard for years," I replied. "My mother's not yet convinced that I'll never come back except to visit."

"This is the first time I've been back since graduation," she said. I raised my eyebrows at this. "I think you're just about the only reason I could think of for coming back."

I looked at her, trying to figure out what she was trying to communicate.

"Why *did* you agree to go to the prom with me, Lyn?" I asked. "You didn't have to, you know."

She regarded me carefully before answering. "It was such a simple decision," she replied, finally. "You supported me unconditionally throughout that ... difficult year for me, and I thought...it would be the least I could do to give something back to you." Still the look of something unsaid crossed her eyes. "You have a place all set at Berea? And you can pay for what you need, and get a foot in the door?"

"There's no tuition at Berea, remember?" She suddenly looked relieved, and nodded. "As for the other expenses, I'll save up some money from *Wilderness Road* this summer, and work on campus during the fall."

"That's good."

It dawned on me that she was concerned that I might not escape Hazard, having no ready-made place to go as she had.

I don't know what she might have done or said if I had said I couldn't leave on my own.

Ever since I knew her, there had always been something flitting behind her eyes, some unspoken secret that I wasn't privy to, that made me feel as if she wanted to tell me something but couldn't for some reason. My ears filled with a roaring noise. What could it be, what was so terrible or difficult about her life that she didn't want to mention it? In all likelihood I would never see her again. If I was going to find out, it was now or never.

"Lyn," I said, my voice suddenly lacking power enough to be heard. I swallowed and tried again while she waited patiently. "Lyn, why was it that you came to Hazard in the first place? Was it really that you were just wanting to be a student of ... Miss Caudill?" I had nearly said *Cheryl* but old habits die hard.

"It's not something I talk about much," she said, finally acknowledging there *was* a secret to be told. "But I think I can tell you now."

She told me of her wayward sister, whom she loved so much, and the trials her sister dragged her family through. She told me about her sister's young husband, and the time he practically assaulted her, and how Cheryl had helped her escape.

"Cheryl seems to always be helping someone escape," I said, thinking of the students who were trapped, one way or another, by circumstance, family, low expectations, and earned their freedom on the stage in room 111.

"That's not really the worst part," Lyn said. "At one point, after I moved to Hazard, I gave up hope of ever really being happy, or finding my own way in the world. I thought no one really loved me even though that wasn't true. I couldn't see it."

I waited, and listened. She sat there regarding me. "I had just about given up ever having a true friend, you know. Until I met you."

A few songs later, some of the class began to drift out of the door, but Lyn and I remained, talking. I stared at her intently, hoping to memorize every moment, and it seemed she stared just as intently back at me. Hours must have passed, but from our perspective, it only felt like a few fleeting minutes. Some of the decorations were being ripped down as souvenirs (also traditional), and I snagged a couple of silver cardboard stars for Lyn and me.

The prom's theme was *Stairway to Heaven*.

It was almost astronomical.

When I returned she pushed my souvenir autograph pad to me. "Read it later," she said. I tucked it into my pocket.

Eventually the room nearly emptied, and I said, reluctantly, "I guess we should go."

"Yeah," she said. "I guess."

Although there was hardly any one there to see it, she walked out still holding my arm as we had arrived.

It was dark outside. I looked upward at the sky framed by the ridge-lines surrounding our school. The velvet blackness of the sky, spangled with the light of distant suns, was softened by the ever-present humidity of springtime in Kentucky.

"Star light," I said. She looked at me. "Star bright, first stars I see to-night. I wish I may, I think I might, have gotten the wish I wished to-night." She grinned and I couldn't help myself–I laughed out loud, a natural laugh that took the chill out of the cooling night air. She knew that I wasn't laughing at her, or at my own cleverness. It was a simple laugh of joy.

"Twinkle, Twinkle little star, how I wonder what you are," she said. Her voice floated upward to nestle in the trees. "Up above the world so high, like a diamond in the sky." She could even make *nursery rhymes* interesting. Miss Caudill said good actors could read phone books and make them sound good. In Lyn's case I believed it.

"My version's different," I said, leaning on her sister's car. "Twinkle, twinkle, little star," I began. "I know exactly what you are. Hydrogen fusing in the sky, no more need to wonder why." She shook her head, smiling. *Such a nerd.*

In the car, we sat and talked before she started the engine. I brushed coal dust from the car off my sleeve.

"You know," she said. "You never told me *why* you liked astronomy and science."

"You must not want to go home," I said. "Don't get me started."

"No, seriously, I want to know," she said. I raised my eyebrows. I'd been down this road before. Sometimes girls went down this trail and didn't make the return trip. I looked at her again. She nodded vigorously.

I looked out the window, but the lights from the parking lot combined with reflections in the glass prevented me from seeing any stars. "I tell everyone it's because I got this great little book in the third grade called '*Fun With Astronomy*,'" I said.

"That's not the real reason?"

"No. Not really. Maybe at first. It's kind of a long answer."

"I'm not in a hurry. Tell."

"Astronomy is the oldest, and the most romantic of the sciences." *Romantic?* her eyes said. I nodded. "What do you know about astronomy?" I asked.

"Not much," she admitted. She looked genuinely interested.

"It's primarily the study of the universe. Lesson one: the universe is *big*, Lyn." I said. "Mind-numbingly big. Almost too big to comprehend."

"I thought it was infinite," she said. Some of the stragglers walked by. I noted chaperones getting in cars, preparing to leave.

"There's a limit to what we can *see*. The nearest star in the sky, at the speed of light, is four *years* away. Between here, and there, there's a vast expanse of ...*nothing*. Beyond that, we live in a galaxy–"

"I've heard of galaxies. Seen pictures," she said. "Big swarms of stars, swirling around like a pinwheel."

"Exactly so. And galaxies are *huge*. They are 100,000 light years wide, and may contain 100 billion stars. And it gets even more spooky."

"How so?"

"There are more galaxies in the universe than stars in our galaxy," I said. "That means something like 100 billion times 100 billion stars in the universe, at a rough estimate," I said. "There are more stars in the universe than grains of sand on all the beaches of the earth, combined." I paused to let this sink in. She gazed at me thoughtfully.

"This is all very interesting," she said. "How do you know all this?"

"Reading," I said. "I read a *lot.*"

"I bet," she said. "But you haven't answered the question yet. So what? Why do you care?"

"Well, someone once said, it's an awful lot of wasted real estate, just for us."

She smiled.

"But that's the point, don't you see?"

She didn't see.

"In all that vastness, through a universe so large it boggles your imagination, there are only a few little flecks, located in an out of the way planet, in an ordinary galaxy, that can wonder *why we are here.*" I looked at the window, fogging up from my breath, and thought, *She's still listening. Incredible.* "You think Devitt H. Caudill High School is small, and provincial. Now you live in Louisville again, in a larger world with more options and more experiences than we can have here. Cheryl worked so hard at expanding our horizons, giving us experiences that none of us might ever have had. There are dozens of things I had never experienced before I met her." *Before I met you.*

"Especially your freshman year."

"Especially then. Who would know that better than you?"

She nodded. "That was quite a year."

"It certainly was that," I said. "For some of us, limited opportunity here means we'll leave for the big city," I continued. "For some of my classmates, *this–*" I said, waving my arm at the darkening building–"*this* is their whole world. And it always will be. And that's O.K. You can be a good person and have a happy and productive life like that. But I can't," I continued.

"I think the whole *Earth* is provincial. We're *all* just local yokels, barely getting our feet wet in the galactic pool. North and South...city and country...black and white...democratic and communist, all those things, all so... *local.*"

I paused and looked at her directly in the eye. "I feel..." I began. *I feel lots of things.* "I feel...*obligated* to study the universe," I concluded. "Just because I *can.* It needs doing."

She looked at me for a while, not speaking. I could see the cogs turning behind those blue eyes. She smiled. "You never wanted to be an actor, did you? It was just a ticket out the door for you."

"I *love* acting. I may be an actor yet. I'm going to do both for a while, and see what happens. There are so *many* things I want to do it'll take me years to cross them all off the list. *You,* on the other hand, never had any doubts about where you were going."

"That's true," she admitted. "I am a child of the stage." She looked at our hands, which, somehow, had wound up together. "You never lacked for ambition. I'm sure you'll make a great astronomer, or a great actor, or a great *something* that hasn't been invented yet." Discussing my future like this brought up truths I didn't want to contemplate just yet.

"There's one more thing."

"Yes?"

OK old son, here comes the punch line. Don't screw it up. "In all the universe," I said, taking a deep breath, "in all the worlds that exist, all the stars and planets and nebulae and galaxies, there's only one person that exists that is uniquely *you.* With *your* mind. Your *heart.* Your *soul.* It's ...*astronomically* lucky that I should know you. But here you are."

"Here *we* are."

"Yes. Here we are."

Time passed. Starlight hundreds and thousands of years old winnowed its way through the earth's atmosphere, and fell upon her face, and from there came to my eyes. She regarded me carefully.

"Only you could turn an astronomy lesson into a romantic speech," she said. "If it had been anyone else trying to tell me about that, I would have called it hokey," she smiled, though. "But it was very interesting, and sweet."

"I'm hopeless. Pathetic, really. "

"Incurable."

"Doomed to a life of rambling romantic speeches."

"I believe you," she said, matter-of-factly, but with an impish grin.

Then she started the car, and we rolled down the windows to let the humidity out. Soon we were winding our way along Ky. State Route 7, heading toward Viper and Maces Creek.

"You never told me how you got started in drama," I said.

"I did some made-up plays when I was a kid," she replied as we drove down the winding road. "Then I saw Aunt Cheryl's students do a play, and decided I could do that too. I read *The Last Flower* for her."

I had seen her perform *The Last Flower* as an example of how to do dramatic readings for the underclassmen. She was good at it.

"Did she like it?" I asked.

"She cried," said Lyn, smiling at the memory. I nodded. I could see Miss Caudill crying over Lyn's performance. It was a story about the end of the world, after all. "I knew then that acting is all I ever wanted to do."

"Do you remember the story?"

"Every word."

"Tell it to me."

"World War twelve," she began without hesitation, "brought about, as everyone knows, the final collapse of civilization..."

She knew the whole thing, and told it like she'd been rehearsing it earlier in the day. While she spoke, her eyes looked off in the distance through the windshield, her body automatically steering the car and driving, her mind alternating between dispassionately observing the rise and fall of civilizations and recognizing the cruelty of the repetitiveness of history.

She finished and I could see just a hint of a tear in her eye, as she blinked. It is a powerful story and a powerful memory for her.

"You *are* good at this stuff, you know." I stared at her as she turned her head, briefly, to see me sitting there, just glad to be there with her.

She smiled, and I saw her eyes shift back and forth as she looked at my eyes. First one, then the other, then back to the road.

The miles rolled by too quickly. Mere moments passed where sometimes it seemed hours would crawl by on a bus. *You're wasting time. Say something. There's only a few minutes left, fool. Speak. Speak.*

"I had a great time. Really great," I said, finally. *You're jabbering,* I thought.

"I hope it was everything you hoped for."

"It was," I said, "as soon as I got in the car with you. The prom itself–that was just a side effect."

When we got to my house, lurching up the short but steep driveway we both nearly bounced out of our seats and looked at each other, nearly losing it from the silliness of being all dressed up in a straining Volkswagen crawling up a mountainside. I glanced out the front window, and directly ahead we could see the gap in the trees leading to my parent's house, and between the trees I saw stars, calling me. Calling *us.* I wondered if we would just keep on driving upward, into the sky, like some modernized version of *Chitty Chitty Bang Bang.*

We somehow reached the top, and I was forced to note the car's wheels still remained on the ground. We got out but she didn't come inside. The house was dark, but I suspected my mother at least would be sitting in the living room, most likely sleeping (and snoring) sitting up. The porch light was on. The hazy humid air made our clothes, damp from dancing and the cool night air, cling to us.

"I have to take my sister's car back tonight," she said.

"Oh. Yeah," I said. "Sure. Thanks. Have a safe trip home. You'll be driving pretty late."

"Don't mention it. It was the least I could do. I'd gladly do it again," she said. *I'd set up another prom just so you could,* I thought.

"I think," I said, looking at my feet, "I may be one of the luckiest guys on the planet. And coming from me, you should know– that's not a trivial compliment."

She smiled again. Took my hands in hers. She looked up the mountainside, at the stars. "It's a literal stairway to heaven," she said.

"They're the same everywhere, you know," I said. "The same ones are over Louisville. Look up at the sky from time to time, and when you do, there's a good chance I'm looking up too, and thinking about you," I said. I let my gaze fall downward until it met her eyes, which were still looking upward at the stars. *Electric blue*, I thought. *Just like a star.* She felt my eyes on her and lowered her eyes to meet mine.

"I won't ever look up at the stars and see just stars ever again," she said.

I couldn't speak. I decided to attempt nodding, and managed to execute one, just one. I saw her mouth open, and draw in a breath, and hold it ever so briefly.

"You're the most intelligent and sensitive man I've ever met," she said suddenly. *Man.* "Passionate. And talented–you're *brilliant*–and caring, creative, fascinating, loving, sincere, and honest." I stood *aghast.* I'd never heard anything like that from *anyone* before. Especially *her.* "It has been such an *honor* knowing you, working with you, and being your friend... and knowing that my being here was so important to you. It means more to me than you can ever know. I think... it might have even been more even important to me than it was to you."

I could hardly fathom how that was possible. As a matter of fact, I still can't.

"I felt so *alone*, Jeff. I'd had some very difficult times in high school. It was so bittersweet. Some of the happiest and most painful memories I have are from Devitt. But there was one person who I could always depend on to support me, no matter what. I wish I could help you understand how important that was to me."

There were tears present. For a wonder, they weren't mine.

Her hands held mine still. She looked at our hands.

"My freshman year," I said, "was *intense.* You don't even know how many things happened to me that year for the first time. I was ... nearly overwhelmed by all of it. And through all of it, you were there, always watching out for me, encouraging me, being my friend... if it hadn't been for you, my life would have been completely different. And not for the better. You– you–"

She pulled me close, and kissed me. For only the second time since I knew her.

I held her, and kissed her back.

When we parted, I had tears in *my* eyes. She wiped them away. I couldn't speak. I couldn't *breathe.* I wanted to, to find *something* to say, to make her stay right there, and never go away again. There were a hundred reasons she should leave, and only one reason to stay. I had lots of words. Words were my friend, had given me success, a small measure of fame, a job, and purpose. I had a dozen memorized scripts to call upon. Hundreds of books. Dictionaries and encyclopedias, novels and texts. I called on them to *help me.* None of them came to my bidding–not even one word. She walked slowly away, letting her hand slide down my arm, across my hand, down my fingers, and then

I wonder if she is facing the same sort of decision I am, I thought. *This might just be the last chance you ever have to tell her how you feel, to offer to go with her to Louisville, to show her you could be a great companion.*

It doesn't matter if I've already been admitted to Berea. I could work for a year or two, save some money. If I had an income, then she wouldn't have to feel guilty about supporting such a young boyfriend.

But even if I talk her into it, what then? She'll be constantly having to explain who the young kid is hanging around all the time.

And what if we had a kid? She'd have to drop out of school to raise it. And she would do it too, even if I offered to stay home and take care of a baby. It would effectively end her acting career.

Maybe for years. Maybe forever.

It's tragic, though. Because I do love her. I DO.

I wonder if she knows.

I hope she does.

I have to let her go, right now.

Or else I might wind up hurting my best friend.

It's so obvious he's in love with me, she thought. *I could offer to take him with me to Louisville. I bet he'd go. But even now, he's still so young compared to me...only 17!*

I've never met anyone who obviously loves me like he does. He practically worships the ground I walk on. And who appreciates me for myself, no questions asked. I may never meet anyone like that again. Maybe I should take a chance...

I'm older. Supposedly more mature. If I were to pursue this relationship beyond tonight, we'd have all sorts of problems. Not the least of which are legal in nature. Can a 21-year old even date a 17 year old?

Probably not.

I love my sister. But I'm not *her. I couldn't put him in that situation. I couldn't bear to hurt him. I do love him. I DO. And because I do, I have to do the right thing. I cannot be this good to myself at the expense of his education and emotional maturity.*

If we started dating he'd never finish college.

I have to turn and walk away. Right now.

Or else I might wind up hurting my best friend.

...we were no longer holding hands.

Everything I could have said, I realized, had already been said three years ago. There were no new arguments in my arsenal, no matter how desperately I searched to find one. The old ones were still there; and they were more true now than before. I was still young enough to be too young, and old enough to know what those few orbits had cost me.

She got in the car. I waved. She waved. She started the engine, turned the car around, and left. I think at some point I must have started breathing again, because I am still here.

I stood there, until the glow of the lights of her car disappeared between the trunks of the trees farther down the hollow. Until the sound of her sister's wheezing little VW couldn't be heard echoing in the canyonlike walls of the hills. Until I could no longer feel the tingling of my lips from where she had kissed me.

For some reason, an image of what Cheryl Ann would say, rolling her eyes, came unbidden. *Sooo melodramatic, Jeff. You're such a loser, so full of yourself. Get a life.*

Perhaps I was full of myself, overly dramatic, not as passionate as I liked to think I was. But I didn't care. I had no regrets. I'd do it all again, and end it the same way, rather than not have had the short time we did share. I only knew her seven months of my freshman year, and one date after that. *'Tis better to have loved and lost, than never to have loved at all.*

As I've said before, it's not such a cliché when it actually happens to *you.*

I put my hands in my pockets. There was the little autograph book Lyn had signed. I opened it. I stood there under the porch light, looking at it as unidentified insects swirled over my head, searching for something, they knew not what.

There were several pages with room for autographs. I had shared the booklet with others during the evening, but hadn't read any of the comments.

> *Jeff- So dreams do come true. Love you- CC.*

So she *did* know, all along.

> *Jeff- What can I say. I had fun and I had fun watching you have fun. Love, Cheryl Ann.*

Which was one of the nicest things she ever said to me. There were like five times she said something nice like that. That was one of them.

> *Jeff-A nice person. Don't forget me. Love, Meredith.*

So were you, Meredith. And I never did forget you.

Then there was the last page.

> *Jeffery-You've grown to be a real man. I'm so proud to know you and be your friend. This was a beautiful evening and I had a great time! Just remember, you can do ANYTHING. I honestly believe that. I'll never forget the time we spent to-gether. Love, Lynnie.*

Oddly, I didn't cry once she had left. I thought I would. I had cried so many other times contemplating what might have been. I had bawled like a baby, alone in my room after we separated during the end of my freshman year. It wasn't because it didn't hurt this time; it did. But this time, I knew it was coming, and knew that she had a life already, independent of me, and I was headed off to college myself.

In all likelihood, I would never see her again; nevertheless, we were *always* going to be friends. *Always. Forever.*

Forever is a long time. When an astronomer says *forever and always*, pay close attention. Something serious is happening.

The prom provided some closure and a last chance to get together, to be near her, which was incalculably valuable to me. But, I thought, my heart wasn't broken despite the beating it had taken just moments before; the world kept turning. The stars above twinkled, familiar and friendly. I had a friend, perhaps the best friend I had ever had, somewhere out there in the world who loved me for *me*, with no expectations or obligations. Knowing who I was, where I came from, where I was going, and still judged me worth knowing and loving. That was the gift she left me; confidence, a sense of self-worth, love, and *hope*. I hoped I left something valuable with her in return. If I could love someone as amazing as Lyn, and be lucky enough to have the love returned, then surely others would follow; someday, I'd find someone I loved as much, even *more* maybe, and who loved me back and wouldn't *ever* leave, always and forever, and I wouldn't be alone in the world, or lonely again.

I hoped, with all my heart and for her sake, Lyn could do the same.

I waved at the stars, and smiled, and tucked the booklet back into my pocket with the remains of my boutonnière and my receipt, and went in the house.

And Everything That Goes With It

Valedictorian was essentially between Tammy Wainwright, and Chris Peterson and me; all of us had straight-A's as far as I knew, so it was going to be up to some senior teacher to split us into order. We didn't have ties, as far as I knew. I think it was because they only had one stole with the word *Valedictorian* printed on it.

We were up for other awards, from the various academic departments, clubs, and so on. I knew either Cheryl Ann or I would get the drama award. The other, more than likely, would get the speech award, judging from past years' traditions.

Mrs. Hayword had to eventually break the tie on one award. With my first summer's earnings, I had bought a tiny portable Royal manual typewriter, and with it, I had typed my senior paper. I don't remember the topic. Whatever it was, I made typing errors (a friend once commented I was the fastest typist he'd ever seen, not counting all the backspacing and correcting I had to do) and fixed them with some newfangled paper tape correction gizmo. "Your paper looks like it has the measles," she wrote. "B-."

I hadn't gotten a B in a class– *ever*– but I knew my test scores would drag up the B- on the paper and make my grade an A in her senior English class, so I didn't worry. However, Tammy Wainwright had the same grade as me in that class, but her paper had gotten an A– so Tammy got the English award.

I did all right though. I had the highest GPA due to some mysterious B in each of their transcripts I never knew about, and trailing ever so slightly behind me was Tammy, followed by Chris. I got the math award, the science award, journalism and drama awards for the class. Today, these are hanging on a chain from my Hall of Fame award from my senior drama banquet. Cheryl Ann (Esprit d' Corps) said the trophy I designed was nearly as big as my head, but not quite, despite the fact trophy was two feet tall. *I don't know whether to love you or hate you,* she wrote in my senior yearbook. *Oh, all right, I guess I love you but honestly, there are times.*

During our senior year Cheryl Ann, Meredith and I decided we wanted to get a letter jacket like the athletes wore–only the principal wouldn't even let us buy a jacket in the school colors.

"The basketball parents would think there's some confusion about who actually *earned* a letter jacket," he said.

By then I had enough nerve to speak up for myself. But my judgment wasn't what it should have been.

"Well we actually *accomplished* something, so shouldn't we get the jackets *before* them?"

The look he gave me told me of my strategic error, and that ended the discussion.

What we did was spend some leftover fundraiser money and bought ourselves jackets *anyway*. Patches for the jackets came from our own pockets, and I used the remaining few dollars of my *Wilderness Road* money to buy a Thespian patch (four stars and a bar, for those of you who know what that means) and one with my name on the back surrounded by a bunch of bright yellow stars.

At graduation it was traditional for the valedictorian to write a speech. It was vetted–no school administration on Earth likes surprises, good or bad, Miss Caudill said– and it was traditional for the graduate to give roses, supplied by the school, to their mother. I was loaned a golden stole to wear over my graduation robes, marking me as VALEDICTORIAN. Actually they had to tell me to give it back; I hadn't realized it was a loaner until someone said they didn't have the budget to buy a new one every year.

Well of *course* they don't, I thought, when I returned it. It's only for being *valedictorian*, not as if I'd been captain of the basketball team or anything.

Graduation was at Leatherwood elementary school, which for some reason had a gymnasium and an honest-to-God *stage.* I wondered why we weren't bussed over *there* for plays and basketball; probably some behind-the-scenes political machination.

During the ceremony, Meredith, Cheryl Ann, and I along with a few others sang a couple of Barry Manilow songs. It's not a popular thing to say amongst the *young'uns* these days, especially for a guy, but I *like* Barry Manilow. His songs always choked me up. I guess guys have to pretend they don't like Barry so they won't get choked up and cry in public. I was a closet Manilow fan for years.

I don't really know why I was selected for that; I wasn't exactly American Idol audition material. Probably they needed a male voice and I had an aversion to saying no to *anything* that put me on a stage. We also sang *The Impossible Dream* from *Man of La Mancha.* That was primarily for Miss Caudill, as we all knew. She sobbed openly in the audience as we sang. I just about cried myself.

Someone offered a protracted prayer, still legal in those days.

Then I gave my speech. Mrs. Hayword had read it and handed it back to me unchanged a couple of days ago. It couldn't be too long; too technical or too silly. I had decided to go with sentimental. I had typed it on my Royal portable. It looked like it had measles. She said it didn't matter. For the first time since I had met her, she had no comment about the content of what I wrote.

They say these are the best years of our lives, I said. I would have said that myself a couple of months ago; now I had a different outlook on life. *I disagree. If this is the best you'll ever have, you'll lead a pretty depressing life. Is everything going to be downhill from here? How sad!*

I looked down at the audience of students in caps and gowns. Meredith was crying already. She was almost as sentimental as I was. It was one of the reasons I liked her.

I think we should look at high school as the opportunity to go even farther than ever before. It's not an end. It's a beginning. That may be a cliché, but that doesn't mean it can't be true. Keep your options open, graduates.

My mother clutched her purse tightly, unsure why I'd asked her to sit so close to the stage.

There are people who will tell you that you can't accomplish much because of who you are, or where you're from. Don't you listen to them! Don't fall into the trap of claiming you can't do this, or can't do that... people say "I can't do math," or "I can't draw," or "I'm no good at sports," and it becomes a little story they tell themselves so often they start to believe it. Or you might think you can't be successful because some schools are bigger or better in some way. I learned lots of things at Colonel Devitt H. Caudill Memorial High School. Every sentence needs a verb–verbs are our friends. The interior angles of a triangle add up to 180 degrees. Never turn your back to an audience if you can help it. Don't aim the rocket at the spectators when you launch it. Turn off the water carefully when the fish tank is overflowing. Never leave a hydrogen generator running in a lab without a fume hood.

Chuckles all around, and from Mrs. Williams especially.

But one thing I have learned above all else. I learned that with hard work, dedication and purpose, you can accomplish anything. And that lesson is more important than any lesson from any book or any lecture or any notes on a chalkboard. Everyone here helped me learn that, but I never figured it out until I took drama.

I grew up in drama class, in every way that matters. I learned about persistence, and vision, and having a Mission.

I started to finish, but noted that even Cheryl Ann, staunch defender of the truth and advocate for moderation in all things, especially my ego, was crying. I smiled at her, and she hid her face from me. "I thought I could tough it out," she said to me after the ceremony. "Good job."

I just want to say thank you to everyone who helped me. Miss Caudill, Mrs. Williams, Mrs. Hayword, and all of you: I appreciate it more than you will ever know. And good friends, past and present, who tolerated me and defended me and made my life here happy.

You may never see some of the people in this room again, for the rest of your lives. That's why it's important to remember your friends.

I said some other things. I looked for Miss Caudill, but for some reason couldn't see her.

And especially I want to say thank you to my mom, who trusted me and always supported whatever harebrained project I had gotten myself into. Thanks, Mom.

Then I gave the roses to my mom, who tried to talk but couldn't.

I leaned over the microphone one last time.

Love one another. Be good people. Have a happy life.

Then my mother started to cry, and I walked her back to her seat before returning to my own. I looked again, but still couldn't locate Miss Caudill. It's possible she had left the faculty area.

Names were called, diplomas handed out. Every graduate got polite applause or better. With only 77 in the graduating class, there's time to celebrate. We were done in an hour and a half.

On the stage, the superintendent, Kevin Caldwell, handed out diplomas. He had been my principal in elementary school just four short years ago. As I worked my way through the district, he had as well.

When he shook my hand, he said, "You get to walk out and get a diploma with your class this time."

I nodded, smiling. I could barely hear him over the applause. All the graduates and much of the audience were clapping. A small contingent of graduates was actually standing and cheering. Including Cheryl Ann and Meredith. The Boy Who Skipped 8th Grade made good on the bet the teachers made recommending me for the job, I guess.

We got our diplomas during the ceremony in those days. I even got a wallet-sized replica of the diploma to carry in my pocket, like an I.D. Carried that thing for years, until it became old and yellowed and brittle and fell apart.

I sought out Miss Caudill, located her outside the gym in the parking lot, and said some things I can't remember. I wish I could. I hope they were dramatic and kind, respectful, appreciative and honest. If you can't remember either, Miss Caudill, let's just pretend I said the right things, and you were happy, and so was I.

The next day, I was driven to Berea by my father (the last time he ever drove me to school) and the next chapter of my life began.

Synodicity

30 orbits later

The wheel of time turned as the players scattered and went their separate ways. From time to time I would glance across its diameter and converse with my past and future selves, questioning my motives, critiquing my decisions, reassuring myself as the occasion warranted. Life went on.

In Ptolemy's view of the universe the planets revolve about us on wheels mounted upon wheels, adjustments made to account for subtle differences in the observed orbits. The deferent of time relentlessly drags us forward despite the distracting epicycles of work and love and time. Just as in the real universe, Ptolemy's attempt to save the appearances of his model by matching it to reality occasionally brought the planets into alignment, temporarily aligning that which was normally torn apart by time and space.

In college, I married a girl who needed me. Her name was Laura, and once upon a time I loved her as much as a man needs to love a woman. I needed her as well. We lived a happy life for many years.

Then, as happens to people, things changed; we grew apart; eventually separated. We are in the process of raising two strapping young boys.

Eventually, I was able to see Lyn again.

Her marriage had already crumbled. Mine had just begun the process of disintegrating, although I wasn't fully aware of it yet.

I didn't teach to please or honor Miss Caudill; I just liked it. I made the decision while acting as a teaching assistant in an astronomy class. I did some plays– a *bunch* of plays, even wrote a musical comedy with a friend of mine. *Wilderness Road* closed permanently due to budget cuts at the state arts agency. I was an acting apprentice for a while, getting dance lessons and diction drills from a professional actress. Later on, I pounced on an opportunity to major in astronomy at the University of Arizona – I even got to use some giant telescopes, some in domes bigger than my parent's old house.

I haven't done plays in a long time. There's too much else to do. I spent some years exploring different careers; in college I worked part time as everything from a computer programmer, janitor, newspaper editor, teaching assistant, actor, to theatre shop apprentice. After graduation I taught high school for a while in Lexington, worked as a consultant for the state department of education, and became a project manager and logistics person for a national test development effort in California. Eventually I returned to the classroom because I missed the interaction with students, and the excitement in their eyes when they learned something new that changed their outlook on life.

Today my students use space probes to study distant black holes, and take pictures of sand dunes on the surface of Mars. We build sundials. They get art lessons on how to draw craters. They learn how to use a spreadsheet, and they know that doing a *real* experiment requires an independent variable, not just a nice poster and some downloaded stuff from the internet.

I still use the skills I learned from Miss Caudill. *Every day.*

I do presentations for science teachers. I like to think I'm pretty good at it. My senior year in high school, for my final speech, I gave a speech about how to give a speech. Miss Caudill still remembers it. She *hooted.*

I go back to visit the folks every year or two, whenever I accumulate enough frequent flyer miles or have a little extra money. It's not as often as I would like.

On our last trip, the entire central part of the town of Viper had been .... *erased,* like some real-world version of the *Hitchhiker's Guide to the Galaxy,* to make room for a new, four lane hyperspace bypass. I thought it was a shock when they closed my high school and consolidated it. Imagine what it's like to see a substantial part of your *home town* erased. The elementary school still exists, but has many additions beyond what I grew up with, including a new playground. Even Beetree Hollow, where Todd had unceremoniously run me off the road into a ditch, was *paved*. Now my father only lives a couple hundred feet from where the pavement ends. My mother died of ovarian cancer some years ago, but not before she met her grandchildren and got to hug them. I am thankful for that. I am thankful, in reflective moments, for a *phenomenal* number of things.

His driveway was much smoother when we drove the rental van up the hillside than when I trundled up the hill in a wheezing VW Beetle a lifetime ago.

A few months ago, I won a teaching award, and had to give a speech. The award was from the Amgen Corporation. They make pharmaceuticals. I was nominated by a friend and had to fill in some paperwork to be eligible. Six of us won awards from California, and we flew down to Thousand Oaks for the ceremony. It was the first time I ever got picked up by a chauffeur holding a little sign with my name on it. I wrote and rewrote the speech several times, but it kept coming back to Miss Caudill.

This is the relevant part of what I said.

> *The lesson I learned that enabled me to make the conceptual leap from reading about science to doing science was not in a science classroom. It was in a theatre—actually, just on a raised platform at one end of study hall in room 111.*
>
> *I had a teacher in high school who inspired me to become a teacher, and taught me that anything was possible with a sufficient application of hard work. That teacher was Cheryl Caudill, who took our small town high school theatre class from the back woods of Kentucky to a state championship in theatre and acting– multiple times. She helped me understand what it means to be a teacher. We worked hard– sometimes till midnight, and later, for weeks and months at a time to prepare for shows. We worked because we knew the payoff was that we would be good, and we would have accomplished something of which we could*

be proud. So we worked–and worked–and worked. And we learned many things. That it is important to finish what we start. And that we can do hard things, and things that are too easy are probably not worth doing. That's more important than the difference between upstage and downstage and who Hamlet's father was and ...what the third moon of Saturn is.

I know what a teacher is. A teacher's job ostensibly consists of grading papers, taking attendance, going to meetings, preparing students for standardized tests. But those are just hoops, waiting to be jumped through. A teacher's real job is to inspire students. Inspiring students, and making it possible that they can believe they are capable of great things, is job #1. Everything else –everything else– is secondary to that. An inspired student comes to school, doesn't get in trouble, tries to excel at everything just to keep the opportunities they hunger for alive.

If I were 1/10 of the teacher Miss Caudill was, my students would be in charge of Intel and Amgen and I could retire. Before it ever occurred to the state to try, Miss Caudill set the standards for us, and she tried like hell not to leave even one of us behind. She didn't leave me behind, I can tell you that.

She taught me what a teacher's real job was because she inspired me.

So I finally did a little detective work, and found Miss Caudill's number. I left messages; eventually she called me back. I told her about the awards, the grants, the kids sent off to college to be astronomers and engineers and actors and how we sent kids with an inflatable planetarium to teach astronomy in grade schools just as we had done plays for children all those years ago.

I mentioned to Cheryl my idea for this book, and she told Lyn.

Cheryl sent me one of those emails you send to your friends, and in it was a cc: list of *her* friends, and it included one name I thought I almost recognized: *Adelyn Anderson*. Cheryl gave me Lyn's email address indirectly, and you know, I wonder if it wasn't intentional, even after all these years. I wouldn't put it past her.

It was a long time before I decided to send Lyn a message. Eventually I did, when I needed to find Cheryl for scheduling a visit during our next trek "back East." I suppose I was just waiting for an excuse. Perhaps I was. Even so, Cheryl wasn't answering her phone. I told Laura about the email, and why I'd written to Lyn.

"Why didn't you just call?" she asked.

"I don't have a phone number," I replied. "Besides, I'm not sure what I would say."

"You're a silly goose," she said. "*Call.*"

I hadn't seen Lyn for something approaching 30 years.

What do you say to a person you loved, a person who changed your life so fundamentally, and with whom you departed on good terms? *How's it going? What've you been up to for the past 30 years? I loved you and here, let me introduce you to my wife.*

Some days later, Lyn wrote back. Cheryl was visiting her sister, Lyn's mother Edie. Lyn had been married, recently divorced. Three wonderful kids. Many plays, a nice house in some trees, and dogs. She writes plays, and they've all been produced. *Dozens* of them. She owns a theatre company, American Dream Theatre. I offered to build a web site for her. She offered to help with this book. We talked about Cheryl.

Cheryl kept teaching. She won many awards. One of the awards was for being in the Hall of Fame for teachers in Kentucky. There's a certain karma there, I think. She gave so many Hall of Fame awards herself. She finally got one of her own.

I spoke to Cheryl on the phone one day. She told me a *bunch* of stories, some of which I remember, some of which I never knew. She spoke of her Mission, and tilting at windmills, and being appreciated by at least one person. Turns out *I* was her person. One of them, at least. I never knew *that*, either.

"Lyn was your Dulcinea, you know," she said to me.

"Of course she was. I eventually considered her my *muse*. It was the only thing that helped me get over her leaving for Louisville. I knew she could be my muse even if she wasn't around me in person."

I asked her if she was disappointed that I didn't pursue acting professionally. She gave me the same answer I've given to my own students so many times. "I don't care what you do as long as you're happy," she said. "Still, you should know, you could have been– could *be* successful as an actor."

"I use what you taught me every day," I said. "It's like I'm on stage, every day, six hours a day, doing improv," I said.

"But are you *happy*?" she asked suddenly.

"You have no idea," I said. "I've fulfilled so many of my childhood dreams. I have sweet children who are fun to be around. I have a fulfilling job–that I *love*–and they actually pay me money to do it. "

"I know what you mean. It would be nice if it were more money, though."

I laughed. I gave up acting partly because it couldn't pay enough, consistently, to raise a family without tremendous sacrifice. In its place? *Teaching*, surely the road to fame and fortune. In Perry County, the largest employer in my high school days had been the school board, and teachers seemed well off compared to what I knew.

"I agree. If I had a way to pay the bills, I'd probably teach for free," I said. "I've gotten to use *space probes*, Miss Caudill. The only thing better would be going into space myself." I looked at her. "I wrote an astronomy textbook," I said. "I use it in my own class. I always wanted to be a writer. Among other things. I read so many books, I always hoped to find a story in me worth sharing. "

She looked at me. "You should write a book about the year we did *Shrew,*" she said. "I never had another year quite like that."

"Neither did I," I replied.

That's when I had to confess, I'd already started one. Or tried to. She encouraged me to take my flimsy outline and 40-odd pages of memories and turn it into a story, in the storyteller's tradition, with a voice, a plot, nice collection of antagonists and protagonists, and a climax, perhaps more than one, and a denouement.

"Don't let the facts get in the way of the truth," she said. "And don't telegraph the ending."

I allowed as how that would be a great idea, and I would let it soak for a while and see what developed.

We talked about this book, and its multiple purposes. I told her, theatre is ephemeral, insubstantial; you do a play and it's *gone*. But the influence of theatre on her life and my life is as real as the bricks and mortar that make up the walls of the building holding a stage within it. We discussed *Shrew* and school-teaching and No Child Left Behind and politics and presidents, administrators and Don Quixote. She's had the most triumphant and tragic experiences a person can have, and it's been a long road. I was motivated to start this work and to finish it, in large part, to honor her vision and to let her know, *Now no one will ever forget what you did for us*. She changed so many lives, and mine, in particular, for the better.

I know for a fact that there are other people who feel the same way, because they told me; Meredith, for example; Cheryl Ann, for another, and Lyn, for another.

Her life was never simple; her relationships, complex and always significant. Nevertheless she has always been, and remains, the inspiration for my professional life and a dear part of my personal life.

Every experienced teacher knows you can't truly, individually, reach every child. Your school's staff has a chance to do it collectively, perhaps, or not at all. But what Cheryl did, and what I try to do, is to let the kids know that we damn well gave it the *best* shot we could, and we never left *anyone* behind on purpose.

"I had an impossible dream," she told me. "I wanted to change Perry County so it could appreciate theatre. But one person can't change an entire culture. It's the very definition of an impossible dream," she said. "That's why it's *impossible*. It can't be done."

"I think you had more influence than you think you did."

"I sometimes wonder if it was worth it."

"It was worth it to *me*," I said. "All the *world's* a stage, Miss Caudill. All the men and women–"

"–merely players," she said, completing the classic line.

"Your stage is *bigger* than Perry County, Cheryl. You just never realized it." That might have been the first time I called her *Cheryl* instead of Miss Caudill.

 She and I sat there, in silence, as the carrier waves from our cell phones whisked back and forth through space.

"You know, Jeffery," she said suddenly, "Quixote thought that if he could make the world better for just one man, the Quest would have been worth it. Did I– " even over the crackly connection I could hear her gasp as she attempted to regain control of her voice. "did I make it *better* for you?"

"Cheryl," I said. "You *changed my life*. Without you I would have been an architect, a newspaper editor, an administrator in a school...who knows? I *might* have led a happy life. I might not have. But instead I've had the chance to do *amazing things.* Listen–I've taught *thousands* of students. Teachers from all over the country. They in turn have reached thousands more. I have a teacher support web site that is read by people all over the *planet.* If I hadn't met you, none of those things would have happened. Teachers want to have a taste of immortality by passing on their wisdom, and hope that it gets passed on to still others. Your influence has spread far *beyond* Perry County. Look at Lyn's plays. All over the country, and seen by thousands, and still growing. Meredith became a teacher to try to have the same kind of influence you did. Cheryl Ann helps people improve their lives every day as a counselor. You don't just get credit for us, you get credit for everyone we've ever taught or written or performed for."

"It's not what I set out to do," she said.

"When you teach a kid you never know how they're going to use what you taught them. Some lessons are bigger and more important than how to move downstage right. Or what the third moon of Saturn is, for that matter. Someone once said that 'no one believes a small group of dedicated people could change the world...indeed, it's the only thing that ever has.' You just changed a different world than you intended."

"Maybe you're right, " she admitted. "I'm glad I talked to you today."

Through some cosmic act of karmic balance, Lyn gave the speech supporting Cheryl at the Hall of Fame award ceremony. She said:

> *Hello and welcome. My name is Adelyn Anderson and I have been asked to speak today about Cheryl Caudill: Teacher, Director, Magic Maker, Mentor and my aunt. I am not surprised at all that she is receiving this award. It is so deserved. She is the type of person I'm sure this honor was conceived for.*
>
> *Theatre and kids: these are the two things that have always been in Cheryl's life, and because of this, it changed my life, and the lives of so many others.*

Aunt Cheryl came to town with some of her students who were competing in a speech competition at the state level. As I watched these students perform, with awe and respect, a little voice deep inside of me thought, "I can do that...and maybe even better." And Cheryl heard that voice.

She gave me a piece to read called "The Last Flower", which I'm certain has been heard by the people in this room more times than you care to remember. As well as Cheryl. Yet, when I finished, she had tears in her eyes. I had moved her, and it was amazing. Then she told me she thought, if I worked hard, that I could be good. Really good. From that moment on , my life was forever changed.

But did her advice stop there? No pat on the head and wish for luck from her. No, she took me to live with her in Hazard, and through hard work, and with the magic of Cheryl, my senior year, 1977, Devitt H. Caudill Memorial High School from Jeff, Kentucky won 1st place in the Kentucky High School Speech League's Drama competition for our production of Shakespeare's Taming of the Shrew, and I took home one of the Best Acting awards.

Perhaps one of Cheryl's greatest gifts is taking a kid in need, assessing that need, and whatever it takes, helping that kid achieve their potential. I have seen her do it countless times. They might need a ride home from rehearsal, to an extremely remote hollow, or an outfit for competition, or, maybe not the whole outfit, but just a rust colored blazer because not only did it fit the character but it was in the students color palette. Or, they might need a meal, or a safe place to be because of a family situation, they might need to do "The Tell Tale Heart" to release some of their inner demons, or Rosalie in "Oh, Dad, Poor Dad..." to release some of their promiscuity, they might need a haircut or to stand up straight or just for someone to tell them that with work, they could be good. Really good. Cheryl has been doing all of this and more for close to 40 years.

And she has done it all no matter what. She has done it regardless of parents who may have been misguided by drugs or alcohol or just plain ignorance, she has done it while being the care giver for her terminally ill brother until his passing…and when she couldn't walk because of knee injuries, she got a wheel chair and wheeled herself in and created her magic and helped her children.

A colleague recently paid me one of the greatest complements I have ever received: he told me that I have the ability to "spin straw into gold." And it's all because of Cheryl Caudill: my teacher, my director, my magic maker, my mentor, my aunt. And I know that I speak for all of her students, through all of the years… having Cheryl Caudill in my life, has been … amazing.

I wish I could have been there to say a few words, or just clap enthusiastically. I had to settle for just crying, quietly, to myself when I read it. I imagine listening to that must have been wonderful and terribly difficult for Cheryl. Wonderful because of the true understanding that both Lyn and I had about her Mission, and our role in it. Terrible because of the painful, and personal memories it must expose to create a coherent story. I suppose she'll feel much the same way about this book. She made many hard choices with us about the roles we played and the situations in which we found ourselves embroiled. She sacrificed much for us… a normal home, her health, a social life, a simple relationship with her employer, any number of opportunities to reach out to a wider world, and more. She never had children of her own, but of course she considered *all* of us her children; and many of us considered her sort of a surrogate mother, friend, confidante, and most importantly, mentor.

I hope she knows that we *appreciate* what she gave up for us, and what she did for us. And for my part, at least, I know it was hard for her, but I'm glad she was there and she did what she did.

Some of Cheryl's students went on to successful and happy lives. Some didn't. She continued to butt heads with obtuse administrators, worked with others that understood her Mission and performed the ultimate act an administrator can perform; they Got Out Of Her Way. She's been depressed, felt like a failure, recovered, and as Lyn noted, never married. She's maintained happy relations with some of her former students, not so much with others. Theatre generates strong emotions, and personal feelings. It's hard to separate your feelings from your job in this line of work. That single fact probably explains the majority of the brief Hollywood romances so important to the paparazzi culture.

There are some more stories from her that didn't fit here, but perhaps I can find a way before the final draft. I'll ask the story, and see what it has to say about it. (Author's note: *Yup. I managed to slip a few of them in.*)

===

We were flying in to Kentucky, I told Lyn via email, to make our annual circuit of the area, doing all the required visits to relatives one must make when going back home once a year. Lyn graciously invited us to her home, to meet her kids. Our flights usually landed in Louisville on these treks, and she lives just minutes from the route we normally take. Cheryl and Edie would be there, she said, and we could visit and eat and the kids could play.

I was so nervous, I had a hard time picking up the phone to ask directions to Lyn's house. My wife noted this, sharp as a tack as usual. Lyn noted it as well. I think, someday, they are going to be good friends. When that day comes, I fear I shall be thoroughly outmaneuvered and unable to win an argument of any sort. *Shall be?* my wife will say when she reads this. *It's too late for that, Darth darling. You're outmaneuvered right now.*

I'll allow as how that is most likely true.

Lyn and I exchanged emails, and ideas, old newspaper clippings, photos, and memories, and suddenly the 40 pages of writing I had started five years ago had a plot, and a purpose, and here we are. *Wouldn't it be fantastic if we could tell this story, and somehow help people become inspired about learning and Shakespeare and space and love and theatre, and maybe even provide a little more security for our kids?* Lyn asked. *Wouldn't it be the most amazing thing?*

I told her what she had meant to me. She told me she already knew, and felt the same way. Friends forever, thankful for the time we had shared together, thankful that we both had helped each other move from where we were to where destiny had flung us.

It's nearly impossible to catch up on 30 years of missed stories in a couple of hours, but we gave it a good try. *An 'A' for effort.*

We talked about the "good old days," as I referred to them, and as my wife chased after our children in the downstairs family room, Lyn said, "They weren't all good for me."

"I knew you weren't happy," I said. "Did you ever go back to Hazard after the prom?"

"No, I never did. I can't think of a reason why I would have. You were the only thing that might have drawn me back, and--"

"--I wasn't there anymore," I said. We sat there looking at each other for a bit. Then Cheryl and Edie arrived at last, and my photographer wife took pictures of all of us together. *All* of us together. Again.

We talked about our various memories. I reminded them of the story about the broken water pipe, and Cheryl *hooted.*

Cheryl told me the story about *her* broken water pipe and I laughed along with everyone else. We talked about the few people we knew from those days whose current whereabouts of which we were aware. Eventually, the discussion turned to my efforts to write this book, and I hauled out a notepad and tried to fill in some gaps in my memories.

I learned about Lyn's first play (in the basement of her house), her intention to move to L.A. or New York in pursuit of acting work and she told me how her plans to depart had been interrupted by illness in the family and how she had never managed to reset the clock, so to speak. I asked Lyn why she had left Louisville as a teenager and she reminded me of the story of her sister, who had passed away some years ago.

"I loved my sister, but it was difficult living with her," she said. "She was just a vacuum that sucked in everyone's energy, time, and attention. That was bad enough, but once she moved back in with her little babies, I went from being the youngest to a middle child, in a way. I felt abandoned."

"These are things we've seldom talked about to people outside the family," said Cheryl. "It was a difficult time for all of us."

You have no idea flitted across Lyn's eyes. "I can tell *you* what happened," she said to me.

"What?" I asked, trying unsuccessfully to read the faces of the three women in front of me. My wife Laura looked at me with one eyebrow slightly canted, spouse-speak for *What is she talking about?* I didn't know, so I widened my eyes slightly in response, in that way spouses have of speaking without words. "What happened after you left home?"

And then, after all these years, she told me.

No Pleasure Cruise

The day that Lyn and Cheryl and Edie and Mamal had argued, the day that Lyn stormed up the stairs and cried, as her elders sat in the room at the bottom of the stairs and talked in low, buzzing, murmuring voices about *Whatever are we going to do about Lynnie,* Lyn's frantic dash gradually dissipated in the confines of the small bathroom and her despair turned to anger.

She seethed with resentment, feeling alternatively smothered and abandoned, these contradictory feelings tearing at her heart. She couldn't exist any more not feeling wanted, or loved, or respected. Her hands gripped the sides of the sink basin, squeezing with all her strength, until the anger within her made her kick the base of the basin in frustration. The rickety basin transmitted the energy of her kick to the medicine cabinet above the sink, where a mirrored door that refused to stay shut rattled and slowly swung open, revealing multiple bottles of medication used, among other things, for pain relief. Lyn stared at them, tunnel vision obscuring all else, the voices downstairs, the faint musty smell from the decaying walls of the house, the flowery print hanging slightly askew on the bathroom wall.

Somehow, without a conscious decision to do so, a bottle of pills appeared in her hand. A similar timeless transition left the lid upside down in the bottom of the basin.

We'll just see how much they love me, she thought.

Lyn swallowed a fistful of pills.

The room seemed to slow down. The voices from downstairs grew distant, muffled. There was a strange sensation as the room began to rotate, all on its own, and rise up in the air–

She collapsed on the floor.

414

She could still hear, and respond somewhat. But she could tell that this was *serious.* The question was, would her mother? her grandmother? her *Aunt?*

An interminable amount of time passed. Although her heart slowed dangerously, Lyn's mind seemed disconnected from the stress her body was going through. Thoughts proceeded through her mind, sounds entered her ears, heard, understood, but unimportant. There were murmurings from below, the soft *thumping* of someone trudging up the stairs to check on her. The door opened.

Someone, possibly her mother, screamed. The door slammed again. *Are they going to leave me here?* passed casually through her brain. More thumps. Yelling. Cheryl shouting for attention, to bring order to the chaos. Accusations flying already. *Hello,* she transmitted to her vocal cords. *I'm on the floor here. Someone help me.*

Aunt Cheryl always said to speech classes that for communication to occur, a message must be transmitted, received, and understood. *One out of three ain't bad,* Lyn thought.

The door banged open and the three women cried out in shock. *Quick, quick, call the hospital,* one voice said. *There's no time,* said another. *We've got to get her in the car and go, now.*

Exhortations and face-slapping and crying accompanied them as they lifted, half-dragged, and pushed Lyn down the narrow stairs. *Quick, quick, we've got to go Now,* she heard, still unable to identify who was speaking. Out the door, she could see the light from the day; it hurt her eyes, so she closed them with an effort. *No! Don't go to sleep! Wake up, wake up!*

She was placed in the car, her head lolling to one side, her muscles not responding to the confused messages her brain was sending.

Now maybe they'll listen, she thought. *I'm not like my sister. I'm not. I'm my own person and can make my own decisions.* Time passed. She waited for the car to start. Her vision dimmed; what she could see constricted to what appeared to be a long tunnel, pointed at nothing in particular. *I think I must be dying,* she thought. *Why aren't we moving?*

"Just a minute, Edie," said Cheryl to the telephone handset, wringing her hands and popping back and forth between her mother and glancing at Lyn. "Mom can't find her shoes. We've got to find her shoes."

I'm dying, thought Lyn. *I am sitting here in this car, about to die, and they won't take me to the hospital because they can't find Mamal's shoes. Hang up. Start driving.*

A tear found its way out of her eye, draining down her cheek, but she couldn't raise her arm to wipe it away.

The tunnel closed, and became dark.

Lyn remained passed out on the trip to the hospital on the other side of town. It was three days before she regained consciousness. When she awoke, at first, no one noticed. She recognized the back of her mother's head. Her grandmother sat in profile, facing the other side of the room. There were flowers on the stand next to the bed. Various devices *peeped* and *chirped.* A television mounted on the wall was tuned to some generic soap opera. A water glass sat half-filled with water, partially suspending some mostly melted ice. *How long?*

And on the bed across from her, Cheryl lay with her arm across her head.

"It's all my fault," said Cheryl. "I was too nice. I pampered the poor child. She had no direction, no real parent here."

"Now, Cheryl," said Edie. "You can't blame yourself for this."

"Oh, I do, I do," wailed Cheryl.

416

"Look at what's become of Teri," said Mamal. "You didn't cause *that*, did you? And you didn't cause this, either."

All seemed unaware that Lyn was conscious. All Lyn could think about, despite her weakened condition, confusion about the conversation, and her mild surprise at finding herself alive was *This means I'll have to go back to Louisville,* she said. *I don't know what's worse. The Prison at Glomawr or the Dysfunctional Family with the Invisible Girl.*

She closed her eyes and didn't bother telling anyone she awoke. They found out later when she stirred.

Lyn remained in the hospital for several days. A visit from a psychiatrist followed. The family asked him what he thought she should do. Lyn wanted to know if her angst was really *her* fault or merely a side-effect of just being in the wrong place. It was apparent, he informed her, everything wrong with her stemmed from her evil sister's ways. If it hadn't been for Teri and her worthless husband, none of this would have happened. Given the situation he could only advise her to remove herself as far from her sister and her abusive husband as possible.

No, she insisted. *I love my sister. She loves me. That's not what I meant to happen.* She realized then that the act of attempted suicide had not simply been one of despair or a real attempt to die but had been intended to *cause an effect.* She didn't know exactly what that effect was, but estrangement from her sister was not on the list of desired outcomes.

Events washed over her like seawater over a beach, eradicating the marks she had made, the plans, her strength and her will. What was she going to do? Which option left more of her identity intact? More power to decide her own fate?

Go home, and surrender. Accept whatever fate had in store and whatever Roy might do to her. Turn into a miniature version of her sister.

Stay and be more restricted than ever before.

Sometimes life presents you with unpleasant decisions, ones you'd rather not make. Avoiding a decision is a decision in and of itself. Lyn vacillated between her options until it occurred to her that despite the fact that she didn't agree with Cheryl's point of view much of the time, at least she had Cheryl's undivided attention most of the time.

I'll ask Cheryl if I can stay anyway despite what I did, she thought. *If she ever stops wailing.*

Apparently, one assumes, she did.

Declension

"I knew something terrible had happened to you in high school, Lyn," I said. "I had no idea what it was."

"We were all terrified. We thought we'd lost her. I've never been so scared in my entire life," declared Cheryl.

"Why didn't you tell me?" I asked. "I-- could have talked about it, listened to you, tried to be a better friend than I was–"

"*No,*" she said. "That was it exactly, don't you see? When you knew me, my... attempted suicide was only a couple of years in the past. I cherished your friendship because you *didn't* know. It said to me that there was something about me that a person could appreciate. I was more than just a collection of things I'd done in the past." She stopped, and looked at her hands. Her mother and aunt fidgeted. Thirty years, and there were still echoes of those painful days resounding off the walls of a house hundreds of miles and a generation away.

My pencil held, suspended, above the notepad. I'd not written anything for several minutes. I looked at it and wondered how I would deal with this revelation, *if* I would deal with it.

"What are you going to write?" asked Edie. It was just like her to remain quietly in the background and spear to the heart of the matter when an opportunity to speak presented itself.

"I don't know." The pencil still wavered. Finally I put it down and folded up the pages of notes over the top of the yellow pad.

"I trust you," said Lyn.

"So do I," said Cheryl. "But send it to me before you publish it."

"Well, the idea is that we want to write a screenplay," I said. "But I thought having an intact story first would be a good way to start."

"I'd pay to see it," said Edie.

"If it ever is made into a movie, Mom, I think we'll probably spring for a ticket," said Lyn.

Then dinner was ready, and the conversation shifted to other things for a while. I noted we were very late for a visit to my sister Jane's house in Paris, Kentucky, and I called to tell her we would be late.

The first time Cheryl and Edie and Lyn and I sat in her living room and our children ran about playing and laughing, as we looked at old photo albums, a yellowed valentine, a press clipping with a picture of Benny and Lyn standing together, a note scribbled on the back of a certificate, and my carefully preserved program from *Charlie Brown '77*, it seemed as if we had all been together just a few weeks ago and we had come back from summer vacation and were almost plotting to start another show right then and there.

Cheryl, a twinkle in her eye, asked if I'd be interested in doing a little touring when I retire from teaching. I haven't answered her, yet. My life's a little more complex than it used to be. But I am tempted.

I told them I felt blessed to be in the same room with almost all of my favorite women in the whole world. What a lucky bastard I've been, to have known and loved and worked with all of these remarkable people.

We resolved to be active, *significant* friends again. We had always been friends, and now we are again. We cried, separately and together, remembering how we helped each other.

Thank you, thank you, my brain kept transmitting. *From the bottom of my heart.*

The planets and people of my life have aligned for me like that only a few times in my life. I suppose this is as appropriate a place as any to tell them how much I appreciate all they've done for me, how I admire each of them, honor them, and love them all, each in their own way.

And I will, forever and always.

[Close curtain. Drop lights.]